In the Shadow of the Incarnation

Brian E. Daley, S.J.
Photo by Bachrach.

In the SHADOW *of the* INCARNATION

Essays on Jesus Christ in the Early Church

in Honor of

BRIAN E. DALEY, S.J.

edited by

PETER W. MARTENS

University of Notre Dame Press

Notre Dame, Indiana

Notre Dame, Indiana 46556
www.undpress.nd.edu

Manufactured in the United States of America

Library of Congress Cataloging-in-Publication Data

In the shadow of the incarnation : essays on Jesus Christ in the early church in honor of Brian E. Daley, S.J. / edited by Peter W. Martens.
p. cm.
Includes bibliographical references and index.
ISBN-13: 978-0-268-03511-2 (cloth : alk. paper)
ISBN-10: 0-268-03511-3 (cloth : alk. paper)
1. Jesus Christ—History of doctrines—Early church, ca. 30–600.
I. Daley, Brian, 1940– II. Martens, Peter William.
BT198.I58 2008
232—dc22
2008027217

∞ *The paper in this book meets the guidelines for permanence and durability of the Committee on Production Guidelines for Book Longevity of the Council on Library Resources.*

Contents

ABBREVIATIONS

Antirrh.	Gregory of Nyssa, *Antirrheticus adversus Apollinarium*
Ar.	Athanasius, *Orationes tres adversus Arianos*
Arian.	Augustine, *Contra sermonem Arianorum*
BA	Bibliothèque augustinienne, *Oeuvres de Saint Augustin,* Paris: Desclée de Brouwer, 1949–
C. Jul. op. imp.	Augustine, *Contra Julianum opus imperfectum*
Carm.	Gregory of Nazianzus, *Carmen*
CCSG	Corpus Christianorum: Series graeca. Turnhout, 1977–
CCSL	Corpus Christianorum: Series latina. Turnhout, 1953–
Cels.	Origen, *Contra Celsum*
Civ.	Augustine, *De civitate Dei*
Comm. Cant.	Origen, *Commentarius in Canticum*
Comm. Jo.	Origen, *Commentarii in evangelium Joannis*

Comm. Matt.	Origen, *Commentarium in evangelium Matthaei*
Comm. Rom.	Origen, *Commentarii in Romanos*
Conf.	Augustine, *Confessiones*
CSEL	Corpus scriptorum ecclesiasticorum latinorum
De Engast.	Eustathius, *De Engastrimytho*
De or.	Cicero, *De oratore*
De Trin.	Hilary of Poitiers, *De Trinitate*
Decr.	Athanasius, *De decretis Nicaenae synodi*
Dial.	Origen, *Dialogus cum Heraclide*
Dial. contra Nest.	Maxentius, *Dialogus contra Nestorianos*
Div. quaest. LXXXIII	Augustine, *De diversis quaestionibus LXXXIII*
Doctr. chr.	Augustine, *De doctrina christiana*
Enarrat. Ps.	Augustine, *Enarrationes in Psalmos*
Enchir.	Augustine, *Enchiridion de fide, spe, et caritate*
Enn.	Plotinus, *Enneads*
Ep. ad episc.	*Epistula ad episcopos*
Ep. Marcell.	Athanasius, *Epistula ad Marcellinum de interpretatione Psalmorum*
Eun.	Gregory of Nyssa, *Contra Eunomium*
Exp. Gal.	Augustine, *Expositio in epistulam ad Galatas*
Faust.	Augustine, *Contra Faustum Manichaeum*
Fid. symb.	Augustine, *De fide et symbolo*
GCS	Die griechische christliche Schriftsteller der ersten Jahrhunderte
GNO	*Gregorii Nysseni Opera,* ed. W. Jaeger et al. (Leiden: Brill, 1952–)

Haer.	Irenaeus, *Adversus haeresus*
Hist. Eccl.	*Historia ecclesiastica* (various authors)
Hom. Exod.	Origen, *Homiliae in Exodum*
Hom. Ezech.	Origen, *Homiliae in Ezechielem*
Hom. Gen.	Origen, *Homiliae in Genesim*
Hom. Jer.	Origen, *Homiliae in Jeremiam*
Hom. Jos.	Origen, *Homiliae in Joshuam*
Hom. Judic.	Origen, *Homiliae in Judices*
Hom. Lev.	Origen, *Homiliae in Leviticum*
Hom. Luc.	Origen, *Homiliae in Lucam*
Hom. Num.	Origen, *Homiliae in Numeros*
Hom. Ps.	Origen, *Homiliae in Psalmos*
Immort. an.	Augustine, *De immortalitate animae*
In Inscr. Ps.	Gregory of Nyssa, *In Inscriptiones Psalmorum*
Inc.	Athanasius, *De incarnatione*
Instr. Ps.	Hilary of Poitiers, *Instructio Psalmorum*
Lib. arb.	Augustine, *De libero arbitrio*
Libell. fid.	*Libellus fidei* (chap. 10)
Mag.	Augustine, *De magistro*
NBA	Nuova biblioteca agostiniana, *Opere di S. Agostino, edizione latino-italiana,* Rome: Città Nuova, 1965–
NPNF	*Nicene and Post-Nicene Fathers*
Or.	Gregory of Nazianus, *Orationes*
Or. catech.	Gregory of Nyssa, *Oratio catechetica*
Orat.	Origen, *De oratione*

Ord.	Augustine, *De ordine*
Pecc. merit.	Augustine, *De peccatorum meritis et remissione*
PG	Patrologia graeca. Edited by J.-P. Migne. 162 vols. Paris, 1857–86
PL	Patrologia latina. Edited by J.-P. Migne. 217 vols. Paris, 1844–64
PLRE	*The Prosopography of the Later Roman Empire,* 3 vols., ed. A. H. M. Jones, J. R. Martindale, and J. Morris (Cambridge: Cambridge University Press, 1971)
Praed.	Augustine, *De praedestinatione sanctorum*
Princ.	Origen, *De principiis*
Prof. brev.	*Professio brevissima catholicae fidei*
Quant. an.	Augustine, *De quantitate animae*
Resp. adv. epist.	Maxentius, *Responsio adversus Epistulam Hormisdae*
SC	Sources chrétiennes. Paris: Cerf, 1943–
Serm.	Augustine, *Sermones*
Serm. Dom.	Augustine, *De sermone Domini in montes*
Sol.	Augustine, *Soliloquiorum libri II*
Spir. et litt.	Augustine, *De spiritu et littera*
Tract. Ev. Jo.	Augustine, *In Evangelium Johannis tractatus*
Tract. Ps.	Hilary of Poitiers, *Tractatus super Psalmos*
Trin.	Augustine, *De Trinitate*
Tusc.	Cicero, *Tusculanae disputationes*
Ver. rel.	Augustine, *De vera religione*

Introduction

Peter W. Martens

The essays in this volume are offered in warm gratitude to Brian E. Daley, S.J. They serve, to be sure, as only a small expression of thanks from a handful of the many who count themselves as Brian's friends. They are centered on the topic of Jesus Christ in the early church and were commissioned on the occasion of our honoree's sixty-fifth birthday.

I cannot introduce Brian Daley more succinctly or more faithfully than by describing him as a Jesuit priest. It is the Jesuit way of life that has ordered and shaped the rest of his life, including his vocation as a scholar. Brian entered the Society of Jesus in 1964, shortly after taking his B.A., *Literae Humaniores* from Oxford University. Long before he joined the Jesuits, however, the Society had already begun to mold him. Brian attended a Jesuit high school, St. Peter's Preparatory School in New Jersey, and he earned his first college degree from another Jesuit institution, Fordham University (B.A. in Classics). After joining the Society, much of Brian's early theological education transpired at the Jesuit *Hochschule,* Sankt Georgen (Frankfurt, Germany), where he served as the research assistant to Aloys Grillmeier, S.J. Brian would return to Oxford, where he was awarded his Doctor of Philosophy for his thesis on Leontius of Byzantium. While at Oxford he lived at Campion Hall, a private house owned and run by the Jesuits.

Much of Brian's academic service and scholarship has been woven into the fabric of major Jesuit institutions. After graduating from Oxford he taught for eighteen years at the Weston Jesuit School of Theology, one of two Jesuit seminaries in the United States. Over the years Brian has also served as a trustee at Le Moyne College, Boston College, and Fordham, and served as a member on the board of directors at Georgetown University. He was also an acting dean at Weston. He has been a member of the editorial boards of the series Studies in Jesuit Spirituality and of *Communio: International Theological Review,* and is an editor for *Traditio*. His Ignatian identity has also been expressed in the larger ecclesiastical community, where his dedication to reconciliation and ecumenism, integral to his understanding of Jesuit ministry, is evident. One of Brian's enduring achievements is his contribution to ecumenical dialogue. Most notably, he has faithfully served for nearly twenty-five years as a member of the Orthodox-Roman Catholic Consultation, a bilateral dialogue sponsored by Orthodox and Roman Catholic bishops of the United States.

Brian's Jesuit commitments overflow into the classroom and print. Perhaps without peer in his generation, Brian has cultivated a lifelong passion for the Christology of the early church. This is certainly not his only interest—the span of topics that he has tackled in print is remarkable, ranging from Origen's scriptural interpretation to the debates surrounding the Filioque, from early Christian eschatology to late medieval iconography of Mary, from the relationship between Boethius and Byzantine scholasticism to Ignatian spirituality, from the episcopacy in the early church to commentary on the Catholic catechism—the list goes on. And none of this exhausts the incredible breadth of topics about which Brian can effortlessly converse, which is fitting for someone who has taken to heart the Ignatian ideal of a rich, cultural humanism. Nevertheless, Jesus Christ in the early church is Brian's central academic passion. At Sankt Georgen he had the privilege of studying under the eminent scholar of patristic Christology, Aloys Grillmeier, and several years later at Oxford, he was awarded his D.Phil. for his thesis on Leontius of Byzantium, a theologian who played an integral role in the post-Chalcedonian debates about the person of Christ. Whether in articles, translations, lectureships, books, or courses offered, Brian has continuously held before his own eyes, as well as those of his peers and students, the Christ who was contemplated, loved, and followed by early Christians.

I have entitled this volume "In the Shadow of the Incarnation." The phrase is inspired by a stirring passage in Origen's *On First Principles* where the Alexandrian turns his treatise with "deepest amazement" toward the mystery of the incarnation and, in particular, to Jesus' soul (*Princ.* 2.6.1). In Origen's cosmic vision, this soul was unique among all other primordial souls since it clung with such an indissoluble love to the Son, Word, and Wisdom of God who had created it that, having received so fully of this Son, this soul became "one spirit" with it and could fittingly be called "the Son of God." Origen then turns toward his reader with a pastoral exhortation. Surely it does not fall to the soul of Jesus alone to become, by imitation, "one spirit" with God's Word, Wisdom, and Truth. After all, it was Paul who also wrote: "he who is joined to the Lord is one spirit" (1 Cor 6:17) (*Princ.* 2.6.3). As the soul of Jesus practiced a loving union with God's Word and Wisdom, so too ought Origen's readers to turn their souls in love toward the pioneer of their salvation.

With these two loves in mind, Origen recollects the poetic lines uttered by the prophet Jeremiah: "The breath of our countenance is Christ the Lord, of whom we said that we shall live under his shadow among the nations" (Lam 4:20). The depiction of Christ as a "shadow" rouses Origen's exegetical imagination. Shadows, he notes, are inseparable from their bodies and unswervingly mimic their movements and gestures. This is perhaps what the prophet had in mind when he was likening Christ to a "shadow"—the prophet was alluding to the action of Christ's soul that was inseparably attached to the Word. And in the verse cited above, Jeremiah also speaks of Christ's followers living "under his shadow among the nations." Jesus' disciples, Origen concludes, live under his shadow to the extent that they "imitate that soul through faith and so reach salvation" (*Princ.* 2.6.7).

This richly allusive title, "In the Shadow of the Incarnation," serves our volume well on several levels. It is inspired by the pen of one of the early church's most distinguished theologians, and it also refers back to these theologians, who themselves sought to live under Christ's shadow among the nations. The title also suggests more specifically the theme of this book: Jesus Christ as he was perceived through the eyes and hearts of the early church's scholars. These were theologians, after all, who were convinced that to live under the shadow of Christ also meant to reflect with unwavering gaze upon Christ.

The title also points beyond this book to our honoree. Brian Daley has not only studied Jesus Christ in the early church, he has also sought to live "in the shadow of the incarnation." Brian's students, colleagues, and friends know him not only as a teacher of Christ but also as a disciple of Christ. Formed by Ignatius of Loyola's *Spiritual Exercises,* whose sole objective is to help a person know and follow Christ more intimately, Brian lives in a religious community founded as the "Company of Jesus." In the Notre Dame community, his academic home since 1996, he presides regularly at Eucharist in the basilica. Brian gives his time generously to the *cura personalis* of students, faculty, and administration and fosters a warm relationship with his graduate students. Some of my best memories in the doctoral program at Notre Dame come from our Monday evening gatherings at a local brewing company. There Brian reserved a large corner booth and read through a Greek text from the early church with a cluster of diligent graduate students (much to the amusement of the restaurant staff). Brian's care for his students extends to his home as well. His hospitality and culinary skills are repeatedly displayed for students and faculty at the aptly-named "De Lubac House," the Jesuit residence off campus named in honor of the prolific Jesuit scholar and student of the early church, Henri de Lubac. Come Easter and Thanksgiving (and a few other occasions as well), invitations to the De Lubac House are held in high regard.

The Ignatian heritage has left an indelible mark upon Brian's life. Within the classroom, his voice is refreshingly free of ironic detachment or abrasive polemic. It is rare, indeed, to find someone today who is willing to hold a conversation with the theologians of the early church under the conviction that they are our equals, worthy of being studied and heard on their own terms, worthy of informing and forming us, worthy of even having, on occasion, the last word. While incessant demands are placed upon Brian outside the classroom, he generously makes himself available to those who request his help and counsel. Despite towering erudition, Brian remains refreshingly unassuming, good-humored, and humble. And while he holds strong convictions, he speaks the truth in love. As others will testify, it is not selfish ambition that drives him, but rather his ever-growing love for Jesus Christ.

So, if Brian is in any way apprehensive about being honored with this volume, my suspicion is that this unease emerges from a conviction, which he has both taught and lived: the servant cannot be greater than his Master. But even servants can be thanked. Nor is there anything incongruous, in speaking of this Master, as this book will do, to acknowledge those who have served him well, whether they are the theologians of the early church or our honoree. If there is even the slightest suspicion that this book might signal the twilight of Brian's scholarly career, then let us clearly announce that this volume is simply a timely expression of thanks and encouragement to our teacher, colleague, and, above all, friend. *Ad multos annos!*

I have arranged the essays that follow in chronological order. The volume opens with D. Jeffrey Bingham's examination of the role that apocalyptic motifs and the book of Revelation played in the *Letter to the Churches of Lyons and Vienne*. The *Letter* was written shortly after the persecution of Christians in Lyons in 177 and is preserved by Eusebius in his *Ecclesiastical History* (5.1.3–5.3.3). Bingham demonstrates that the martyr accounts in the *Letter* give voice to a wide range of apocalyptic motifs and draw extensively upon themes voiced in John's Apocalypse. From these apocalyptic perspectives on the martyrs' deaths arises a Christology that depicts the martyrs as followers of Christ the "Lamb" (Rev 14:4). Bingham argues further that the *Letter* portrays Christ the Lamb and his martyr-followers as sacrificial victims, whose self-offerings had a militaristic tenor: the martyrs shared in Christ's own combat against the Adversary, a combat that was apologetic and revelatory as Christ's martyrs demonstrated the solidity of their faith to their onlookers.

Khaled Anatolios ushers us into the early fourth century with his gentle critique of Karl Rahner's critical assessment of "classical Christology." Rahner contended that patristic Christology was overly preoccupied with ontological and not functional concerns, that is, it offered a

Christology concerned with Christ's "nature" and "person" but insufficiently attentive to the salvific work of Christ in his life, death, and resurrection *pro nobis*. With Athanasius's *On the Incarnation* in mind, Anatolios shows that in many ways this early theologian's exposition of "classical Christology" was more "functional" than even Rahner might have suspected. Anatolios concludes by taking up Rahner's recommendation to translate the basic insights of Athanasius's Christology into simple statements that have a straightforward relevance to the experience of the Christian faith today.

The next two essays explore the "Athanasius of the West," Hilary of Poitiers. Michael C. McCarthy, S.J., offers an eloquent piece on Hilary's interpretation of the Psalms. McCarthy reminds us that ancient interpreters of the Psalms, Hilary included, viewed them as the Word of God operating at a particular moment in the history of the church and the life of the individual Christian. For Hilary, McCarthy contends, the Psalms did not simply provide locutions for healing present maladies but also offered a future orientation. In particular, the return of Christ, the judgment, the final transformation, and the handing over of the kingdom to the Father formed the outermost frame of the narrative wherein Hilary interpreted the Psalms in his *Tractatus super Psalmos*.

Carl L. Beckwith, in his essay on Hilary of Poitiers, argues against the school of scholarship that maintains Hilary was a Docetist because he claimed that Christ suffered without pain. Beckwith contends that when we read Hilary's comments on Christ's suffering in the larger context of his *De Trinitate,* bearing in mind both his philosophical commitment to Stoic moral psychology and his theological adversaries, his Christology not only escapes suspicion but also emerges as a significant contribution to fourth-century patristic thought.

We return to the Greek world with Christopher A. Beeley's essay on Gregory of Nazianzus. Beeley asserts that Gregory's doctrine of Christ is wrongly summarized in the standard accounts as "dualist." Beeley argues for the predominantly unitive character of Gregory's Christology by offering a sensitive examination of whether biblical references to Christ's actions refer to one or two acting subjects, and by exploring the ramifications of a purported dualist Christology for Gregory's own understanding of salvation and the Christian life. Beeley also raises (and dismisses) the claim that Gregory of Nazianzus was in any way fundamentally anti-Apollinarian.

Eustathius of Antioch, an early opponent of Arius, receives considerable attention in Kelley McCarthy Spoerl's essay. Spoerl offers a detailed examination of the trinitarian and christological features of Eustathius of Antioch's thought and compares his views with those of another early opponent of Arius, Marcellus of Ancyra. Spoerl highlights the kinship between these two pro-Nicene theologians, as well as their notable differences. She concludes by suggesting that their trinitarian and christological affinities provide clues to the emergence of Apollinarius's Christology, a later and very different Christology from within the same pro-Nicene coalition.

The next four essays touch on various facets of Augustine's Christology. Basil Studer compares Origen and Augustine on the theme of loving Christ, emphasizing the love and friendship that exists between believers and Christ. Studer focuses in particular on the practice of theology. He canvasses a wide spectrum of texts that indicate that for both Origen and Augustine, the discipline of theology was an exercise practiced in the presence of Christ and in dependence on him as the theologian quested after the vision of God.

Studer refers in his essay to a paper delivered by the Archbishop of Canterbury, Rowan Williams, at an International Patristics Conference (Oxford, 2003), which Williams has also contributed to this volume. Williams offers an insightful account of the *persona* of Jesus Christ in Augustine's major writings. For Augustine, the divine *sapientia* is first and foremost the joyful contemplation of God by God, but in so doing, this *sapientia* also realizes itself as *caritas,* a radically disinterested love that seeks the fruition of others in the same joy it knows. In Jesus Christ, then, we see the person of divine Wisdom-in-action, the humility of identification with the created order through the incarnation, Wisdom engaging with what is not by nature God so as to incorporate it into the divine life and make it capable of seeing what Wisdom sees. This humility is precisely what the created order needs, since our prideful self-assertion is the root of our alienation from God, and only a humility that reflects Wisdom's *caritas* can again reconcile us with God and one another. The incarnate Christ, so Williams argues, with J.-M. Le Blond, serves as our path to and the form of the transfiguring and participatory knowledge of God for Augustine. However, the concept of Christ as *sapientia* is linked as much to spirituality as it is to Christology proper. Williams proposes that the rhetoric of Augustine's Christology sounds "Cyrilline" or unitive (as opposed to Antiochene, where the concern is to distribute the *dicta* of Jesus between the Word and the human individual Jesus) because of Augustine's own sense of the absolute dependence of the incarnate one's human speech on the single act of divine Wisdom. There is no dialogue of resistance or submission between Jesus and the Word, as there is between the Word and other human beings. Rather, the incarnation is the act of divine self-offering that concretely animates the soul-body humanity of Christ. The entire earthly life of the incarnate Son is a speaking or acting in the person of divine Wisdom, who is freely engaged in the world of historical suffering and struggle.

Williams's essay has clear links to the two that follow it. Lewis Ayres examines Augustine's *Letter* 137, in which for the first time the Bishop of Hippo uses the noun *persona* to describe Christ ("uniting both natures in the unity of his person") and likens the union between the two natures in Christ to the union of soul and body in the human being. Ayres argues that questions about the doctrine of the incarnation are for Augustine inseparable from questions about the more basic theological context in which Christian doctrine is explored and questioned. In particular, Augustine encourages his readers to cultivate a special practice of thought and contemplation as they consider the constitution of Christ's person, a practice shaped by how creation exists within God's presence and ought to exhibit the humility modeled by the incarnate Christ. The ensuing contemplation of Christ's person is less concerned with making the union of the natures comprehensible than it is with defining and reflecting upon the incomprehensibility of this union.

David R. Maxwell continues an examination of Augustine's notion of Christ's *persona* by turning to the Scythian monks' reception, or lack thereof, of Augustine's Christology as it was voiced in his *De Trinitate*. Why did the theologians of the Theopaschite controversy in the sixth century, who in most regards were ardent Augustinians, fail to draw on Augustine in their Christology? Maxwell contends that when Augustine's Christology was located in a new context (namely, the sixth-century Nestorian controversy), his formulations took on a different meaning because they bore in several respects a superficial resemblance to certain "Nestorian" formulations, even though they were never intended to address the questions posed by the later controversy. As such, Maxwell's argument runs, the theologians of the Theopaschite controversy, otherwise enthusiastic Augustinians, explicitly embraced a Cyrilline Christology.

This collection concludes with essays by John J. O'Keefe, John A. McGuckin, and Andrew Louth. O'Keefe examines an overlooked facet of Cyril of Alexandria's later Christology—its "low" side. O'Keefe argues that Cyril's Christology, viewed against its Irenaean and Athanasian backdrop, was profoundly driven by a particular human experience and a particular human hope: the human Christ gave Cyril the hope that the human race would one day be able to escape the violent force of bodily corruption, putrefication, and decay. O'Keefe urges caution on two fronts. Not only should we attend to the "low" side of Alexandrian Christology alongside its undeniably "high" concerns, but we must also distinguish between varieties of "low" Christologies in the Christian theological tradition—what registers as "low" for a Christian of antiquity like Cyril might not register as low for someone with a modern, Western sensibility.

John A. McGuckin offers a focused rereading of the Chalcedonian creed, in search of its essence. He advances the thesis that this creed can easily be misread if undue accent is placed on its anathemas and on the literary and cultural remains of Leo's *Tome* that reside within it. McGuckin argues that we need to attend with greater care to the ancient patterns of thinking characteristic of the many synodical processes of the Eastern church prior to the Chalcedonian statement. These ancient patterns shaped the Chalcedonian creed into an instrument of sublime christological praise, of celebration of the good news of Christ, and of pure doxology. This creed was not primarily about the resolution of a theological condundrum, but rather, McGuckin maintains, the restatement of the soteriological mystery in doxological form that provided the correct lens for approaching such problems.

Finally, Andrew Louth turns us to Maximus the Confessor's reflections on the transfiguration of Christ. Louth shows that Origen's reflections on the transfiguration were taken up by Maximus, but were also transformed by their twofold location—both within the developed Byzantine Christology of the sixth century, as set out in the decrees of the fifth ecumenical council, and within a modified Dionysian distinction between kataphatic and apophatic theology (i.e., the theologies of affirmation and denial). In the tradition of Origen, the ineffability of God was reconciled with his manifestation in the incarnation by emphasizing the manifold ways in which Jesus' disciples apprehended the manifestation of God; as a consequence, the notion of the inexhaustibility of God ruled out any one, true, iconic depiction of the incarnate one. For Maximus, on the other hand, this encounter with the transfigured Lord was the acknowledgment of the reality of the divine person of God, rather than a denial that qualified and limited our affirmation of the revealed images of God. God's inexhaustibility was actually found in the person-to-person experience with the dazzling radiance of the face, or divine person, of the transfigured Christ. In beholding this face or person there was a movement beyond utterance—the realm of the kataphatic and doctrinal—into silent wonder—the realm of the apophatic and iconic. Maximus's approach to the transfiguration, Louth argues, did not discard the icon as inadequate, but rather affirmed its importance by underlining the central significance in theology of not simply affirming but also beholding and contemplating.

An underlying concern of several of the essays in this volume is to correct particular misconceptions that have arisen around individual Christologies in the early church. As a group, however, all attempt to correct a larger misconception that still exists within, as well as outside of, our discipline. One of Brian Daley's deeply held convictions is that the Jesus Christ of the early church cannot be reduced to what can be gleaned from early credal statements. Brian has repeatedly stressed the need to contextualize patristic Christologies within their larger doctrinal matrices, and this is a task that we have taken to heart. The essays that follow explore, among other things, how early Christian theologians connected Jesus Christ to their other doctrinal concerns about God, the gift of salvation, and the eschaton, and how convictions about Jesus Christ informed numerous practices, including discipleship, martyrdom, scriptural interpretation, and even the practice of thinking well about Christ.

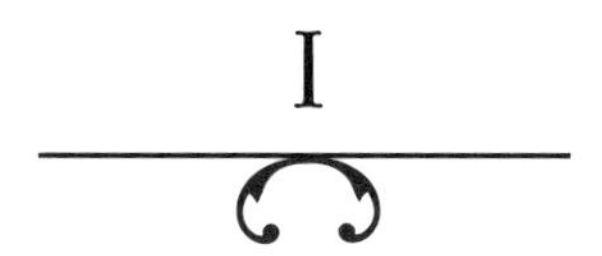

The Apocalypse, Christ, and the Martyrs of Gaul

D. Jeffrey Bingham

In 43 B.C., Lucius Munatius Plancus, the governor of Further Gaul and a faithful servant of Julius Caesar in the Gallic wars, founded Roman Lugdunum, as the Senate had directed. He established the city on the hill of the *Forum vetus,* the old forum, or the *fourvière* hill, the origin of modern Lyons. Lugdunum, located at the intersection of the Rhone and Saône rivers, became the capital of the three Provinces of Gaul. On the hill the Romans built two theaters, which overlook the modern city. The larger, wondrously preserved Gallo-Roman theater could seat upwards of 10,000 spectators, while the smaller, enclosed Odéon seated only 2,500. Across the Saône to the north of the *fourvière* and dedicated to Augustus in 19 B.C. by the provincial priest C. Julius Rufus lay the "Amphitheater of the Three Gauls," nestled on the slopes of the Croix-Rousse hill of Lyons. Modified later under Hadrian's rule (A.D. 117–38), the amphitheater hosted the usual exhibitions, contests, games, and combats.[1] Today, only meager, somewhat disappointing, portions of barely a third of the original amphitheater can be seen. This amphitheater is also the accepted location of the torture and execution of the Christians from both Lyons and the neighboring city of Vienne, sixteen miles south of Lyons on the east bank of the Rhone.

Our witness to this persecution is the *Letter of the Churches of Lyons and Vienne,* a selection of which is preserved in Eusebius's *Ecclesiastical History* (5.1–3). The *Letter* is an account of the persecution that befell these churches in the summer of A.D. 177.[2] Written by one or more of the survivors of the Gallic community—some have even argued that Irenaeus was its author—the *Letter* was sent to Asia and Phrygia.[3] Attempts to demonstrate that the *Letter* was a later forgery and that the persecution took place in Galatia, not Gaul, have found little sympathy.[4] The tragedy began, perhaps, on 2 June and lasted until 1 August, the feast of the Three Gauls, commemorating the day in 12 B.C. when the altar to Rome and Augustus had been established. On this date, each year, representatives of the sixty Gallic *civitates* gathered to celebrate the cult of Rome and Augustus in Lugdunum.[5]

The *Letter* tells of the social rejection, the abuse, the accusations, arrests, and imprisonment of the Gallic believers.[6] It recounts the public trial, the familiar charges of incest and cannibalism, and the long-drawn-out attempts to secure denials of faith. Here we learn of the firmness in faith and martyrdom of Vettius Epagathus and the torture of Sanctus, Maturus, Blandina, and Attalus; of Biblis, who having once denied Christ, died for him; of the persecution of the Phrygian Christian physician Alexander, a Roman citizen; of the brutality experienced by Ponticus, a fifteen-year-old boy; and of the martyrdom of the bishop of Lyons, Pothinus, who died in the jail at the age of ninety.

In this essay I investigate the apocalyptic motifs and role of John's Apocalypse in the *Letter of the Churches of Lyons and Vienne* and explore, against this backdrop, the relationship between martyrdom and Christology.

Apocalyptic Themes in the *Letter*

The apocalyptic themes in this *Letter* are particularly fascinating because of the way they shape the various accounts of martyrdom of Christians from Asia and Phrygia. These martyrdoms are repeatedly viewed as a composite, anticipatory experience of the endtime, and as an apocalyptic event of the persecution of God's people by Satan and his assistants.[7] Mary Hope Griffin has shown that there is a tendency for apocalyptically oriented communities like that of the Christians of Lyons to use military or battle imagery when depicting martyrdom. For these communities, martyrdom was clearly seen as combat with the Devil. "The Devil was incarnate in the state."[8] William C. Weinrich has referred to this as the "programmatic motif for the entire letter." P. Lanaro sees the *Letter* as describing an episode in Satan's great hostile combat against God. The persecution makes visible in the present, through human drama, the conflict which has its climax in eschatological catastrophe.[9] In the *Letter*'s own words, "The adversary swooped down upon us with full force, giving us now (ἤδη) a foretaste (προοιμιάζω) of his unrestrained (ἀδεῶς) future coming."[10] Charles E. Hill has helped us in his analysis of this passage to recognize the force of the rare word ἀδεῶς.[11] By assigning it a meaning of "freely, without restraint," as we find in the entry in Lampe (on the basis of a word group association with δέω rather than with ἀδεής),[12] the difference between the two stages of the adversary's coming is highlighted. The first coming is restrained, incomplete—a foretaste. The second is unrestrained and cataclysmic. The author(s) of our text places the narrative within an apocalyptic framework, one which understands the apocalyptic nature of the events in the sense of a restrained, first installment. The text employs the term "foretaste" (προοιμιάζω) with the sense of "to introduce beforehand, foreshadow."[13] This same term also occurs helpfully in Irenaeus. When discussing the intermediate state of the righteous, such as Enoch and Elijah, who were translated to paradise prior to death, Irenaeus writes that "there [in paradise] shall they who have been translated remain until the final consummation [*consummation; συντελείας*] as a prelude [*coauspicor;* προοιμιάζω] to incorruptibility."[14] In Lyons there is an appreciation for the concept of experiencing aspects of apocalyptic eschatology in stages; prolepsis followed by consummation, foretaste followed by fulfillment.

In regard to the martyrs of Lyons and Vienne, it is not surprising to find such a connection to apocalyptic events. The association between martyrdom, persecution, and apocalyptic worldviews is well attested.

We need only recall G. W. E. Nickelsburg's discussion of religious persecution in apocalyptic texts.[15] For example, Nickelsburg treats the themes of persecution and vindication of the righteous in 2 Maccabees 7 and relates them to features of apocalyptic eschatology found within apocalypses.[16] In Maccabees the brothers die because of their obedience to the Torah, yet they predict that Antiochus will acclaim the one true God and that ultimately he will be punished. In contrast, they predict that they will be rescued from death through resurrection and that their righteousness will thereby be vindicated.[17] Though this is a text of history and not an apocalypse, Nickelsburg argues for its grounding in apocalyptic ideas. His evidence demonstrates that

> the story preserved the hope that God would avenge [the brothers'] unjust deaths by means of an *apocalyptic* catastrophe. This story is then supplemented by the Isaianic exaltation tradition, which was also used in Antiochan times. It, too, announced an *apocalyptic* judgment on Antiochus, but it delegated the execution of his judgment to the righteous whom he persecuted, thus adding to the original story the hope of post-mortem vindication for the righteous. In 1 and 2 Maccabees, this double *apocalyptic* tradition is adjusted to certain facts of history.[18]

Elsewhere Nickelsburg discusses the apocalypses in Daniel, Jubilees 23, and the *Assumption of Moses*. Each is composed under persecution. In each, persecution is resolved only with God's imminent judgment. But their apocalyptic concern does not cause a departure from the historical. Instead, "by describing history in such a way that they place themselves and contemporary events at the fulcrum of history and eschatology, they offer assurance to the faithful that God will indeed act and that he will act quickly."[19] The apocalypses through vision, then, describe history by joining it to eschatology and by connecting the contemporary to the future, thus providing assurance to the persecuted.

The apocalyptic themes in the *Letter of the Churches of Lyons and Vienne* are not exhausted in the concept of the proleptic experience of the adversary's coming. Denis M. Farkasfalvy's treatment of the *Letter*'s Christology brings important additional elements to the foreground.[20]

One of them is clarified by the *Letter*'s introduction to its citation of Romans 8:18 and its use of that verse. In this passage of the *Letter* the martyrs hasten to Christ in their deaths, and this haste "demonstrates [ἐνδείκνυμι] that the sufferings of the present times are not comparable to the future glory which is to be revealed in us."[21] The general apocalyptic notion of future glory drives the martyrs as they embrace suffering. This idea of glory is common in accounts that join persecution and apocalyptic themes, and is listed by K. Koch as one of the typical motifs of apocalyptic texts.[22] As already noted, the brothers of 2 Maccabees endured death after predicting their eschatological vindication and delivery. What is remarkable about the *Letter*'s use of Romans 8:18, however, is its emphasis that "the suffering of the martyrs *manifests* the truth of the saying that the future glory is incomparable to our present suffering. This *manifestation,* of course, displays an anticipated glory amidst actual suffering, glory perceivable only to the eye of faith."[23] Here Farkasfalvy orients us, through another aspect of the *Letter,* to an idea already addressed above. The believers of Lyons and Vienne understood their period of persecution as a prolepsis of apocalyptic events. The adversary's coming is upon them, though in a restrained manner, and the future glory is being manifested in events of the flesh, though in a manner visible only to the spiritual eye. The *Letter* certainly brings the adversary into the present. And the *Letter* "brings both the expected glory and the truth of Scripture into evidence, almost within reach, although without suppressing its eschatological dimension."[24]

Two other apocalyptic themes in the *Letter* deserve mention. First is the theme of the victor's crown, "the crown of incorruptibility," a reward that appears three times in the *Letter*.[25] Recognizing that this imagery has both Jewish and Hellenistic roots, Farkasfalvy draws attention to its New Testament background (1 Cor 9:25; 1 Pet 5:4; 2 Tim 4:6–8; Rev 2:10; James 1:12). The language of 1 Peter 5:4 makes the eschatological identity of the crown explicit—its reception is linked to the Chief Shepherd's appearance, an important apocalyptic motif of the mediator who appears to accomplish final redemption.[26] The *Letter* alludes to this verse when it specifically mentions that the maiden Blandina, the victorious athlete in her martyrdom, had defeated Satan who had come: she "had overcome the adversary in many contests, and through her conflicts had won the crown of incorruptibility."[27] It is particularly stunning to note the language of 1 Peter 5:4 and that of the *Letter* as it relates to the story of Blandina. In 1 Peter we find: "you *will* obtain the unfading crown of glory" when Christ appears, emphasizing the future reality. Not so for Blandina. She "was crowned" with the crown, emphasizing the already received award. Once more, we see that apocalyptic events are viewed proleptically in Lyons at the time of the persecution.

Second is the theme of renewed life. This repeatedly occurs in the epistle, and we find it associated with the motifs of restoration, rebirth, and resurrection. To begin with, the martyrs hope for the eschatological resurrection or bodily restoration. At one point in the narrative the Romans refuse to allow the bodies of the dead martyrs to be buried. Instead, they eventually cremate them and scatter the ashes in the Rhone. The *Letter* reports that the Romans "did this as though they could overcome God and deprive the martyrs of their restoration."[28] Here the *Letter* attests to the hope of resurrection that strengthened the martyrs' advance toward the end. But, the concept of life is not exhausted in the notion of eschatological resurrection. Quite pointedly, the *Letter* expressed the conviction that the martyrs received life from God at their death,[29] and that in the renewed faith of those who had previously borne no witness, those who had been dead in their denial were restored to life in their confession and martyrdom.[30] In other imagery within the *Letter,* the martyrs have not been victimized in their deaths but rather transported to a "bridal banquet" and "eternal fellowship with the living God."[31] For the martyrs of Gaul, the motif of renewed life, common to apocalyptic eschatology, is not purely future. Life is found in bearing witness, in martyrdom. In the Amphitheater of the Three Gauls, apocalyptic eschatology has disrupted the violent games of the Romans.

While it may, then, have been an exaggeration for Ernst Käsemann to have stated that "apocalyptic was the mother of all Christian theology," it seems appropriate to say that for the Christians of Lyons and Vienne, apocalyptic was the mother of martyrdom, of witness.[32] It brought forth the living. In the *Letter* this is made very clear in striking terms, immediately after the stories of the deaths of Maturus and Sanctus and the seemingly never-ending suffering of Blandina. These stories make repeated references to the eschatological crown, indicating that the apocalyptic event of the mediator's coming to reward the faithful had imparted courage to them. Because of these martyrs the faithless became faithful and the dead were brought to life: "The dead were restored to life through the living; the martyrs brought favour to those who bore no witness, and the virgin Mother [the Church] experienced much joy in recovering alive those whom she had cast forth stillborn."[33]

The Apocalypse of John in the *Letter*

Motifs of apocalyptic eschatology are clearly present in the *Letter,* and their important function repeatedly emerges. But apocalyptic eschatology is present in the *Letter* in a way other than by motif. John's Apocalypse also plays a role in its composition. While the *Letter*'s use of Scripture has received some attention,[34] to my knowledge no one has treated in a concentrated fashion the role of the book of Revelation within it.

The first citation from John's Apocalypse occurs in an account concerning Vettius Epagathus (*Hist. Eccl.* 5.1.9–10). He is a young man who, we are told, loved God and neighbor and walked blamelessly, and he is even compared to Zechariah, the father of John the Baptist (Luke 1:6). Vettius Epagathus, though not yet arrested himself, spoke in defense of Christians, was interrogated by the prefect, confessed his own Christianity, and, full of the same Holy Spirit who had filled Zechariah (Luke 1:67), was martyred. By fullness of love he manifested the filling of the Spirit and with pleasure laid down even his own life in defense of his fellow Christians. This, of course, calls forth the words of John in 1 John 3:16: "By this we know love, that he laid down his life for us; and we ought to lay down our lives for the brethren." Immediately following the implicitly drawn parallel between Vettius Epagathus and Jesus Christ comes the citation from Revelation 14:4 making the parallel explicit: "He was and is a true disciple of Christ, 'following the Lamb wherever he goes.'"

Those of whom John speaks in Revelation 14 are the 144,000 standing with the Lamb on Mount Zion. They are chaste, blameless, tell the truth, and have not received the number of the Beast on their foreheads (Rev 13:16–17). Instead, they have the name of the Lamb and the Father (14:1–5). Vettius Epagathus is set before the reader as the one who imitates the Lamb in his death on behalf of others and as a member of the eschatological community of the blameless, who are aligned not with the Beast but with the Lamb. That community is not merely eschatological, however. Its membership already includes the faithful of Lyons and Vienne. Mount Zion upon which the Lamb and the 144,000 stand has become, in this proleptic moment, the Croix-Rousse hill.

That the community of the Gallic martyrs is associated with the apocalyptic 144,000 is also made clear at the beginning of the *Letter,* which describes how the believers were barred from the baths, public square, and all other social places and markets (*Hist. Eccl.* 5.1.5). Revelation 13, in parallel, describes how the people of the apocalyptic times cannot trade in the marketplaces unless they have the Beast's mark (13:16–17). Furthermore, "the whole earth" follows the Beast in Revelation 13:3, while in the *Letter* (*Hist. Eccl.* 5.1.5) the Adversary who swoops down upon Lyons and Vienne prepares his own people to be poised against God's people. The Beast's abusive community is described as "the whole people," and the Christians are brought before "the entire population."[35]

Continuing to associate the Gallic martyrs with the apocalyptic community of blessing, the *Letter* contrasts the faithful with the unfaithful believers and states that the former manifested countenances of joy, majesty, and beauty, to the degree that they bore their shackles as if they were lovely ornaments fit "for a bride adorned" with golden embroidery.[36] This language is dependent on the epithalamium of Psalm 45:12–15 and the apocalyptic use to which John puts that imagery in Revelation 19:7 and 21:2, 9. The one who is "as a bride adorned" for her husband, the Lamb in John's Apocalypse, has clothed herself with the fine, bright, pure linen of righteousness. She is the New Jerusalem who descends from heaven upon the new earth with the radiance and clarity of precious jewels and crystal. Her descent marks the blessed apocalyptic presence of God with humanity that vanquishes sorrow, death, and suffering. Already in A.D. 177 this city had descended upon the earth of the Amphitheater of the Three Gauls and included within its population the martyrs whose blood stained its dust. Of Blandina, it is said, in a manner which maintains the imagery, that she rejoiced and glorified in her death as if she had been invited to a "bridal supper." An angel in Revelation 19:9 proclaims to John that those invited to "the marriage supper" of the Lamb are blessed. Blandina in her death has already been seated at the Lamb's apocalyptic nuptial feast. The martyrs of Lyons are those who know and already wear the "wedding garment" and experience blessings associated with it.[37] Though the martyrs experience inexpressible torment, they also, remarkably, experience relief from their suffering. Their association with the marriage and its feast, with its victory over suffering, brings to them anesthetic strengthening, refreshment, and even a cure (cf. *Hist. Eccl.* 5.1.19, 22, 23, 24, 28).

Toward the end of the *Letter* (*Hist. Eccl.* 5.1.57–63) another reference to the end of John's Apocalypse appears. The accusers of the Christians are described as exercising wanton violence, hatred, and cruelty against the Christians in the manner in which they treat the bodies of the martyrs after their deaths. The bodies of those who had been strangled in the prison were thrown to the dogs (Ps 79:2), while the bodies of those who had been burnt and torn apart were left unburied and guarded for six days. Eventually they were cremated and the remains cast into the Rhone. Drawing on the language of Psalm 79:3–4, some of the Romans are described as raging and gnashing their teeth at the bodies in a continuation of their vengeance. Within this context the *Letter* loosely cites Revelation 22:11: "Let the wicked be wicked still and the righteous righteous still."[38] The Gallic Christians viewed this passage as a prophecy that was fulfilled in the desecration of the bodies of their martyrs.

But there is more to the Romans' defilement of the bodies of the martyrs than this. In Revelation 11:1–13 the prophecy of the two witnesses is recorded. For 1260 days they will be given power to prophesy with great testifying powers. When they finish their testimony the apocalyptic beast who arises from the pit will kill them, "and their dead bodies will lie in the street" (11:8). For three and a half days an international procession of people will view their bodies and refuse to bury them, rejoicing and celebrating in apparent vengeance the death of the prophets who had tormented them. After three and a half days the two prophets are raised by God from the dead and are translated to heaven.

The author(s) of the *Letter* wants the reader to understand that the Gallic "martyrs" are, in a proleptic manner, the apocalyptic witnesses and martyrs prophesied in Revelation 11. They share the bodily desecration and endure together the rage, celebration, and mocking of the people. They also share the apocalyptic beast as the leader of the wickedness. The *Letter* states, prior to its account of the desecration and citation of Revelation 22:11, that the people were led forward by "the wild beast," a synonym for the adversary who appears at the beginning of the *Letter* (*Hist. Eccl.* 5.1.5); this adversary shows up again as "the Devil" and "the evil one" (*Hist. Eccl.* 5.1.6; 5.1.25, 35), and makes a final appearance at the end as the beast (*Hist. Eccl.* 5.2.6). It is with reference to the apocalyptic beast who governs the whole persecution that the multiple references to the beasts that maul the martyrs are to be understood.[39] The beasts are the tools of *the* beast.

Finally, we should make mention of the apparent discrepancy between the prophecy given to John and the Gallic persecution. While it could be argued that the martyrs of Lyons and Vienne were not raised *bodily,* and as such, this marks a decisive difference between the *Letter* and Revelation 11, it could also be argued that such a discrepancy is beside the point. The Gallic martyrs are, after all, given life, because faithful witness *is* life, while faithless denial is death. They have been crowned and seated at the feast. With such a reading, moreover, eschatological tension is heightened. The Gallic martyrs still await bodily resurrection in parallel with the two mysterious witnesses in Revelation 11. As was the case with those witnesses, who remained dead for three and half days before God breathed life into them (cf. 11:7–11), so too with the Gallic martyrs, who await consummative resurrection and restoration.

The *Letter to the Churches of Lyons and Vienne* clearly demonstrates, then, the centrality not only of apocalyptic motifs but also of the Johannine Apocalypse in the lives and deaths of the martyrs of Gaul. The perspectives and motifs in John's text undoubtedly strengthened those who underwent the tortures, as well as helping the survivors interpret what had taken place. Apocalyptic motifs and literature affect communities both prospectively as they undergo martyrdoms and retrospectively as they attempt to come to terms with them.

Christology: The Sacrificial Lamb

But what of the Christology of the *Letter* that arises out of its apocalyptic motifs and its particular dependence on the Apocalypse of John? Of course, it includes the notion of Jesus Christ as Lord in fellowship with God the Father and his Spirit (*Hist. Eccl.* 5.1.3, 34), who, to return to Farkasfalvy, "is actively present in the life of the Church and the individual Christian."[40] He is the Lord who is "both crucified and glorious, both present in history and still to come, 'a noble and victorious athlete' who continues to be involved in bloody fighting, repeated trials, and unceasing tribulations."[41] His "glorious life belongs to a realm other than this earth," but in martyrdom there is already participation in that glory.[42] Undoubtedly, Farkasfalvy's great contribution has been to orient us to "the image of Christ, present on every page of the document" from Lyons, which is the image not "of the suffering but of the glorious Christ."[43] More can be said, however.

In his magisterial study on martyrdom and persecution in the early church, W. H. C. Frend comments that behind the practice of martyrdom was a theology that proclaimed that the martyrs "were seeking by their death to attain to the closest possible imitation of Christ's passion and death. This was the heart of their attitude, Christ himself suffered in the martyr."[44] This comment is the springboard for my present discussion of the Christology of the *Letter of the Churches of Lyons and Vienne,* and in particular, its use of Revelation 14:4, where it speaks of those who follow Christ, the "Lamb." There are two such references in the *Letter*. Frend has already identified the first, where Vettius Epagathus is depicted as one who conducts himself as a disciple, a follower of Christ, the Lamb, by imitating him in death.[45] The second, not mentioned by Frend, is the imagistic depiction of Blandina as the bride of the Lamb (Rev 19:7; 21:2, 9) at the apocalyptic wedding feast of the Lamb.[46] The image of Blandina the bride evokes the image of the groom, the Lamb, just as the image of Vettius Epagathus, the follower, evokes the image of the Lord, the Lamb, who gives himself to death. The question is the significance of these references to the Lamb and his followers in the *Letter*. Do they suggest a sacrificial aspect to Christ's death?

I propose that the communities of Lyons and Vienne must have read the text in a way that understood the Lamb of the Apocalypse as a sacrificial victim. By depicting a martyr such as Vettius Epagathus as following the "Lamb," all martyrs are being depicted as sacrificial victims approaching their martyrdom. By implication, such an understanding of the followers of the Lamb as sacrificial victims also sheds light on how the "Lamb" itself was understood: its slaughter is a sacrifice. There is additional evidence for this reading of the Lamb imagery in the *Letter*. In particular, by dying for God in imitation of Christ, the martyrs of Lyons and Vienne believed their deaths were sacrificial.[47] For instance, the *Letter* (*Hist. Eccl.* 5.1.40–41) speaks of Maturus and Sanctus as those who, in the end, were "sacrificed" (θύω), and of Blandina hanging from a "tree" (ξύλον) seemingly in the form of a "cross" (σταυρός). In this scene, those witnessing her death recognized in her a sacrifice, like Christ, "who was crucified for them." This description of Blandina on the tree (which usually, unfortunately, is translated as "post") of course looks back to Deuteronomy 21:23 and reflects a Christian interpretation evident in Acts 5:30 and Galatians 3:13.[48] Both Peter and Paul apply the prophecy of the curse that comes to all who hang "on a tree" (Deut 21:23) to Christ and his crucifixion. Christ became "a curse for us," thereby accomplishing redemption. Finally, we should also note the passage (*Hist. Eccl.* 5.1.52) that describes Attalus's flesh as roasting. The odor that arises is described as that of a burning sacrifice (κνίσα).[49] Both Attalus and Alexander "were sacrificed" (θύω) at the end.[50] Blandina, the *Letter* says, was also "offered in sacrifice" (θύω).[51]

Exactly how martyrs perceived their sacrificial offering is not entirely clear. Scholarship over the last thirty years has suggested diverse emphases and taxonomies.[52] Frances M. Young, in her brief comments on Blandina, may point us in the right direction.[53] Young categorizes her death as "Martyrdom as Aversion Sacrifice," that is, the martyr shares in Christ's combat against the Adversary and his agents. This taxonomy fits well with the evidence gathered in this essay, since the community that produced the *Letter* interpreted its persecution in terms of the drama of eschatological conflict between Satan and God. Overcoming the Devil was assured in dying for God (cf. *Hist. Eccl.* 5.1.23, 27). This had been the pattern established by Christ, and the pattern was now continued by his followers, with one notable exception: in the deaths of Christ's followers we are no longer on Golgotha but on the Croix-Rousse within the eschatological battle described in John's Apocalypse.

This eschatological battle was largely about ideology: about faith against sight, virtue against evil, reality against illusion. The battle was, to be more precise, apologetic and revelatory. Several times in the *Letter,* martyrdom is presented as an argument by Christians against the worldly ideology of the persecutors and the Adversary. Martyrdom *proves* (ἐπιδείκνυμι) that temporal suffering does not compare to eschatological glory (cf. Rom 8:18; *Hist. Eccl.* 5.1.6). Vettius Epagathus gives his life in *defense* (ἀπολογέω) of his fellow Christians, who are falsely charged with atheism and impiety (*Hist. Eccl.* 5.1.9, 10). Through Blandina's witness Christ *proves* (ἐπιδείκνυμι) that those things viewed contemptuously by the Adversary's agents are actually glorious (*Hist. Eccl.* 5.1.17). The suffering of Sanctus, which is the suffering of Christ in him, *shows* (ὑποδείκνυμι) that nothing frightening or painful occurs where the Father's love and Christ's glory are present (*Hist. Eccl.* 5.1.23). Again, Blandina's sacrifice is equated to Christ *convincing* (πείθω) believers that martyrs "will have eternal fellowship with the living God" (*Hist. Eccl.* 5.1.41). In this way, then, in their suffering and their deaths they are already participating in something otherworldly, something eschatological, something beyond the bitter confines of the temporal moment under the scorching rays of the Gallic summer sun and the vile contempt of the Romans. The victorious age to come, although masked and costumed in defeat, makes a measured, uninvited appearance at the Romans' bloody feast.

Conclusion

The tortures that took place in second-century Lyons were certainly, from the perspective of the Christian communities involved, events associated with athletic competition (*Hist. Eccl.* 5.1.42) and gladiatorial combat (*Hist. Eccl.* 5.1.40), both of which were seen as anticipatory eschatological struggles against the Evil One. But in the Amphitheater of the Three Gauls we are not only seated within a stadium or around a field. We are within a temple.

The followers of the Lamb placed the passion and death of Christ at the center of their Christology and discipleship. By employing their own understanding of sacrificial suffering as imitation of Christ, we can see that for them, Christ was fundamentally the slaughtered, sacrificial lamb whose death was expiatory but also revelatory and apologetic. Christ's sacrificial offering of himself manifested surprising, shocking, and apparently irrational, unsubstantiated claims to a world deceived by the powers of darkness. Martyrdom and sacrifice brought light within that darkness.

For the martyrs of Gaul, the Apocalypse and leading apocalyptic motifs portray an existence in which the eschatological conflict has been made, in some measure, present, and which requires for victory a return to the model of warfare established in Jerusalem three generations before. This Lamb was slain in sacrifice, and it was this Lamb who appeared to John the Seer (Rev 5:6) and whom the martyrs followed (Rev 14:4). Such a portrayal of the death of the martyrs of Lyons and Vienne clearly exhibits an early Christian exegesis of the Apocalypse and an early Christology centered upon sacrifice.

Notes

I offer this essay in celebration of Brian Daley's immense contribution to patristic eschatology and Christology. In particular, I am grateful for his *Handbook of Patristic Eschatology,* which has immeasurably formed my own understanding of the early Christian hope.

1. J. Guey and A. Audin, "L' Amphithéâtre des Trois Gaules à Lyons," *Gallia* 20 (1962): 177–45; 21 (1963): 125–54; 22 (1964): 37–61; A. Audin and M. Le

Glay, "L' Amphithéâtre des trios Gaules, première campagne," *Gallia* 28 (1970): 67–89; A. Audin and M. Le Glay, "Decouvertes archéologiques récentes à Lyons, métropoles des Gaules," *Bulletin Société nationale des Antiguaires de France* (1966): 96–109; J. Guey, "Les inscriptions (et à propos des inscriptions) de l' Amphitheater," in *Les Martyrs de Lyons (177): Centre national de la recherché scientifique, Lyon, 20–23 septembre 1977,* ed. J. Rougé and R. Turcan (Paris: Éditions du CNRS, 1978), 107–9. For the critical edition of the *Letter* I have used *Eusébe de Césarée Histoire Ecclesiastique Livres V–VII,* SC 41, ed. G. Bardy (Paris: Cerf, 1955), 6–23. English translations include H. Musurillo, *The Acts of the Christian Martyrs* (Oxford: Clarendon, 1972), 62–85 (with Greek text), and *Eusebius: The History of the Church from Christ to Constantine,* trans. G. A. Williams, rev. and ed. A. Louth (London: Penguin, 1989), 139–49. All biblical quotations are from the RSV; emphases are mine.

2. For discussions of dating which range from A.D. 175 to several years after 177 (but within the reign of Marcus Aurelius), cf. T. D. Barnes, "Eusebius and the Date of the Martyrdom," in *Les Martyrs de Lyons (177),* 137–41, and P. Nautin, *Lettres et écrivains chrétiens des iie. et iiie. siècles* (Paris: Cerf, 1961), 62–63. The date of 177 appears to most scholars to be given in a straightforward manner by Eusebius in *Hist. Eccl.* 5, pref.

3. Cf. the arguments of Nautin, *Lettres et écrivains chrétiens,* 54–59; R. M. Grant, *Eusebius the Church Historian* (Oxford: Clarendon Press, 1980), 118–19; A. Rousseau, *Irénée de Lyons Contre les Hérésies Livre IV,* SC 100.1 (Paris: Cerf, 1965), 258–61; R. M. Grant, "Eusebius and the Martyrs of Gaul," in *Les Martyrs de Lyons (177),* 132; Oecumenius (PG 119.536C–D).

4. Cf. J. W. Thompson, "The Alleged Persecution of the Christians at Lyons in 177," *American Journal of Theology* 16 (1912): 358–84; P. Allard, "Une nouvelle théorie sur le martyre des chrétiens de Lyons," *Revue des Questions Historiques* 93 (1913): 53–67; J. Colin, *L'Empire des Antonius et les martyrs gaulois de 177* (Bonn: R. Habelt, 1964); idem, "Martyrs grecs de Lyons ou martyrs galates? (Eusebe, Hist. Eccl. v. 1)," *L' antiquité classique* 33 (1964): 108–15; J. Jouassard, "Aux origins de l'église de Lyons," *Revue des Études Augustiniennes* 11 (1965): 1–8; A. Audin, "Les martyrs de 177," *Cahiers d'Histoire* 11 (1966): 343–67; cf. William C. Weinrich, *Spirit and Martyrdom* (Washington, D.C.: University Press of America, 1981), 207, a.1.

5. Cf. W. H. C. Frend, *Martyrdom and Persecution in the Early Church: A Study of a Conflict from the Maccabees to Donatus* (Oxford: Blackwell, 1965), 8. Cf. the argument of J. H. Oliver and R. E. A. Palmer, "Minutes of an Act of the Roman Senate," *Hesperia* 24 (1955): 320–49, that an act of the senate in 177–78 substituted Christians as sacrificial volunteers or gladiators at the festival in Lyons. The deaths of the martyrs of Lyons and Vienne are commemorated by Jerome and Ado on 2 June.

6. Cf. Frend, *Martyrdom and Persecution,* 1–30, for a convenient summary.

7. Cf. K. Koch, "What Is Apocalyptic? An Attempt at a Preliminary Definition," in *Visionaries and Their Apocalypses,* ed. P. D. Hanson (Philadelphia: Fortress, 1983), 26.

8. Mary Hope Griffin, "Martyrdom as a Second Baptism: Issues and Expectations for the Early Christian Martyrs," Ph.D. Thesis (Los Angeles: University of California, 2002), 169.

9. Weinrich, *Spirit and Martyrdom,* 187; P. Lanaro, "Temi del martiro nell' antichita Christiana. I martiri di Lione," *Studia Patavina* 14 (1967): 206.

10. *Hist. Eccl.* 5.1.5.

11. Charles E. Hill, *Regnum Caelorum: Patterns of Future Hope in Early Christianity* (Oxford: Clarendon Press, 1992), 109–10. One need not, however, join him in the connection he makes with Rev 20:2. The sense in which the adversary is restrained in his first coming is that of a prolepsis. It is an anticipation of a future eschatological/apocalyptic event. The adversary promises through proleptic experience, but does not fulfill or consummate, his ultimate brutality.

12. G. W. H. Lampe, *A Patristic Greek Lexicon* (Oxford: Clarendon Press, 1961), s.v. "ἀδεῶς."

13. Lampe, *Lexicon,* s.v. "προοιμιάζω."

14. Irenaeus, *Haer.* 5.5.1 (SC 153, 66.28–29).

15. George W. E. Nickelsburg, *Resurrection, Immortality, and Eternal Life in Intertestamental Judaism* (Cambridge, Mass.: Harvard University Press, 1972). Here, at least, is where Frankfurter also sends us when he wishes to substantiate his claim that "[t]he extreme behavior of the Christian martyr-sects certainly reflects an ideology based in Jewish apocalyptic traditions of righteous sufferers and the heavenly favors they earned" (D. Frankfurter, "The Legacy of Jewish Apocalypses in Early Christianity: Regional Trajectories," in *The Jewish Apocalyptic Heritage in Early Christianity,* ed. J. C. Vanderkam and W. Adler [Assen/Minneapolis: Van Gorcum and Fortress, 1996], 168).

16. Nickelsburg, *Resurrection, Immortality, and Eternal Life,* 93–111.

17. Cf. Koch, "What Is Apocalyptic?" 26.

18. Nickelsburg, *Resurrection, Immortality, and Eternal Life,* 109. Emphasis added.

19. Ibid., 42.

20. Denis M. Farkasfalvy, "Christological Content and Its Biblical Basis in the Letter of the Martyrs of Gaul," *Second Century* 9 (1992): 5–25.

21. *Hist. Eccl.* 5.1.6.

22. Koch, "What Is Apocalyptic?" 28–29. Cf. Weinrich, *Spirit and Martyrdom,* for further treatment of the theme of glory in the *Letter* (188–91).

23. Farkasfalvy, "Christological Content," 21–22. Emphasis his.

24. Ibid., 10. A. Breckelmans's argument that the *Letter*'s use of Rom 8:18 presents Paul's eschatological notion of glory in a non-eschatological sense and views it instead as merely present or immediate reward, fails to account for the way in which apocalyptic eschatology operates in accounts of persecution. Cf. A. Breckelmans, *Martyrerkranz: Eine symbolgeschichtliche Untersuchung im frühchristlichen Schrifttum* (Rome: Liberia Editrice dell' Università Gregoriana, 1965), 59. Cf. also Weinrich, *Spirit and Martyrdom,* 188–89, 191.

25. *Hist. Eccl.* 5.1.36, 38, 42.

26. Cf. Koch, "What Is Apocalyptic?" 27–28.

27. *Hist. Eccl.* 5.1.42. Again, the point needs to be made that in the worldview of the *Letter,* the apocalyptic event of the Redeemer's coming to reward the faithful is already taking place in the martyr's experience in 177 in the Amphitheater of the Three Gauls. As Farkasfalvy says, "While their share seems to be death and defeat, they obtain glory and life" (Farkasfalvy, "Christological Content," 12).

28. *Hist. Eccl.* 5.1.63.

29. *Hist. Eccl.* 5.2.7.

30. *Hist. Eccl.* 5.1.45.

31. *Hist. Eccl.* 5.1.41, 55.

32. Ernst Käsemann, *New Testament Questions of Today,* trans. W. J. Montague (London: SCM Press, 1969), 102; cf. 137.

33. *Hist. Eccl.* 5.1.45.

34. Farkasfalvy, "Christological Content," has treated the biblical basis for its Christology.

35. *Hist. Eccl.* 5.1.7–8.

36. *Hist. Eccl.* 5.1.35.

37. *Hist. Eccl.* 5.1.48.

38. *Hist. Eccl.* 5.1.58.

39. E.g., *Hist. Eccl.* 5.1.38, 41, 42, 47, 50, 55, 56, 59; 2.2.

40. Farkasfalvy, "Christological Content," 23.

41. Ibid.

42. Ibid.

43. Ibid., 27.

44. Frend, *Martyrdom and Persecution,* 15.

45. *Hist. Eccl.* 5.3.10, in Frend, *Martyrdom and Persecution,* 15.

46. *Hist. Eccl.* 5.1.35.

47. Cf. E. A. Castelli, *Martyrdom and Memory: Early Christian Culture Making* (New York: Columbia University Press, 2004), 54–55.

48. Musurillo, *Acts of the Christian Martyrs,* 75; Williams and Louth, *Eusebius,* 14.

49. Musurillo, *Acts of the Christian Martyrs,* 29, and Castelli, *Martyrdom and Memory,* 54, catch the correct meaning, but Williams and Louth, *Eusebius,* 146, with "reek," miss it, as does Bardy, SC 41:20.

50. *Hist. Eccl.* 5.1.51.

51. *Hist. Eccl.* 5.1.56; cf. Musurillo, *Acts of the Christian Martyrs,* 81.

52. Cf. Robert J. Daly, *Christian Sacrifice: The Judaeo-Christian Background before Origen* (Washington, D.C.: Catholic University of America, 1978); Frances M. Young, *The Use of Sacrificial Ideas in Greek Christian Writers from the New Testament to John Chrysostom,* Patristic Monograph Series, no. 5 (Philadelphia: Philadelphia Patristic Foundation, 1979); T. Hermans, *Origène: Théologie sacrificielle du sacerdoce des chrétiens* (Paris: Beauchesne, 1996).

53. Young, *Use of Sacrificial Ideas in Greek Christian Writers,* 227–28.

2

Athanasius's Christology Today

The Life, Death, and Resurrection of Christ in *On the Incarnation*

Khaled Anatolios

In his essay "Christology Today?"[1] Karl Rahner begins with an acknowledgment that the articulation of a Christology adequate to our time must be in fundamental continuity with that of "classical Christology." The rationale for this assertion is that classical Christology is formative of the consciousness of the church, which is where God's definitive and irrevocable Word in Christ is continually actualized. It is also because "classical Christology" gives normative expression to what is most essential in the *kerygma* of the gospel, that in Christ humanity is gifted with an unsurpassable communion with God through God's own human self-expression in Jesus Christ. At the same time, Rahner believes that such faithfulness to "classical Christology" must be open to an acknowledgment of its limitations vis-à-vis our modern sensibilities. In outlining these limitations, Rahner characterizes "classical Christology" as preoccupied with "ontological" categories (such as "person" and "nature") that are located within a descending "incarnational" framework. Such an ontological Christology needs to be supplemented by a "functional" Christology that draws attention to the salvific work of Christ *pro nobis,* in his life, death and resurrection. This supplementation, articulated in "simpler statements which we find more accessible today and yet which underlie those of classical Christology,"[2] is the task of Christology today.

As is typical with Rahner, his essay strikes a carefully poised balance between a discerning fidelity to what is most essential in the tradition and a creative openness to the requirements of proclaiming the gospel in our own time. Yet, it is also typical in manifesting certain problematic features in modern "systematic" readings of the "classical christological" tradition. The heart of the problem is uncovered as soon as we pose the question: what exactly is meant here by "classical Christology"? For the most part, it seems that by this phrase Rahner is alluding to the formulae of church councils, such as Nicaea, Ephesus, and Chalcedon.[3] There are at least two significant drawbacks to this approach. The first is that the terse formulae of such councils cannot be made to bear the weight of representing in themselves wholly elaborated theological systems; they are merely attempts to provide the most basic guidelines in adjudicating debates that predate and postdate them, and these guidelines cannot be understood apart from the contextualization of such debates. Perusing conciliar formulae cannot of itself give us complete access to "classical Christology." The second drawback is that a narrow focus on conciliar formulae, especially Chalcedon, easily leads us to an anachronistic conception of the category of "Christology" itself. "Christology," read backwards from a post-Chalcedonian perspective, tends to refer to an analysis of the "composition" of the identity of Jesus Christ: one person in two natures. Thus by defining "classical Christology" with primary reference to conciliar formulae, Rahner is understandably led to the conclusion that it is a "descending" Christology of the incarnation, which favors ontological vocabulary rather than functional, soteriological, and existential categories. Yet Rahner's project of a creative fidelity to the church's tradition of christological proclamation with a view to its modern appropriation is better advanced if we ask these soteriological and existential questions precisely of "classical Christology," considered more widely than Rahner typically does.

In this essay, I make this endeavor with regard to Athanasius, a figure who is typically regarded even by patristic scholars as representative of a Christology that favors the category of "incarnation" over "death and resurrection." For the sake of brevity and a close adherence to the text, I confine myself here to the second part of Athanasius's classical double treatise, *Against the Greeks–On the Incarnation*. I begin by asking in what sense we can speak of Athanasius's "Christology," as it appears in this treatise. I then try to show how the "functional" categories of the life, death, and resurrection of Christ figure within Athanasius's christological vision.[4] Finally, I try to follow Rahner's recommendation of translating the basic insights of Athanasius's "Christology" into simple intelligible statements that have a concrete bearing on the experience of the Christian faith. The goal of such an analysis is not to claim that, after all, the "classical Christology" elaborated by Athanasius is completely sufficient for all ages and requires no modern supplementation. Rather, in agreement with Rahner's own principle that Christology requires an integration of ontological and functional categories, the goal is to discern how Athanasius attempts this integration himself. Hopefully, such discernment will provide resources for attempting this task in our own context.

Can We Speak of a "Christology" in Athanasius?

It might seem self-evident that we can speak of a "Christology" in the work of Athanasius, or in any of the classical theologians of the early church. After all, the term can be simply defined as "discourse about Christ," which is not lacking in any of these theologians. But it should give us some pause that the term is not used by Athanasius, nor is it used generally in the early church. Moreover, as noted above, we tend to construe the signification of the term in a post-Chalcedonian framework in which it refers principally to an ontological analysis of the identity of Jesus Christ as divine and human. In that sense, however, it is important to recognize that we do not find a full-fledged "Christology" in the work of Athanasius. It is true that Athanasius does make statements in this treatise that tend in that direction. He makes statements about the integral humanity and divinity of Christ, about how the humanity is "appropriated" by the divinity, and about how human and divine attributes are predicated of one and the same subject.[5] But if we look at his classical work, *Against the Greeks–On the Incarnation,* we do not find that the overarching framework is that of a "Christology" in the narrow sense of an ontological analysis of the identity of Christ.[6] Rather, the overarching framework is a narrative account of human reality in which the Christ event is the salvific climax and hermeneutical key. Insofar as it is an apologetic work, it is intended to make an intelligible defense of the Christian faith as centered on the worship of a crucified God.[7] Non-Christians mock this cornerstone of the Christian faith as irrational, *alogon*. Athanasius therefore intends to render an account of the rationale of this faith. He does this not from the perspective of a neutral standpoint of presuppositionless reason but by showing how the Christian faith, centered on the crucified *Logos,* represents a coherent and intelligible account of reality. If we speak, then, of Athanasius's "Christology" in this work, we must give it that signification which arises from the text itself, where what is primarily at stake is not an explanation or analysis of the internal composition of the person of Christ, but rather an account of how the humanization of the Word and the life, death, and resurrection of Christ *make sense* of human reality. It is a project that is very much in line with Rahner's call for an existential and functional Christology, and thus invites an appropriation in the idiom of our own times.

The Salvific Value of the Life of Christ in *On the Incarnation*

In his account of the limitations of "classical Christology," Rahner complains that it "does not sufficiently and directly make clear the connection between the incarnate Logos and his function as the mediator of salvation."[8] Rahner immediately qualifies this statement by conceding that such a connection was in fact made, albeit inadequately. This inadequacy is due to the supplanting of the concrete reality of the life and death of Jesus in favor of abstractly Platonic and speculative categories which posit a divine-human subject assuming the entirety of human "nature":

> But above all a vertical incarnational and "descent" Christology of this kind, considered in isolation, involves a limitation and a danger. For it first talks only about the adoption of a human nature which remains abstract. It does not simply begin from the very outset with the actual, specific reality of Jesus' life and death. Yet after all it is this which we experience first of all, and it is this that we grasp in faith and hope as what is saving and liberating for ourselves.[9]

On this point, Rahner's general critique of classical Christology can be reinforced by certain assessments of patristic scholars about Athanasius's Christology. His Christology and soteriology are sometimes held to involve a "physical" transaction between the Logos and human nature as a whole, considered as a Platonic "form."[10] In the context of this critique, the project of looking for resources within patristic Christology for a modern updating leads us to ask the question whether in fact the specificity of Jesus' life and death was a significant feature of Athanasius's Christology.

To begin with, what did the human life of Jesus mean for Athanasius's Christology and soteriology in *On the Incarnation*? We can start with what it did not mean. Nowhere do we find any evidence in this text for a notion of a Platonic "form" of humanity salvifically assumed by the Logos, despite the following assessment by J. N. D. Kelly: "Athanasius's language often suggests that he conceived of human nature, after the manner of Platonic realism, as a concrete idea or universal in which all individual men participate. From this point of view, when the Word assumed it and suffused it with his divinity, the divinizing force would be communicated to all mankind, and the incarnation would in effect be the redemption."[11] Such a reading would justify the double critique that Athanasius overlooks the specificity of Jesus' life as well as the soteriological value of his death. It is not a reading, however, that is supported by the text. Athanasius typically speaks of the incarnation in terms of the Word's assumption not of a human "nature" but specifically "a body," and, to be more precise, "one body, like our own."[12] A telling analogy that he employs in articulating the salvific effect of the incarnation is that of a criminal-infested city which experiences a new level of safety when the king takes up residence in its midst: "When a great king enters a large city and takes up residence in *one of the houses in it,* such a city becomes worthy of great honor and is no longer assaulted by any enemy or bandit descending upon it, but is rather deemed worthy of every attention because of the king residing in *one of its houses*. So it is with the king of all."[13] The analogy here does not seem to be based on a conception of the Word uniting himself with the totality of human nature but rather with a singular instance of human reality ("one body") which makes him accessible to relation with other human beings. Such a conception is further reinforced by Athanasius's typical manner of referring to the salvific value of our "kinship" or "similitude" to Christ's body.[14] Rather than looking to a Platonic theory of incarnation, such language is much more readily explicable with reference to its eucharistic connotations.[15] In his *Life of Antony,* as well as in his anti-Arian polemic, we have abundant indications that Athanasius considered such kinship to be not an automatic process, Platonic or otherwise, but a discipleship that involved appropriation of the "ecclesiastical" kerygma and a life of imitation of Christ.[16]

It could be argued, of course, that we still have here a "descending" Christology, in which the value of Christ's embodied life is conceived largely in terms of its union with the Word. Indeed, it must be conceded that Athanasius always conceives of Jesus Christ as the enfleshed Word, and to that extent his is always a descending Christology. But it is not thereby an abstract conception that jettisons functional categories in favor of ontological ones that do not have a bearing on Christians' concrete experiences. If we are correct in presuming the eucharistic connotations of Athanasius's use of the motif of Christ's body, we can understand his emphasis on the human bodiliness of Christ precisely as an affirmation that a significant salvific "function" of the incarnation is to provide human beings with access to direct bodily kinship with God, now mediated by the sacramental life of the church.

The functional or soteriological value of Christ's bodiliness is further explicated by Athanasius in an epistemological key, when he discusses how the embodied life of Christ provides accessible knowledge of the transcendent God. Athanasius elaborates this theme by inserting the Johannine motifs of Jesus' "works" (*erga*) and "signs" (*sēmeia*) within a reading of salvation history as the interplay between God's efforts to share knowledge of himself with humanity and humanity's frustrations of these efforts.[17] Prior to the incarnation, God had endeavored to impart knowledge of himself to humanity through humanity's being created according to the image of the Logos and through the revelation mediated by the law and the prophets.[18] But humanity still largely failed in the project of knowing God; they "did not look toward the truth" but became "irrational" and imprisoned in the merely immanent and sensible.[19] In departing from communion with God, humanity was deprived of the knowledge of God, thus perpetuating a vicious circle in which lack of the knowledge of God further detracts from communion with God. Such a chasm between God and humanity entailed a deconstruction of humanity's being "in the image" and an affront to divine glory, since the lack of humanity's knowledge of God entailed a failure to properly "honor" God.[20] Both God's glory and humanity's salvation required a divine intervention of an altogether different order than that of creation and divine instruction through the law and the prophets. This intervention is enacted in the incarnation of the Word. The salvific value of the concrete human life of Jesus Christ is that it accommodates to human sensibilities and reveals the knowledge of the Father:

> As was fitting, he wished to benefit humanity and so he came as a human being, taking to himself a body like other human beings, so that from the things below—that is, from the works of the body—those who did not wish to know him through his providence and rule over the universe, might come to know through the works of his own body the Word of God who was in the body, and through him, the Father.[21]

The Incarnation of the Word then represents God's own self-communication "from below," his pedagogical condescension in accommodating knowledge of himself to humanity's preoccupation with the sensible. In Christ, therefore, the contemplation of God is no longer a matter of simply abstracting from the sensible, as it generally is in Greek thought. The incarnation of the Word means that the contemplation of God is now anchored in the human bodily reality of Jesus of Nazareth. In this way, the concrete life of Jesus Christ has soteriological significance for Athanasius. That is why, explains Athanasius, the Word did not simply become incarnate and then die on our behalf, but spent a human lifetime accomplishing the "works" and "signs" that rendered visible the knowledge of God.[22]

So we find in *On the Incarnation* that a key functional category for articulating the salvific value of Jesus' humanly embodied life is that Jesus' bodiliness provides a humanly accessible locus for God's self-communication. It is implied that we have this tangible access to the humanity of Jesus through participation in the eucharist, whereby we become incorporated into Christ's humanity. Moreover, because of the incarnation of the Word, our knowledge of God is no longer a matter of abstracting from the immanent human milieu, but is rather anchored in contemplation and imitation of the human "works" of Jesus.

The Salvific Value of the Death of Christ

For Rahner, it is precisely the death and resurrection of Jesus that reveals him to be God's irrevocable Word who has a unique relationship to God. Jesus is revealed to be God's all-encompassing Word to humanity insofar as he is the one in whom the extreme limit of human annihilation is taken over and replaced by the extreme limit of divine affirmation: "But when the whole of our existence and history is all at once withdrawn from us and struck out by what we call death—when such an all-annihilating 'nay' is heard and this, just this and nothing else, becomes the divine 'yea'—then such a divine Word must necessarily be irrevocable and definitive."[23]

Certainly, we do not find in Athanasius the same explication of the signification of "Logos" as the enunciation of God's absolute affirmation through the reversal of Jesus' death in resurrection. Yet, we do find a stress on the revelation of Jesus as Word through his death, which effects a human victory over annihilation. Here again, we encounter a distortion of Athanasius's theological vision due to a long-standing interpretation in which he is associated with a soteriology, supposedly shared by the Greek fathers in general, that focuses on the category of "incarnation" rather than "the cross."[24] In fact, Athanasius holds that the atoning death of Jesus is the primary reason for the incarnation and the "chief point of our faith."[25] That would seem to assimilate him, in Rahner's categories, to the "Western" view, which understands "the Incarnation as the establishment of a divine-human subject who, by obediently accepting the death for which he was destined, can offer God in his holiness expiation and satisfaction for the guilt of mankind."[26] For Rahner, this Western perspective "make[s] use of the solution that adopts the categories of Germanic legalistic thinking in the theory of satisfaction."[27]

While we may safely presume that the fourth-century Alexandrian bishop was innocent of "Germanic legalistic thinking," he does use the categories of "debt" and "substitution." But rather than involving a "satisfaction" theory as such, in the Anselmian vein, we find that these categories are integrated into a vision of human death as the ultimate "deconstruction" of God's creative work, and of Christ's death as the divine reversal of this negation. Such an interpretation admittedly is enabled by Rahner's own theology of death and resurrection, but we can show that it is sufficiently anchored in the actual text of Athanasius to be allowed as a legitimate hermeneutical "fusion of horizons." The explication of Athanasius's understanding of the salvific value of Jesus' death must begin with his anthropology, which is based on a strong emphasis on the notion of creation from nothing. Human existence is conceived as a movement from nothing into being, through participation in the Word. This movement is initiated by God and sustained through the adherence of the human will to the continuing divine offer of grace. In Athanasius's account, God's original intention for human existence included the endowment of immortality. But the effect of sin was to reverse the direction of the movement of human existence, from participation in divine life to death and nothingness. In this sense, Athanasius understands the category of death not merely as signifying the end of vital bodily functions, but as inclusive generally of the breakdown of divine-human communion by which the integrity of human life is sustained: "Death became powerful and corruption took firm hold against humanity. The human race was perishing; the human being who was made rational and according to the image [of God] was being wiped out; the work created by God was being destroyed."[28]

An acknowledgment of Athanasius's double starting point of creation from nothing and sin as reversion to nothingness enables us to situate properly his understanding of Christ's salvific death. This understanding presumes a certain integration, embedded in his theological anthropology, of the categories of nature and law as applied to human death. With respect to the category of nature and from the perspective of his ontology of creation, Athanasius understands human death and the decline into nothingness as the inescapably necessary and natural consequence of humanity's volitional withdrawal from participation in divine grace. Since human existence is a movement from nothing into participation in the Word, humanity's rejection of such participation ineluctably leads it back to nothingness. At the same time, Athanasius speaks of the death-nothingness that is consequent upon sin as instituted by divine law and as incurring a debt against God which must be repaid. But in interpreting his use of these primordially biblical rather than Germanic categories, it is crucial to note how the language of law and debt is derivative of the language of grace and mercy. We find this significant ordering of these notions exemplified in *De incarnatione* 3–5. Here Athanasius speaks of creation from nothing with primary reference to the categories of divine goodness, mercy, and grace:

> God is good—or rather, he is the source of goodness. But the good is not begrudging of anything. Because he does not begrudge being to anything, he made all things from non-being through his own Word, our Lord Jesus Christ. Among all the things upon the earth, he was especially merciful toward the human race. Seeing that by the logic of its own origin it would not be capable of always remaining, he granted it a further gift. He did not create human beings merely like all the irrational animals upon the earth, but made them according to his own Image, and shared with them the power of his own Word, so that having a kind of reflection of the Word and thus becoming rational, they may be enabled to remain in blessedness and live the true life of the saints in paradise.[29]

We glean from this passage that the fundamental structure of the divine-human relation is that of gift-giving on the part of God. That creation came to be from nothing bespeaks the radicality of this gift; that humanity is made according to the Image who is the Word bespeaks the extremity of the gift, the "added grace." Athanasius speaks of the law and its accompanying threat within this framework of gift and grace. Indeed, this law is conceived precisely as an instrument for safeguarding the divine gift:

> Moreover, knowing that the human power of free will could incline both ways, and anticipating this, he made the grace given to them secure by a law and a place. For he led them into his paradise and gave them a law, so that if they guarded the grace and remained good, they would retain the life of paradise, without sorrow, pain, or trouble, along with the promise of incorruption in heaven. But if they transgressed and turned away and became evil, then they would know that they would suffer in death the corruption consistent with their nature and would no longer live in paradise but in future they would die outside it and remain in death and corruption.[30]

In light of this passage, it is justifiable to speak of the place of the "law" of death in Athanasius's conception as a divinely instituted symbol and, as it were, a compass of humanity's relation to God. That relation is radically constituted by divine gift, and the law is meant to secure this gift by manifesting to the human will the two radical options available to it: either adherence to the gift through obedience to the divine commandment, or rejection of the gift through disobedience, in which case the transgression of the law manifests humanity's decline from participation in divine life and lapse into nothingness. Situated in this conceptual framework, the "debt" incurred by radical human transgression turns out to be not so much an affront to divine honor, as in the Anselmian satisfaction theory, but a rejection of the gift of the divine loan of being and well-being.

It should be explicable by now why the notion of humanity's debt is never correlated by Athanasius with the terminology of punishment. If Christ's death is salvific, it is not by a repayment of the debt through his undergoing punishment. Rather, the primary category used by Athanasius to speak of the salvific efficacy of Christ's death is that of "offering," as that notion is employed in the Letter to the Hebrews.[31] Again evoking eucharistic overtones, Athanasius repeatedly makes the point that human death is reversed when Christ makes an "offering" or "sacrifice" of his own body.[32] If Christ's death is "in behalf of all," that is not merely a matter of his being a substitute victim of divine wrath, but rather a matter of his ability to incorporate all of us into his stance of self-offering. This understanding can be gleaned from the way that Athanasius correlates the categories of "death for all" and "offering for all":

> The death of all was fulfilled in the Lord's body, and death and corruption were obliterated because of the Word who was united with it. For death was necessary and it was needful that there be death on behalf of all in order that the debt owed by all might be repaid. Therefore, as I said before, the Word himself, inasmuch as he could not die, for he was immortal, took to himself a body which could die so that he may offer it as his own on behalf of all.[33]

In reading this passage, we must be careful to interpret the categories of "debt" and "repayment" in light of the text before us and not through the anachronistic lens of some later atonement theory. We have already seen that the "debt" is really an ontological one that is incurred when humanity declines the gift of participation in divine life, while "repayment" is here understood in terms of Christ's self-offering. Following the logic of the Letter to the Hebrews, Athanasius understands this offering on behalf of all not in terms of being a "substitute victim" but, more positively, as the opening up of a passageway into the divine realm. "Self-offering" is here understood not primarily as self-immolation but as re-entrance into communion with the divine: "For it was not the Word himself who needed the opening of the gates . . . . We were the one who needed this and he carried [*anepheren*] us up through his own body. For as he offered it to death on behalf of all, so through it he again prepared the way into heaven."[34]

We are now in a position to bring to Athanasius's understanding of Christ's death Rahner's challenge of explicating "the connection between the incarnate Logos and his function as the mediator of salvation."[35] Simply put, for Athanasius, Christ's death is a reversal of our death. Such a statement is conventionally understood as signifying the result of Christ's death (i.e., Christ's death leads to the overcoming of human death) but needs to be more radically interpreted as applying to the very form of Christ's death: Christ, as it were, changes the direction of human death by reorienting even the annihilation of death Godward. Our death is the actualization of our natural propensity to lapse into the abyss of nothingness when we decline the gift of God's life-sustaining grace. With this decline comes a "debt" that amounts to nothing less than ontological insolvency; our credit line of being and well-being goes into the red, as it were. Christ repays our debt inasmuch as the movement of our withdrawal from God is reversed by the movement of his self-offering into which we are incorporated and through which we enter again into the divine realm. In the biblical idiom, a "sacrifice" or "offering" is a gift that accompanies or symbolizes one's entrance before the Sovereign Lord.[36] Applying this notion to Athanasius's understanding of the salvific efficacy of Christ's death, we can say that through Christ's self-giving on our behalf and his extension to us of this posture of self-giving through our communion with him, our refusal of the gift of divine life is reversed to the point of our receiving this gift and responding to it with our own gift of ourselves to God through Christ. Through death, Christ enters into the extreme limit of humanity's withdrawal from God and reverses this withdrawal by making it a gift-offering to the Father.

The Salvific Value of Christ's Resurrection

For Rahner, as we have seen, grasping the significance of the resurrection of Christ is consequent upon seeing his death in its stark reality as the annihilation of Jesus' human identity and his experience of utter God-forsakeness. Jesus' resurrection is the divine reversal of this limit point of human failure. The risen Jesus is manifest as the divine Word precisely inasmuch as he embodies the victorious and unsurpassable utterance of God when the utterance of human existence has been extinguished:

> This word has been uttered in the death and resurrection of Jesus. It is definitive because after death no history continues and no new possibilities offer themselves. But it is irrevocable because in death, if it is really taken seriously, only God can offer himself unless nothingness is to engulf us. Jesus was crucified and is risen into the incomprehensible darkness of God. This means that he is *the* Word of God to us, not simply *a* word. But if in this Word-for-us God promises himself to us irrevocably, then that Word has a unique relationship to God himself.[37]

Elsewhere, Rahner explains that the encounter of the believing Christian with the risen Christ is radically structured by the transcendental hope of resurrection that is native to human subjectivity.[38] Every human subject seeks assurance of the "abiding validity" of his existence, not merely in its physical embodiment but also in its meaningfulness. From the perspective of religious experience, such assurance seeks the acceptance and affirmation of one's existence by God. The kerygma of the risen Jesus provides the possibility of such assurance inasmuch as it claims for Jesus this absolute affirmation. This kerygma raises the existentially crucial question "of whether this transcendental hope in resurrection is still simply *looking* in history to see whether it can encounter a risen one, or whether he 'already' exists and as such can be experienced in faith."[39] The affirmation of the latter claim stakes its foundation on the apostolic preaching as well as on the personal experience of the risen Christ in the Spirit, both of which are experienced as manifesting an inner correspondence "between transcendental hope in resurrection and the categorical and real presence of such a resurrection."[40]

The appeal to transcendental structures of human subjectivity is obviously not within the ken of Athanasius. Yet, with regard to his explication of Christ's resurrection, as in other aspects of his christological thinking, it will not do to reduce his Christology to a merely "vertical" Christology of incarnational descent. Indeed, it is not too far-fetched to suggest that Rahner's recourse to the dialectical correspondence between transcendental hope and categorical claims to fulfillment of this hope is substantially paralleled in Athanasius's method of correlating Christology with a theology of creation. At the beginning of *On the*

Incarnation, Athanasius signals the centrality of this strategy to his argument: "As we embark on our exposition, it is appropriate for us to begin by speaking of the creation of the universe and of God, its Creator."[41] A little later, as his theology of creation focuses on theological anthropology, Athanasius once again asserts his method: "Perhaps you are wondering why we are now dealing with the origin of humanity when we proposed to speak about the incarnation of the Word. But this is not outside the scope of our exposition."[42] Clearly, Athanasius himself is pursuing a strategy of explicating the intelligibility of the message of Christ in terms of an inner correspondence. But in place of an inner correspondence between transcendental and categorical experience, we have in *On the Incarnation* an attempt to depict an inner correspondence on the level of narrative, between the stories of creation and redemption. Yet, within this narrative mode, the reader is led to an encounter with substantially the same inner realities that Rahner hopes to expose with his transcendental perspective: that humanity is ordained to immortality and a secure participation in the life of God. In the very telling of the story of human creation in these terms, Athanasius is evoking precisely the transcendental hope of which Rahner speaks. Conversely, in Athanasius's telling, all the counterevidence in human history and experience to this reality is summed up in the category of "corruption," humanity's decline from its original participation in divine life. The faith claim of Christ's resurrection fits into this story as the reversal of that corruption: Christ brings corruption to an end by the "grace of the resurrection."[43] Through his juxtaposition of narratives of creation and redemption, Athanasius thus depicts the noncorrespondence between the human aspiration to fullness of life (participation in the divine) and the tragedies of the human condition as overcome through the resurrection of Christ.

What are the indications of this overcoming? In the essay by Rahner that is the immediate focus of our attention, this question is not broached. Elsewhere, Rahner points to the inner witness of the Spirit as the nexus between the transcendental hope of resurrection and the categorical claims of the gospel.[44] Athanasius's *On the Incarnation* largely abstracts from reflection on the work of the Spirit, though this lacuna is filled elsewhere. But in this work, there is another intriguing and challenging depiction of the reasons for hope in the resurrection of Christ, and that is the living witness of the church. This witness is depicted not so much in terms of a deliberate proclamation *ad extra* as it is in terms of the inner vitality of the members of the church and the evidence of the transformation of their lives:

> For if it is true that someone who is dead is not active but the Savior acts in so many ways every day, drawing people to piety, persuading to virtue, teaching immortality, instilling desire for heavenly things, revealing knowledge of the Father, implanting power against death, showing himself to each one . . . whom then can be said to be dead? Christ who acts in all these ways? But it does not belong to the dead to be active . . . . For the Son of God is "alive and active" and works every day, effecting the salvation of all.[45]

This argument for the plausibility of the resurrection of Christ was as daring and fragile in Athanasius's own time as it is in ours. Then as now, the community of Christ's disciples manifested not only a witness of luminous transformation but also many of the features of the human condition that Athanasius refers to as "corruption." The "Arian controversy," in which Athanasius was embroiled, gives ample evidence of this. But the essential point in Athanasius's discourse is not the indefectibility of the church, as if there were merely a simple continuity between the risen Christ and the church, but rather the witness that there are some within this community who manifest a transformation whose agency must be attributed to the living God. Since this transformation is undertaken in the name of the crucified Jesus, it is he who is the living God and divine Word. What concerns us here is not so much the apologetic efficacy or logical consistency of this argument as the combination of theological reasoning and existential application. Far from a merely Platonic and ontological Christology of descent, what we have here is the positing of a strict correlation, at least in principle, between Jesus' risen life and its concrete manifestation in the church. The realization of this correlation in fact remains the task of an existential Christology incumbent upon every disciple of the risen Christ.

Concluding Theses

Having outlined the "functional" aspects of Athanasius's understanding of the mystery of Christ in terms of his conception of the salvific meaning of Jesus' life, death, and resurrection, we are now in a position to adopt Rahner's suggestion that the principles of "classical Christology" need to be rearticulated in a contemporary idiom. The following are ten theses that recapitulate some of the fundamental features of Athanasius's classical *On the Incarnation:*

1. The heart of the Christian faith is the affirmation that the crucified and risen Jesus is unqualifiedly the Word of God and thus, God.[46]
2. The central task for the proclamation of this message in the mode of reasoned discourse (theology) is to make intelligible the plausibility of this assertion that the crucified Jesus is God: "so that from the apparent abasement of the Word your piety toward him may be enlarged and multiplied."[47]
3. The construction of the plausibility of this assertion involves accounts of an "inner correspondence" between human experience and the message of the gospel (creation and redemption). Such an account involves claims about human capacity, human incapacity, and God's affirmation of human capacity and reversal of human incapacity. This divine work is salvation.
4. The Christian account of human capacity posits the human being as *capax dei:* in Athanasius's terms, ordained to participation in divine life; in Rahnerian terms, having an obediential potency and a transcendental hope for resurrection.
5. The Christian account of human incapacity adopts a perspective of tragic realism in an unflinching awareness of the degradation of human life, whose absolute and universally inescapable limit is the annihilation of death.
6. The Christian account of the saving God claims that God takes responsibility for the flourishing of human capacity and the reversal of human incapacity because of his sovereign love and the honor of his own glory.[48]

7. Jesus is Savior inasmuch as he manifests God's saving work through the "works" and "signs" of his earthly life, through his partaking of the annihilation of human death, and through his transformation of the content of death from being a withdrawal from divine life to being a self-offering to God. The fulfillment of this reversal is the resurrection of Christ.
8. Jesus, as the unqualified and absolute Word of God, manifests his humanity in the sharing of human incapacity and his divinity in the reversal of this incapacity that is maximally symbolized in death. Both Jesus' humanity and his divinity cohere in a stance of self-offering to the Father.
9. Jesus' stance of self-offering to the Father incorporates those who believe in him into the same stance. The incorporation of the followers of Jesus into this stance is the church.
10. The experience of Jesus as the unqualified Word of God thus essentially involves a corporate (ecclesial) experience of the reversal of human incapacity, alienation, and annihilation in a stance of living unto God. Existential manifestations of this stance include a doxological ethos, moral and social regeneration, and hope in the face of death.[49]

Notes

1. Karl Rahner, "Christology Today?" in *Theological Investigations,* vol. 17 (New York: Crossroad, 1981), 24–38.

2. Ibid., 31.

3. In particular, "classical Christology," at least in this essay, seems interchangeable for Rahner with the Chalcedonian formula; cf. "Christology Today?" 26–27.

4. An exemplary instance of this approach of contextualizing patristic "Christology" within the overall framework of a theological vision is Brian E. Daley's "Divine Transcendence and Human Transformation: Gregory of Nyssa's Anti-Apollinarian Christology," in *Studia Patristica,* ed. Elizabeth A. Livingstone, vol. 32 (Peeters: Leuven, 1997), 87–95; cf. also his "A Humble Mediator: The Distinctive Elements in St. Augustine's Christology," *Word and Spirit* 9 (1987): 100–117.

5. Cf. Athanasius, *On the Incarnation* (*Inc.*) 18; *Orations against the Arians* 3.31.

For a wider treatment of this point, cf. K. Anatolios, *Athanasius,* Early Church Fathers (London: Routledge, 2004), 66–74.

6. For this reason, I believe it misguided to make much of Athanasius's failure to speak of Christ's human soul in this treatise. Focus on this issue can be explained by a doubly anachronistic projection onto Athanasius's texts: that of the problematic of Apollinarius, who denied that Christ had a human soul, and that of a later analytical christological perspective preoccupied with the ontological composition of the person of the God-Man. The latter approach dominates the highly influential presentation of the issue by Alois Grillmeier, who also gives an overview of the pertinent scholarship (*Christ in Christian Tradition,* 2nd ed., vol. 1, *From the Apostolic Age to Chalcedon (451),* trans. John Bowden [Atlanta: John Knox Press, 1975], 308–28). There are three reasons that can help explain Athanasius's neglecting to mention the human soul of Christ: first, Athanasius is more concerned with how the relation between God and creation is changed by Christ than with analyzing how Jesus' humanity and divinity fit together; second, precisely for that reason, he emphasizes the extremes united in Jesus (the Word and the body) rather than an analysis of how these extremes are mediated (e.g., by a human soul). (On these two points, cf. K. Anatolios, *Athanasius: The Coherence of His Thought* [London: Routledge, 2004], 67–78, 127–28.) And third, the doctrine of Christ's human soul had at that time been problematized because of its associations both with the teaching of Paul of Samosata, who was reported to have held that Jesus Christ was a "mere man," and with Origen's doctrine of the preexistence of souls. (Cf. R. Williams, *Arius: Heresy and Tradition,* rev. ed. [Grand Rapids: Eerdmans, 2002], 176.) Athanasius might well have thought it best to set aside these questions. An important hermeneutical principle to observe in this context is that we have to limit ourselves to the text as it stands, in which the human soul of Christ is neither affirmed nor denied. We are not entitled to fill in this gap with esoteric readings of what Athanasius really and secretly thought about what he did not write.

7. Cf. *Against the Greeks* 1; *Inc.* 1.

8. Rahner, "Christology Today?" 29.

9. Ibid., 30.

10. Cf. J. N. D. Kelly, *Early Christian Doctrines,* rev. ed. (San Francisco: Harper & Row, 1978), 378–79; Cf. Grillmeier, *Christ in Christian Tradition,* 1:308–18.

11. Kelly, *Early Christian Doctrines,* 378.

12. *Inc.* 9.

13. *Inc.* 9. Emphases mine. All translations are my own. Greek text in Athanasius, *Contra Gentes; and De Incarnatione,* ed. and trans. Robert W. Thomson, Oxford Early Christian Texts (Oxford: Clarendon Press, 1971), 154. Cited hereafter as Thomson.

14. Cf. *Inc.* 14, 20; *Orations against the Arians* 2.63, 2.74.

15. Thus, we find a similar vocabulary, in an explicitly eucharistic context, in Athanasius's contemporary, Cyril of Jerusalem, *Mystagogic Catechesis* 4.

16. Cf. *Inc.* 57; Athanasius, *Festal Letter* 4.4.

17. These two motifs are just as central to the Gospel of John as they are in *Inc.* For the use of *erga* in John, cf. John 3:19, 3:24, 4:34, 5:20, 5:36, 7:3, 9:3, 9:4, 10:25, 10:32, 10:37, 10:38, 14:10, 14:11, 17:4; for *sēmeia,* cf. John 2:11, 2:23, 3:2, 4:48, 4:54, 6:2, 6:14, 6:26, 6:30, 11:47, 20:30. For examples of the usage of these terms in *Inc.,* cf. 6, 16, 18, 31, 32, 38, 43, 48, 53.

18. *Inc.* 12.

19. *Inc.* 12, 13.

20. *Inc.* 13.

21. *Inc.* 14 (Greek text in Thomson, 168).

22. *Inc.* 16.

23. Rahner, "Christology Today?" 33.

24. For a particularly trenchant statement of this critique, cf. R. P. C. Hanson, *The Search for the Christian Doctrine of God: The Arian Controversy 318–381* (Edinburgh: T. &T. Clark, 1988), 450.

25. *Inc.* 19.

26. Rahner, "Christology Today?" 30–31.

27. Ibid., 30.

28. *Inc.* 6 (Thomson, 146).

29. *Inc.* 3 (Thomson, 140).

30. *Inc.* 3 (Thomson, 140, 142).

31. For further explication of this point, cf. Richard Clifford and Khaled Anatolios, "Christian Salvation: Biblical and Theological Perspectives," *Theological Studies* 66 (2005): 756–60; Anatolios, *Athanasius,* Early Church Fathers, 56–61.

32. E.g., *Inc.* 8, 9, 10, 16, 20, 21, 25; *Orations against the Arians* 1.41, 2.7, 2.14, 2.69; Athanasius, *To Adelphius* 6.

33. *Inc.* 20 (Thomson, 184).

34. *Inc.* 25 (Thomson, 196).

35. Rahner, "Christology Today?" 25.

36. Cf. Cifford and Anatolios, "Christian Salvation," 752–56; Gary Anderson, "Sacrifice and Sacrificial Offerings," in *Anchor Bible Dictionary,* ed. D. N. Freedman (New York: Doubleday, 1992), 5:870–86.

37. Rahner, "Christology Today?" 33.

38. Karl Rahner, *Foundations of the Christian Faith* (New York: Crossroad, 1978), 268–74.

39. Ibid., 269.

40. Ibid., 275.

41. *Inc.* 1 (Thomson, 136).
42. *Inc.* 4 (Thomson, 142).
43. *Inc.* 9.
44. Rahner, *Foundations,* 275.
45. *Inc.* 31 (Thomson, 208, 210).
46. *Inc.* 1.
47. *Inc.* 1.
48. *Inc.* 6.
49. *Inc.* 57. The format of this essay is indebted to the pedagogy of Brian E. Daley, S.J., who typically concludes his courses on early Christian theology by offering summarizing thesis statements that compare patristic theology with modern thought.

3

Expectatio Beatitudinis

The Eschatological Frame of Hilary of Poitiers' *Tractatus super Psalmos*

Michael C. McCarthy, S.J.

Eschatology as an Index of Scripture

Recent scholarship on patristic commentaries of the Psalms emphasizes the close correspondence between the exegetical method and the theological vision of the author. Karen Jo Torjesen, for instance, notes that Origen regarded exegesis as Christian *paideia*.[1] For this ancient Alexandrian, the interpretation of a psalm renders Christ present by transposing the reader into the world of the psalm, so that, from repentance through divinization, "the experiences of the Psalmist become [the reader's own] experiences."[2] To a person thus placed imaginatively and affectively *within* the Word of God, Christ the Word addresses himself. A similar dynamic prevails in the thinking of many fourth- and fifth-century commentators on the Psalms. Because of the regular use of Psalms in Christian worship, their centrality in ascetical practices, and their general accessibility as prayers to be memorized, recited, or sung, exegetes viewed the Psalter as uniquely situated among books of the Bible. Ancient Christians could appropriate verses so easily into their own lives. Augustine's early-fifth-century exhortation to his own congregation exemplifies an attitude we find in many writers, who emphasize that reciting the Psalms with understanding constitutes an actual participation in the Word: "If the Psalm is praying, pray yourselves; if it is groaning, you groan too; if it is happy, rejoice; if it is crying out in hope, you hope as well; if it expresses fear, be afraid. Everything written here is like a mirror held up to us."[3]

The perceived ease, therefore, with which early Christians might link a psalm's verses to their own experience makes early exegesis of the Psalms an interesting case study for investigating how patristic commentators understood Scripture in a theological sense: how, that is, they conceived Scripture operating as the Word of God at a particular moment in the history of the church or in the life of an individual Christian. In his frequently quoted *Letter to Marcellinus,* for instance, Athanasius observes that a person reads the words of the Psalms immediately "as one's own words" and that they possess a therapeutic quality for every psychic malady.[4] As medicine, the Psalms recreate the interior image of God within a person in a manner that corresponds to the salvation effected by the Word's becoming flesh.[5] When commenting on the Psalter, therefore, the exegete places himself within that process of redemption. Thus Brian Daley notes that, for the early church, to expound upon the Psalms was not simply to explain Scripture as an exterior phenomenon. Rather, "it was to draw the mind of the believer more deeply into the process by which the Word of God, working in the deep recesses of the human heart and mind, continues to restore the harmony and health of creation."[6]

To speak of the restoration of creation, however, particularly in late ancient Christianity, implies the expectancy of an eschatological consummation. Here I will argue that such anticipation of final things constitutes a crucial index of how exegetes treated the Psalms as Scripture. If an interpreter intends to transpose the reader into the world of a psalm, wherein Christ, the Word, speaks, then the horizons of such a world will fix the boundaries of its meaning. For patristic writers, the Psalms did not simply provide locutions for healing present maladies but offered a future orientation.[7] Although early Christian commentators regarded the Psalms as prophecy whose fulfillment lies in the person of Christ, not everything in Scripture had yet been completely fulfilled. Expositors of the Psalms remained deeply conscious that history had not come to a close and that the full scope of Scripture's promise extended to some point in the future. The return of Christ, judgment, the final transformation, and the handing over of the kingdom to the Father form the outermost frame of the narrative wherein patristic writers interpreted the Psalms. Whereas a modern exegete, for instance, would explain the rather odd translation of Psalm 127:2 ("You will eat the labors of your fruits [*Labores fructuum tuorum manducabis*]") by suggesting a textual emendation, Hilary of Poitiers explains the verse by placing it against the horizon of eternity. While on earth, he says, you must do good works of mercy, patience, and chastity to nourish your soul. "The fruit of these labors is in eternity, but here the labor of eternal fruits must first be eaten."[8]

Such an eschatological framework so deeply informs Hilary's theology that it largely determines his exegesis. His *Tractatus super Psalmos,* most likely written in the final years of his own life (ca. 365) and representing "the fruits of a grand doctrinal effort,"[9] dwells on the beatitude to be gained by reflecting on the Psalms. Yet Hilary tends to defer the realization of blessedness to the future life. If the *beatus uir* of Psalm 1 is the person who strives to be conformed to Christ, such conformation is necessarily incomplete. "The fact that he has not walked in the counsel of the wicked," says Hilary, "nor stood in the way of sinners nor sat in the seat of pestilence does not yet [*nondum*] consummate the blessedness of the man."[10] This eschatological consummation obtains only when he has arrived among the saints, who have put off the corruption of flesh and blood. In Hilary's final words on Psalm 150, he refers to the proper end of human beings as the eternal praise of God. "They have been reformed into the image of their creator," he says, "because they have begun to be conformed to the glory of God's body, because they are filled with every fulness of God."[11]

Hilary's strong sense of futurity grounds both his conception of the Psalter as a whole and his reading of individual psalms. If the Psalter is God's Word having become our Word, then the particular eschatological framework within which one interprets the Psalms will have a unique efficacy in the lives of those who try to make those verses their own. Many ancient commentators, for instance, showed deep interest in the order or sequencing of the Psalms as itself significant, as itself reflecting the gradual restoration and ultimate reformation of creation. A decade after Hilary, Gregory of Nyssa notes that there is a "natural and necessary order which progressively achieves that which is pursued."[12] As a sculptor does not begin a work "at once with the end," so the Word hews us and carves us methodically and orderly so as to arrive at the end of forming the divine likeness in us.[13] Gregory's interest in the order and aim of a work may reflect ancient grammatical concerns, but it also foreshadows the insights of literary theorists on the dynamics of narrative. For such theorists, logical relations among elements of a narrative give meaning to the whole, and it is usually within a temporal sequence of events that one seeks understanding. As Paul Ricoeur notes: "time becomes human time to the extent that it is organized after the manner of a narrative; narrative, in turn, is meaningful to the extent that it portrays the features of temporal experience."[14]

When a Christian author such as Hilary, then, takes a non-narrative genre such as the Psalms and places them against the larger Christian narrative pointing toward the final transformation of the world, he situates the reader of the Psalms within a sequencing pattern that has not yet achieved closure. Only such closure, however, will give the Psalms their full meaning. From the very beginning of his *Tractatus super Psalmos,* Hilary explicitly sets the Psalter within an eschatological horizon that is crucial to his understanding of what Scripture is and does.

Hilary's *Instructio Psalmorum*

Before he starts to comment on individual psalms, Hilary provides a general commentary on the Psalter as a whole. He begins this *Instructio Psalmorum* by arguing that the Psalms form a unity as a book. Although other writers want to divide the Psalms into five books or treat them simply as discrete, individual "Psalms of David," Hilary follows Origen in finding authority in Peter's reference in the Acts of the Apostles to a single book of Psalms (Acts 1:20).[15] Therefore "it is more rightly called a 'book of Psalms,'" says Hilary, "with different prophesies of different people and authors and times gathered into one volume."[16] Yet the principle of this unity among the Psalms remains its inspiration by the Holy Spirit, who intends the understanding of the total Christian narrative: "Without doubt what is said in the Psalms must be understood according to the proclamation of the Gospel, so that in whatever *persona* the spirit of prophecy speaks, it refers as a whole to the understanding of the glory and power of the coming of our Lord Jesus Christ, his incarnation, his passion, his kingdom, and our resurrection."[17] The Psalter's classification as a single book, therefore, depends on its future orientation and sense of narrative progression from Christ's coming to Christ's glory and our final resurrection. Such progression is essential to understanding what Hilary calls the whole weaving of types and allegories in the Psalms. "Through all of them," he asserts, "are spread out the mysteries of the only-begotten Son of God being born in the flesh and suffering and dying and rising and ruling into eternity with those believers together glorified with him and judging the rest."[18] The same expectation of Christ's future rule and of the glorification of believers with him appears throughout the *Tractatus super Psalmos* as a key to Hilary's interpretation.

Like so many patristic commentators on the Psalter, Hilary notes that the psalms are ordered, not in historical sequence, but so that the virtue and mystery of the number may perfect each psalm in their mutual arrangement.[19] So, for instance, while historically David's penitential prayer in Psalm 50 comes after the episode related in the inscription to Psalm 51, referring to Doeg the Edomite, the actual order in the Psalter places the psalm about the remission of sins before the psalm which shows the punishment that will ensue if one does not seek remission. By Psalm 51, "both the time and the number of penance had been lost," says Hilary, for the number fifty, as a "sabbath of sabbaths" or the number of the jubilee year, corresponds to the remission of sins.[20] Roughly a decade after Hilary's work, Gregory of Nyssa repeats virtually the same point when he notes that the "spiritual Word [*logos pneumatikos*]" in Psalm 50, not being concerned about chronological order, contains the "antidote given for the destruction of the adversary . . . the antidote of repentance."[21] The similarity in explanation may well derive from a common dependence on Origen.

Although Hilary does not include in his introduction a thorough discussion of sequence among individual psalms, he does divide the book into three parts whose trajectory clearly represents a progression of stages to an eschatological consummation. "The book," he says, "is contained in three groups of fifty Psalms; and this is so in relation and proportion to that expectation of our blessedness."[22] Such reference to relation and proportion (*ex ratione ac numero*) may faintly echo the harmonic theory we find more explicitly in Athanasius.[23] What is most striking in this passage, however, is how the theme of eschatological fulfillment dominates Hilary's conception of the Psalter as a whole:

> For whoever pays close attention to the consummation of the first fifty and then the second fifty and again the third fifty, in which is the end of the book, will understand that the providence of Psalms arranged in this order matches the dispensation of our salvation. For since the first step to salvation consists in being reborn into a new man after the remission of sins, and the step after the confession of one's repentance consists in serving the Lord's kingdom until the time of that holy city and heavenly Jerusalem, and after that, with celestial glory having been consummated in us, we proceed through the kingdom of the Son into the kingdom of God the Father, in which the whole universe of spirits will proclaim the praises owed to God, we will easily understand that the mystery of this arrangement in fifty is contained in the individual virtues of the Psalms collected under the number fifty.[24]

Each psalm, then, somehow moves us from repentance to the expectation of eschatological fulfillment. At the very end of the *Tractatus* Hilary repeats this division in his brief commentary on Psalm 150, where he notes that psalms reflect the step-by-step approach into communion with God (*gradatim per hoc ad dei consortium ueniretur*), moving through baptism, resurrection, and final transformation of one's nature, where one may enjoy the consummation of glory.[25]

The prevalence of this eschatological vision is even more pronounced in Hilary's discussion of the ogdoad as a kind of organizing principle of the Psalter. Like Origen and many other patristic exegetes, the number eight signifies both the final transformation of creation as well as the practice of Christian worship on the "Eighth Day" of the week, whereon they celebrated the resurrection as the first day of their new creation.[26] Most interpreters of Psalm 6, for instance, with its inscription "for the eighth," find in it various kinds of eschatological significance.[27] In the *Instructio Psalmorum,* however, Hilary has a far more extensive discussion of how the Psalter itself, not just the sixth psalm, comports with the ogdoad. After giving the usual explanation of the ogdoad as that day when, according to the fulness of the Gospel (*secundum euangelicam plenitudinem*), Christians would celebrate in complete beatitude the fulfillment of time, he turns to the three psalms that bear the inscription "for the presses":

> It is worthwhile to reflect upon this virtue of the ogdoad, perfect with heavenly mysteries, placed eighth in number, to which the title "for the presses" has been added, that is, vessels prepared for new fruit and made new for containing the heat of seething juice. That number has been fixed in accordance with the evangelical ogdoad, for collecting the fruits of the Gospel, when these corruptible vessels of our bodies have been reformed. The text and language of this Psalm bears witness.[28]

The very pattern of the Psalter underscores the anticipation of final consummation in the Trinity: "For the eighth and eightieth and eighty-third Psalms have this title ['for the presses'], so that in perfect numbers the order of this perfect beatitude may be present to the extent that the mystery of the triad, which we call Trinity, may complete the simple ogdoad and the decade of the ogdoad."[29]

Hilary sees in the lengthy Psalm 118 the perfection of the ogdoad, both in meaning and form, since it comprises twenty-two sets of eight verses, one for each letter of the Hebrew alphabet. Thus Hilary argues that Psalm 118 brings to completion the perfect man according to the teaching of the Gospel (*Psalmus iste perfectum uirum secundum doctri-*

nam euangelicam consummat).[30] Immediately after Psalm 118, however, follow the fifteen psalms of ascent (Pss 119–34), a grouping that itself reflects the progression from the earthly to eternal life, because it comprises the sum of the numbers seven and eight. "For through the observance of the law, which is established in the hebdomad, and the accomplishment of the Gospel, which is perfected both in our present religion and in the hoped-for expectation of the ogdoad, one ascends in the song of the steps to heavenly and eternal things."[31] By attending to this song of fifteen steps, Hilary notes, the number of the hebdomad and the ogdoad together, one will be placed among the perfect, the blessed, and the holy of holies.

At several points in his introductory instruction on the Psalms, Hilary indicates that the purpose of the Psalter is to lead a soul finally to this state of blessedness. In his discussion of the inscription "unto the end," such a concern is particularly obvious. In a passage that bears rather close literary parallels to Origen, Hilary writes:

> The end is that on account of which other things exist; the end itself, however, existing on account of nothing else, provides its own cause. For all things exist on account of an end; nothing else exists beyond that end. For things tend toward an end but they reach their destination in an end. So the end is both the completion of what comes before it and is itself the proper possession of itself, since it puts forth from itself nothing for the sake of something else. Therefore the Psalms that are inscribed "unto the end" must be understood as consisting of perfect and absolute doctrines of eternal goods, as well as of hopes, because the course of our faith extends itself to those things taught in these doctrines, and in these, with no further advance, in the same end of beatitude hoped for and attained, it finds rest.[32]

As for many patristic commentators, the title "to the end" reflects the summary of all Christian teaching. Half a century later, Augustine repeats in many of his sermons that the title "unto the end" refers to Christ as the end of the law, not in the sense of finishing it off but of bringing it to perfection.[33] Hilary's own explanation of the end, however, bears greater resemblance to Origen's understanding of the aim (*skopos*) or end (*telos*) of Scripture as the "connection that exists among spiritual events, those that have already happened and those that are yet to come to pass."[34] Gregory of Nyssa appropriates this idea in his own treatment of the Psalms. Gregory identifies the end or aim of the Psalter with the end of the virtuous life, which is beatitude.[35] He thus explains the inscription "unto the end" as the prophet's showing us the final rewards of our labors in the virtuous life, "so that, by looking to the 'end,' you might entrust yourself to 'the one who gives victory' and procure the announcement 'of victory' for yourself."[36]

That Hilary in his general instruction consistently places the Psalms within the horizon of final things confirms the importance of his theological vision to his practice of exegesis. But the clear eschatological frame also stresses what literary theorists tell us about the importance of closure for the coherence of any narrative. Expectations built into a narrative must be satisfied by the end.[37]

In his series of lectures entitled *The Sense of an Ending,* Frank Kermode notes that people in the middle of events "make considerable imaginative investments in coherent patterns which, by the provision of an end, make possible a satisfying consonance with the origins and with the middle."[38] Throughout his commentary on the Psalms, Hilary locates this coherence in the progressive divinization of humanity through the person of Christ. But the "end" for Hilary is always at some point hereafter. Such divinization is only complete when all things are conformed to Christ's glorified body and brought into eternal communion in the kingdom of the Father. The expectation of blessedness finds satisfaction only with that ultimate closure.

Tractates on Psalms 1 and 2

Although Hilary agrees with other Christian exegetes that the whole of the Book of Psalms must refer to Christ, he differs from those who say that the "happy man" of Psalm 1 must describe Christ.[39] The opening words of the Psalter, "Happy is the man who . . . ," suggest the process of growth into blessedness, which cannot be predicated of Eternal Wisdom itself, existing before the ages. Here Hilary draws an important contrast between God's constant existence and creation's formation into the fulness of existence. "That which will be through the expectation of some future time, cannot be seen either as having been nor as being already in the nature of things."[40] Accordingly, Hilary argues that the blessed man of the first psalm is one who understands his own life in terms of cultivating a future perfection. We must interpret the whole psalm as referring to one who "strives to conform himself to that body which the Lord assumed and in which He was born as a human man, with eagerness for justice and perfect fulfillment of all righteousness."[41] The whole Psalter, it seems, is composed precisely to help weak people hope for a final beatitude by indicating the whole scope of salvation. In a brief passage that suggests Hilary's understanding of the Psalms' purpose, he writes:

> The Holy Spirit takes up this most beautiful and worthy beginning of the Psalms, so as to stir up human weakness through hope of beatitude to the pursuit of blameless piety, to teach him the mystery of God Incarnate [*sacramentum dei corporati*], to promise participation in heavenly glory, to announce the penalty of judgement, to show the two kinds of resurrection, to show the providence of God in just rewards.[42]

Hilary also notes that the prophecy of the Psalms is set forth in "perfect and complete design [*perfecta consummataque ratione*]" so that the reader will cultivate the hope of the blessed man in eschatological fulfillment.[43] On the verse "his will is in the Law of the Lord, and on the law shall he meditate day and night," Hilary stresses that such constant meditation forms the will for the attainment of perfect happiness, wherein one is conformed to God.[44] Although Hilary's language throughout the tractates hints at an Eastern model of salvation as divinization,[45] prior to the fulfillment of time, one advances only in the "expectation of blessedness." Thus Hilary interprets the verse "He shall be like a tree planted beside flows of water, which shall yield fruit in due season and whose leaf shall never fade." The tree itself is the Tree of Life, to which the blessed man will be assimilated. The due season of yielding fruit comes after a delay in time (*mora temporis*). "For the dispensation of giving fruit," he says, "waits upon the fulness of time."[46] And what is the fruit?

The transformation of our vile body (as Philippians says) into conformity with his own glorious body in the resurrection:

> Therefore, Christ will give us his fruits, which he has perfected in that one he has assumed to himself and who is signified in that tree, the one he has transfused into the nature of his own immortality, with his mortality having been absorbed. Thus will the blessed man be as this tree, when he himself shall stand conformed to his Lord in the glory of God.[47]

So too Hilary reads the verse "whatever he does shall prosper." By virtue of Christ's passion, he avers, "whatever happens in us is eternal and eternal with an awareness of beatitude [*aeternum cum beatitudinis sensu*], since we will ourselves be like the tree of life . . . for incorruption will swallow corruption, eternity infirmity, and the form of God the form of this earthly flesh."[48]

Hilary's exegesis of Psalm 2 relates the blessed man's eternal beatitude even more directly to its christological context. Because the Acts of the Apostles quotes this psalm, Hilary, like many other Christian exegetes, claims clear apostolic authority for relating it to the person of Christ, especially verses 6–7: "I have been established by him as king over Mount Zion, announcing his decree. The Lord said, 'You are my Son, today I have begotten you.'" Although Hilary notes that the day of begetting must be an eternal day before all time,[49] he also declares that the Son's establishment as king over Zion refers to an eschatological reality made possible only by the temporal dispensation of the incarnation, resurrection, and bodily glorification: "Because he was Son of God before and then also Son of man, that which in time is the son of man through the power of the resurrection gives birth to the perfect Son of God, that is, to regain and bestow to the body the glory of the Son's own eternity, which glory he, in bodily form, claimed from the Father."[50]

Accordingly, Hilary reads the following verses of Psalm 2 in terms of the final consummation and the transformation effected in the firstborn from the dead. "Ask of me," says the psalm, "and I will give you the nations as your heritage, and the ends of the earth for your possession. You will rule them with an iron rod and dash them as a vessel of clay" (vv. 8–9). Throughout this section of his commentary, Hilary's chief concern is to show how Christ's inheritance lies in giving eternal life to all flesh.[51] Although many regard these verses as contrary to the goodness of God, Hilary emphasizes that Christ's rule is pastoral, not tyrannical,[52] and that the dashing of clay vessels refers to the transformation of our characters through repentance and ultimately our bodies in the general resurrection. Quoting the prophet Jeremiah, who speaks of God treating Israel as a potter treats his clay (Jer 18:1ff.), Hilary notes that God dashes and wears away in order to reform us, so that "after our vices, we might live again in virtue."[53] But the breaking up of clay vessels must also refer to the refashioning of our bodies into vessels of glory:

> That is understood to be signified which, according to the will of God, is the future restoration of risen bodies. For since it pleases God and is worthy in his sight, he will repair what is broken, not from some other thing but from the same old material of its origin, imparting upon them the form of beauty pleasing to him, so that the resurrection of corruptible bodies into the glory of incorruption will not annihilate its nature by dissolution but will change in the condition of its quality . . . . Therefore, change occurs, an abolition is not applied . . . . So let us rejoice, either now or then, to be broken like vessels of clay.[54]

Thus Hilary urges the reader of the Psalms to focus on the eschatological goal of transformation made possible by virtue of the incarnation and resurrection. The note of salvation as a kind of divinization is very clear. Because the Son of God has become what we are, says Hilary, and taken hold of what we are, let us take a hold of him, so that we may attain the nature of God, with God first attaining the nature of humans.[55]

The Eschatological Scope of Divinization in *Tractatus super Psalmos*

At least since Emile Mersch's work on the "Mystical Body of Christ," Hilary's understanding of redemption has been classified as sharing a great deal in common with a more Eastern, "physical" model of redemption, which emphasizes less the atoning death of Christ than the change effected in humanity by virtue of the incarnation.[56] Hilary, the "Athanasius of the West,"[57] is cited as the first theologian in the Western world to suggest an eschatology of "divinization."[58] Christ's assumption of human nature begins a process wherein humanity comes to be transformed and finally shares in God's immortality, namely, so that a human being "may become God."[59] Thus, in his commentary on Psalm 91, Hilary notes that we are reconciled in the body of Christ's flesh: "therefore, through our joining with the flesh that he assumed, we are in Christ." In Christ we are "coheirs and concorporate and coparticipants in his promise [*coheredes et concorporales et conparticipes pollicitationis eius*]. Through its joining with his flesh, the whole universe is in Christ."[60] Christ's bodily transformation into glory inaugurates the possibility of our own bodily transformation into glory. So, "by establishing us in his body, he renovates us into new life and transforms us into a new person."[61] Hilary's contentions follow quite closely the famous Athanasian dictum that "the Word became human so that we may become divine."[62]

In places throughout the *Tractatus super Psalmos* Hilary almost suggests that in the incarnation, the Word itself assumed a universal rather than an individual human nature. If that were the case, then divinization would appear to result simply from the juxtaposition of humanity and divinity in Christ. In his commentary on Psalm 51, for instance, Hilary states that the Son of God born from a woman "assumed in himself the nature of all flesh [*naturam in se uniuersae carnis adsumpsit*]"[63] and that, when the Word became flesh and dwelt among us, "he surely assumed in himself the nature of the human race [*scilicet in se totius humani generis adsumens*]."[64] In his own fine work on divinization according to Hilary, Philip T. Wild expresses certain embarrassment not only at the suggestion that the Word of God may be incarnate in all human persons but also that the transformation of humanity into God is automatically effected by the incarnation.[65] Thus, he distances himself from Mersch's claim that Hilary's "physical theory" of redemption can be separated from his eschatological views.[66] According to Mersch, Hilary understands our incorporation into Christ to be just as real in this life as in the life to come.[67] By contrast, Wild argues that by "universal human nature" Hilary means the weaknesses associated with human nature: the Word, that is, did not take on a nature unlike ours, but assumed the infirmities associated with the human flesh without himself becoming infirm.[68] The human nature that the Word assumes becomes fully divinized with the resurrection of Christ, and those conformed to Christ too shall be divinized at their own resurrection. Such divinization, however, is not guaranteed to all men and women. In a commentary on Christ's statement that "I am the vine: you are the branches," Hilary remarks that by taking on human nature, the vine contains in himself all branches, but a branch that does not bear fruit will be trimmed.[69] So, if humanity is changed on account of the incarnation, only faith in the vine will yield divinization of an individual.

Hilary reveals his sense of the eschatological scope of divinization, as well as its connection with Christ's own resurrection, in his commentary on Psalm 141:8 ("The just shall await me, until you give me my reward"). Prior to the resurrection of the Lord, the faith of the apostles wavers, but after his death and resurrection such fear ceases and they are secure. So, then, do the just wait until Christ is ultimately given his reward by God. And what is that? Exaltation in the glory of God the Father:

> This retribution is given to him by God, so that the eternity of his Father's glory will be given to his body, which he assumed. The same is the expectation, however, of the just, as the apostle teaches when he says: "Our way of life is in heaven, whence we also expect our savior Jesus Christ, who will transform the body of our humility conformed to the body of his glory" (Phil. 3:20). Therefore the just look forward until it will be given to him: that is, that they become conformed to the glory of his own body, which is blessed forever and ever, Amen.[70]

Before their own resurrection believers may be "with Christ" in heaven, but they await the transformation of their own bodies to become glorified.[71] While that will happen in the future, the condition that makes possible such transformation is our sharing in the conjunction with the flesh that Christ assumed.[72]

The tension between our being with Christ and our waiting for our final transformation finds expression toward the end of the tractates, where Hilary draws the distinction between Jerusalem and Zion. On Psalm 147:1 ("Praise the Lord, Jerusalem. Praise your God, O Zion") Hilary argues that, while Jerusalem does not differ from Zion, the former is the actual city of peace, the congregation of the saints conformed to the glory of God. Zion, on the other hand, refers to those who look forward in expectation of that eschatological reality.[73] "Sion means 'watching for [*speculatio*]'. Thus, in this body of the Lord, in which he rose from the dead, in which he sits at the right hand of power, in which is the glory of God the Father, we watch for our hope and our life."[74] The first verse of Psalm 14 represents a crucial text indicating Hilary's understanding of the church as the body of Christ on earth: "Lord, who will inhabit your tabernacle, or who will rest on your holy mountain?" Hilary notes that this body is nothing besides the body the Word takes from us, but it is also the church: *ecclesia corpus est Christi*.[75] Zion is the church, either the one that exists now or the company of saints to come, "which is full of the throng of those glorified through the resurrection and the joyful angels."[76] As we can see, although Hilary does not draw a vast distinction between the earthly church and the heavenly church, the *ecclesia sanctorum* is that which will be frequented through the resurrection of those who are conglorified with Christ. Wild highlights the "eschatological turn of mind" in Hilary's ecclesiology: "he sees everything about man's elevation as one, as consummated in heaven, and hence he glosses over the earthly aspects of our divinization."[77]

If Hilary's understanding of divinization takes an "eschatological turn," however, his exegesis presumes that Scripture's very purpose is to reform the image and likeness of God in which a person has been created, so as to attain that final consummation. Toward the beginning of his long commentary on Psalm 118, Hilary says that the psalmist forms us to be pleasing to God by giving us an education.[78] In explaining Psalm 118:73 ("Your hands have made me and prepared me: give me understanding and I will learn your mandates") Hilary notes that the prophet understands the special honor of his original condition and wants to express this dignity with these words.[79] He goes on to explain the following verses, "Your word will remain into eternity, O Lord," by asserting that the prophet, "while initiating us into the observance of a pure life, lifts up the humility of our nature to the understanding of divine and invisible sacraments."[80] Although the Word abides forever in eternity, it is with us, says Hilary, when we are sober and in peace and temperate and merciful: when we are so disposed, the Word of God abides in us, and the old man is replaced by the new. It is those "who having died and been buried with Christ, have risen into the newness of life and are placed with him in heaven. In these the Word of God remains, as if in heaven."[81] To meditate on verses such as Psalm 118:96 ("I have seen the end of every consummation") is to find oneself within the narrative sweep that the psalmist sees with great clarity: "For he sees, the consummation of the resurrection . . . he recognizes the day of the kingdom of our Lord Jesus Christ, by whom we will be carried into the kingdom of God the Father and be transferred into those inscrutable and unsearchable judgements of God."[82]

Conclusion

In his handbook of patristic eschatology, Brian Daley has argued that Christian faith "in the resolution of the unresolved" takes a wide range of articulations, depending on the context and particular mind of a believer.[83] Not only does a thinker's eschatology express, in future terms, the underlying assumptions of his or her thought, but it represents the logical conclusion of a doctrine of creation and Christology.[84] If Christ is conceived not simply as the incarnate Word but as the revelation of "what was from the beginning" (1 John 1:1) God's plan for the world, then one will find in a thinker's meditation on Christ a future trajectory for the world. As we have seen, in the case of Hilary of Poitiers, Christ's taking flesh is not itself salvation but makes salvation possible. The transformation of his body in glory will yield the transformation of those conformed to that body, not at the present moment, but when God becomes all in all. Hilary clearly betrays an understanding of redemption as divinization rooted in the incarnation of the Word,[85] but he always situates such redemption within a future-oriented eschatological horizon.

Eschatology, however, is not only implicit in a theology of creation and Christology: it also functions as the frame wherein patristic exegesis is carried out. The "meaning" of the Bible, that is, only becomes clear in light of final things. Even the Psalms, which patristic exegetes had seen as fulfilled in the life of Christ, fit within a broader Christian narrative, which looks forward in expectation of final beatitude. In an essay in which Brian Daley argues for the continued utility of patristic exegesis, he notes that the early church saw the Bible as a unified work suggesting a large narrative, whose mysteries always remain to be discerned.[86] Like the *beatus uir* of Psalm 1, the good exegete of the Psalms, in Hilary's mind, is the one who remains humble, reverent, and studious before such mysteries while day and night he hopes, in Christ, to be transformed finally into the perfect image of God. Those who have known, worked with, lived with Brian Daley are grateful for such a *beatus uir* in our own times.

Notes

1. Karen Jo Torjesen, "Origen's Interpretation of the Psalms," in *Studia Patristica,* vol. 17, pt. 2, ed. E. A. Livingstone (Elmsford, N.Y.: Pergamon Press, 1982), 957.

2. Ibid. Also cf. Karen Jo Torjesen, *Hermeneutical Procedure and Theological Method in Origen's Exegesis* (Berlin/New York: Walter de Gruyter, 1986).

3. Augustine, *Enarrationes in Psalmos* 30(2) s. 3.1 (CCSL 38.213). Trans. Maria Boulding in *Expositions of the Psalms* (New York: New City Press, 2000–2004), 1.347.

4. Athanasius, *Epistula ad Marcellinum* 10–11 (PG 29.19–22).

5. For a discussion on the correspondence between the exterior and interior aspects of grace, with respect to Athanasius's understanding of Christ's work in the Psalms, cf. Khaled Anatolios, *Athanasius: The Coherence of His Thought* (London: Routledge, 1998), 195–202.

6. Brian E. Daley, S.J., "Training for 'the Good Ascent': Gregory of Nyssa's Homily on the Sixth Psalm," in *In Dominico Eloquio, In Lordly Eloquence: Essays on Patristic Exegesis in Honor of Robert Louis Wilken,* ed. Paul Blowers et al. (Grand Rapids: Eerdmans, 2002), 189.

7. For a study of the Psalter as a "training-ground" of the affections, cf. Günter Bader, *Psalterium Affectuum Palaestra* (Tübingen: J. C. B. Mohr, 1996).

8. Hilary of Poitiers, *Tractatus super Psalmos* 127.6 (CSEL 22.631–32): "horum laborum fructus in aeternitate est: sed labor hic aeternorum fructuum ante comedendus est." The numbering of Hilary's psalms generally follows that of the LXX.

9. J. Doignon, ed., in Hilarius Pictaviensis, *Tractatus super Psalmos I. Instructio Psalmorum, In Psalmos I–XCI,* CCSL 61 (Turnholt: Brepols, 1997), x.

10. *Tract. Ps.* 1.11 (CCSL 61.25).

11. *Tract. Ps.* 150.2 (CSEL 22.872).

12. Gregory of Nyssa, *In Inscriptiones Psalmorum* 2.11 (*GNO* 5.115, 23–25). As translated in Ronald E. Heine, *Gregory of Nyssa's Treatise on the Inscriptions of the Psalms* (Oxford: Oxford University Press, 1995), 163.

13. Ibid.

14. Paul Ricoeur, *Time and Narrative* (Chicago: University of Chicago Press, 1984), 3.

15. Hilary, *Instructio Psalmorum* 1 (CCSL 61.3). Since Jerome, the influence of Origen on Hilary's Psalms commentary has frequently been noted. For a study of Hilary's dependence on Origen, cf. Émile Goffinet, *L'Utilisation d'Origène dans le Commentaire des Psaumes de saint Hilaire de Poitiers* (Louvaine: Publications Universitaires de Louvain, 1965), and more recently M.-J. Rondeau, *Les commentairs patristique du Psautier (III–Ve siècle),* 2 vols., Orientalia Christiana Analecta 219/220 (Rome: Pontificium Institutum Studium Orientalia, 1982–85), 1:47–49. Note esp. p. 148 n. 22, where Rondeau suggests that Goffinet's work is disqualified because of its reliance on the problematic Migne edition of Origen.

16. *Instr. Ps.* 2 (CCSL 61.4): "Et 'liber Psalmorum' rectius esse dicatur, diuersis in unum uolumen prophetiis diuersorum et auctorum et temporum congregatis." Cf. Goffinet, *L'Utilisation d'Origène,* 21–22.

17. *Instr. Ps.* 5 (CCSL 61.5–6): "Non est uero ambigendum ea quae in Psalmis dicta sunt secundum euangelicam praedicationem intellegi oportere, ut ex quacumque licet persona prophetiae spiritus sit locutus, tamen totum illud ad cognitionem aduentus Domini nostri Iesu Christi et corporationis et passionis et regni et resurrectionis nostrae gloriam uirtutemque referatur."

18. *Instr. Ps.* 5 (CCSL 61.6): "Sunt enim uniuersa allegoricis et typicis contexta uirtutibus, per quae omnia unigeniti Dei Filii in corpore et gignendi et patiendi et moriendi et resurgendi et in aeternum cum conglorificatis sibi, qui in eum crediderint, regnandi et ceteros iudicandi sacramenta panduntur."

19. *Instr. Ps.* 9 (CCSL 61.9).

20. *Instr. Ps.* 10 (CCSL 61.10).

21. Gregory of Nyssa, *In Inscr. Ps.* 2.13 (*GNO* 5.133 [Heine, *Inscriptions of the Psalms,* 178]).

22. *Instr. Ps.* 11 (CCSL 61.10): "Tribus uero quinquagesimis Psalmorum liber continetur; et hoc ex ratione ac numero beatae illius nostrae expectationis existit."

23. Athanasius, *Ep. Marcell.* 27–28.

24. *Instr. Ps.* 11 (CCSL 61.10–11).

25. *Tract. Ps.* 150.1 (CSEL 22.870–71).

26. Origen has a long discussion of the ogdoad. Cf. G. Rietz, *De Origenis prologis in Psalterium* (Jena: Pohle, 1914), 1–2.

27. Cf. Daley, "Training for the 'Good Ascent,'" 197.

28. *Instr. Ps.* 13 (CCSL 61.11).

29. *Instr. Ps.* 13 (CCSL 61.12).

30. *Instr. Ps.* 14 (CCSL 61.12). In the section immediately following, Hilary notes that, for the Hebrews, there are twenty-two books of the Law (matching the number of letters in the alphabet), whereas in Greek (adding Tobit and Judith) there are twenty-four (to match the Greek alphabet). The Latin alphabet, having twenty-three, stands between, as is appropriate, since Pilate had Jesus named on the cross

31. *Instr. Ps.* 16 (CCSL 61.13–14).

32. *Instr. Ps.* 18 (CCSL 61.15). For parallels with Origen, cf. Goffinet, *L'Utilisation d'Origène,* 20–21.

33. For instance, Augustine, *Enarrat. Ps.* 30(2) s. 1.1 (CCSL 38.191).

34. Origen, *De principiis* 4.2.9, trans. G. W. Butterworth (Gloucester, Mass.: Peter Smith, 1973), 286.

35. Gregory of Nyssa, *In Inscr. Ps.* 1.1.5 (*GNO* 5.25 [Heine, *Inscriptions of the Psalms,* 84]). For a discussion of the complex relationship between Origen and Gregory of Nyssa, with some reference to Hilary, cf. Heine, *Inscriptions of the Psalms,* 25–29, 37–40.

36. Gregory of Nyssa, *In Inscr. Ps.* 2.2.16 (*GNO* 5.73 [Heine, *Inscriptions of the Psalms,* 127]).

37. For a useful discussion of "closure" as the satisfaction of expectations engendered in a literary text, cf. H. Porter Abbott, *The Cambridge Introduction to Narrative* (Cambridge: Cambridge University Press, 2002), 51–61.

38. Frank Kermode, *The Sense of an Ending: Studies in the Theory of Fiction* (New York: Oxford University Press, 1967), 17.

39. *Tract. Ps.* 1.2 (CCSL 61.20): "omnis ad eum prophetia est referenda Psalmorum; sed ubi et quando ad eum prophetiae ipsius sermo se referat, rationabilis scientiae discernendum est ueritate."

40. *Tract. Ps.* 1.3 (CCSL 61.21).

41. *Tract. Ps.* 1.4 (CCSL 61.21–22).

42. *Tract. Ps.* 1.5 (CCSL 61.22): "Speciosissimum autem hoc et dignissimum incipiendorum Psalmorum sanctus Spiritus sumpsit exordium, ut humanam infirmitatem per spem beatitudinis ad innocens religionis studium adhortaretur, ut sacramentum Dei corporati doceret, ut communionem gloriae caelestis polliceretur, ut poenam iudicii denuntiaret, ut differentiam resurrectionis ostenderet, ut prouidentiam Dei in retributione monstraret."

43. *Tract. Ps.* 1.5 (CCSL 61.22).

44. *Tract. Ps.* 1.11 (CCSL 61.26).

45. On Hilary as the first Latin writer to suggest a soteriology as "divinization," cf. Brian E. Daley, S.J., *The Hope of the Early Church: A Handbook of Patristic Eschatology,* 2nd ed. (Peabody, Mass.: Hendrickson, 2003), 96.

46. *Tract. Ps.* 1.15 (CCSL 61.29): "Dispensatio dandi fructus plenitudini temporum reseruatur."

47. *Tract. Ps.* 1.15 (CCSL 61.29–30).

48. *Tract. Ps.* 1.18 (CCSL 61.29–30).

49. *Tract. Ps.* 2.23 (CCSL 61.53–54).

50. *Tract. Ps.* 2.27 (CCSL 61.56).

51. *Tract. Ps.* 2.31 (CCSL 61.58): "Haec ergo hereditas eius: ut omnia carni det uitam aeternam."

52. *Tract. Ps.* 2.35 (CCSL 61.62).

53. *Tract. Ps.* 2.39 (CCSL 61.65).

54. *Tract. Ps.* 2.41 (CCSL 61.66).

55. *Tract. Ps.* 2.47 (CCSL 61.71).

56. Emile Mersch, S.J., *The Whole Christ: The Historical Development of the Doctrine of the Mystical Body in Scripture and Tradition,* trans. John R. Kelly, S.J. (Milwaukee: Bruce Publishing Co., 1938), 288–306.

57. Mersch, *The Whole Christ,* 289.

58. Daley, *Hope of the Early Church,* 96.

59. Cf. Hilary, *De Trinitate* 9.38 (CCSL 62.412).

60. *Tract. Ps.* 91.9 (CCSL 61.329).

61. *Tract. Ps.* 125.6 (CSEL 22.609).

62. Athanasius, *De incarnatione,* 54 (PG 26). For a classic discussion of divinization in Athanasius, cf. Jules Gross, *The Divinization of the Christian according to the Greek Fathers,* trans. Paul A. Onica (Anaheim, Calif.: A & C Press, 2002), 163–75. Gerhard B. Ladner places Hilary in his Latin context in *The Idea of Reform* (Cambridge: Harvard University Press, 1959), 141–42.

63. *Tract. Ps.* 51.16 (CCSL 61.104).

64. *Tract. Ps.* 51.17 (CCSL 61.104).

65. Philip T. Wild, *The Divinization of Man according to Saint Hilary of Poitiers* (Mundelein, Ill.: St. Mary of the Lake, 1950), 70–71.

66. Ibid.

67. Mersch, *The Whole Christ,* 297.

68. *Tract. Ps.* 138.3 (CSEL 22.746): "adsumptio autem infirmitatis non fecit infirmum, quia aliud est naturam esse, aliud adsumpsisse naturam."

69. *Tract. Ps.* 51.16 (CCSL 61.104).

70. *Tract. Ps.* 141.8 (CSEL 22.804).

71. Cf. Wild, *The Divinization of Man,* 69.

72. *Tract. Ps.* 91.9 (CCSL 61.329): "per coniunctionem carnis adsumptae sumus in Christo."

73. *Tract. Ps.* 147.2 (CSEL 22.855). On the theme of Zion in Hilary's work, cf. Jean-Pierre Pettorelli, "Le thème de Sion expression de la théologie de la rédemption dans l'oeuvre de saint Hilaire de Poitiers," in *Hilaire et son Temps* (Paris: Études Augustiniennes, 1968), 213–33, at 214.

74. *Tract. Ps.* 68.31 (CCSL 61.316).

75. *Tract. Ps.* 14.5 (CCSL 61.84).

76. *Tract. Ps.* 136.6 (CSEL 22.689).

77. Wild, *The Divinization of Man,* 77.

78. *Tract. Ps.* 118.2.1 (CCSL 61A.18).

79. *Tract. Ps.* 118.10.3 (CCSL 61A.90).

80. *Tract. Ps.* 118.12.1 (CCSL 61A.108).

81. *Tract. Ps.* 118.12.4 (CCSL 61A.109–10). On the teaching of the "old man" and "new man" in Hilary's commentary on Psalm 118, cf. the introduction by Mark Milhau in Hilaire de Poitiers, *Commentaire sur le Psaume 118,* SC 344/347 (Paris: Les Éditions du Cerf, 1988), 1.42–52.

82. *Tract. Ps.* 118.12.14 (CCSL 61A.117–18).

83. Daley, *Hope of the Early Church,* 1.

84. Ibid., 2.

85. For an essay on the christological substructure of redemption in early theology, cf. Brian E. Daley, S.J., "'He Himself is our Peace' (Eph 2:14): Early Christian Views of Redemption in Christ," in *The Redemption: An Interdisciplinary Symposium on Christ as Redeemer,* ed. Stephen T. Davis, Daniel Kendall, and Gerald O'Collins (Oxford: Oxford University Press, 2004), 149–76.

86. Brian E. Daley, S.J., "Is Patristic Exegesis Still Usable? Reflections on Early Christian Interpretation of the Psalms," *Communio* 29 (2002): 185–216.

SUFFERING WITHOUT PAIN

The Scandal of Hilary of Poitiers' Christology

Carl L. Beckwith

In the final books of *De Trinitate,* Hilary of Poitiers argues that Christ suffered on the cross without experiencing pain. This argument has endured more criticism throughout the history of the church than any other aspect of Hilary's theology. Within a hundred years of Hilary's death, Claudianus Mamertus accused him of undermining the truth of Christ's passion and threatening our redemption.[1] In the thirteenth century, Bonaventure was so troubled by Hilary's comments on Christ's suffering that he suggested they might be *contra fidem*.[2] Bonaventure, sharing Mamertus's concerns, argued that if anyone asserts that Christ suffered without pain, that person "not only evacuates the faith of Christ and the gospel of Christ but also evacuates our redemption and says that Christ is not the Christ."[3] Similar attempts to reconcile Hilary's infelicitous statements with the church's teaching were made by Albert the Great and Thomas Aquinas. Frustrated with efforts to recover an orthodox understanding of Hilary's Christology, someone, perhaps Bonaventure himself, relieved the situation by circulating a pious rumor. According to the rumor, William of Paris had seen a statement of retraction in which Hilary corrected his unorthodox statements on Christ's suffering.[4] This rumor freed the medieval writers from defending Hilary's seemingly untenable christological position and preserved his orthodoxy and theological integrity for the medieval church. The usefulness of this rumor persisted well into the sixteenth century and is found, among other places, in the writings of the Lutheran theologian Martin Chemnitz.[5]

During the twentieth century, the pious rumor was put aside and the orthodoxy of Hilary's Christology once again endured suspicion and scrutiny.[6] Two distinct approaches emerged. E. W. Watson, the *NPNF* translator of Hilary's *De Trinitate,* took a cautious approach. He writes, "Hilary has been accused of 'sailing somewhat close to the cliffs of Docetism,' but all admit that he has escaped shipwreck."[7] Watson's cautious approach was also taken up by C. F. A. Borchardt, who concluded that Hilary is "not a docetist in the *strict* sense of the word."[8] Indeed, he could not be a Docetist, notes Pierre Smulders, because he "emphasized that Christ had a true body and even that Christ died."[9] Paul Burns, working on Hilary's earlier *In Mattheum,* writes, "By locating the sufferings of Christ within a human psychology, I suggest that Hilary cannot be accused of maintaining a *purely* docetic Christ."[10] Finally, Mark Weedman, who places Hilary's comments in *De Trinitate* in their wider fourth-century trinitarian context, characterizes the charge of Docetism as "artificial."[11]

Rather than wrestling with the seemingly contradictory christological statements present in Hilary's writings and concluding, as the scholars above have done, that he ultimately avoids error, R. P. C. Hanson has taken a dismissive approach, contending that Hilary was "nakedly Docetic" but in a "sophisticated way."[12] Reminiscent of Claudianus Mamertus and Bonaventure, Hanson argues that Hilary's Christology is so unorthodox that it brings our redemption under question and makes us wonder if Christ was truly our Mediator.[13] He writes,

> This [i.e., Hilary's Docetism] was partly because he went into greater detail in his Christology, partly because in spite of his disavowal of philosophical influences his mind was deeply dyed with

> the axiom that God is impassible (and that Jesus Christ was fully God), but partly too because he made the disastrous mistake of allowing the story of the Virgin Birth, which plays so insignificant a part in the New Testament, to control the whole of his Christology. In effect he concluded that at the very point where Christ's solidarity with humankind is most crucial, in his suffering, Christ was not really human. Not only does this bring our redemption under question and do away explicitly with that central conviction of St. Paul, the scandal of the cross, but it leaves us uncertain as to whether such a figure can seriously act as our Mediator.[14]

Hanson's assertions raise a number of questions. How do we account for Hilary's continued emphasis on soteriology throughout *De Trinitate* and his repeated appeals to the saving work of Christ? How could Hilary advance a nakedly docetic Christology, as Hanson argues, and yet assert that God suffered and died for our salvation—a point observed by the scholars taking the cautious approach? Hilary's repeated emphasis on our salvation and the need to confess that Christ is true God and true man, who assumed our sin, suffered on the cross, and rose again from the dead for our salvation, seems inconsistent with the conclusions drawn by Hanson.[15]

In the following essay, I will determine in what sense Hilary sailed close to the cliffs of Docetism and whether he shipwrecked, as Claudianus Mamertus, Bonaventure, and Hanson suggest, or avoided disaster, as Watson, Burns, and Weedman argue. I do this by reading Hilary's comments on the suffering of Christ as he wished his readers to do, namely, against the background of his lengthy discussion of the two natures in Christ, the character of Christ's human soul, and the various divisive Christologies promoted by his opponents.

The Purpose of the Incarnation

Hilary begins book 9 of *De Trinitate* by reminding the reader of the exegetical tendencies of his opponents and how a proper interpretation of Scripture is to be achieved.[16] He accuses his opponents, as many of the church fathers before him had done, of taking words spoken in one context and for one purpose and rearranging them for use in a different context for a different purpose.[17] He then reminds the reader of "the universal faith" that must be confessed for eternal life. Hilary writes,

> He who does not know that Christ Jesus is true God and true man is thoroughly unacquainted with his own life—indeed knows nothing. It is equally dangerous to deny that Christ Jesus possesses the divine *spiritus* as it is to deny that he possesses the flesh of our bodies.[18] "Therefore everyone who shall confess me before men, I shall confess him before my Father who is in heaven. But whoever shall deny me before men, I shall deny him before my Father who is in heaven" (Matt 10:32–33). The Word made flesh spoke these words and the man Jesus Christ, the Lord of glory, taught them. He has been appointed mediator in his own person for the salvation of the church, and the very mystery of being the mediator between God and man means that he is at the same time one and the other. From the natures united in him, he himself is the same person [*res*] in both natures, in such a manner that he is wanting in neither, lest he cease to be God by his birth as man or fail to be man because he remains God. Accordingly, this is the true faith for human blessedness: to acknowledge him as God and man, to confess him as Word and flesh, neither rejecting God because he is man, nor ignoring the flesh because he is the Word.[19]

Hilary's commitment to a two-natures Christology is guided by Philippians 2:6–7, "Christ Jesus who though he was in the form of God . . . took the form of a slave," Colossians 2:8–9, "in him dwells all the fullness of the Godhead bodily," and John 1:14, "the Word became flesh." For Hilary, Jesus Christ is truly and completely God and truly and completely man, or, put simply, *verum Deum et verum hominem*. Moreover, despite the limitations of Hilary's theological vocabulary, Christ, as man and God, is yet one acting subject. Since Christ is one acting subject in two natures, it is correct, proper, and necessary to attribute the properties of one nature to the other by virtue of their union (*communicatio idiomatum*). Therefore, on account of the incarnation, we rightly say that the Impassible suffers (*inpassibilis patitur*) and the Living dies (*vivens moritur*).[20]

For Hilary, these are not abstract musings about the two natures in Christ. Rather the confession that he is *verum Deum et verum hominem* is necessary to understand the mysteries of our salvation.[21] At the beginning of book 9, Hilary explicitly states the reasons for the incarnation:

> Now these are the mysteries of the heavenly plans determined before the foundation of the world: the only-begotten God chose to be born as man and man was to abide eternally in God . . . . And so God was born to assume us, then suffered to make us innocent, and finally died to avenge us. For our humanity abides in God, the passions of our weaknesses are associated with God, and the spiritual forces of evil and malicious powers are subdued by the triumph of the flesh since God dies by means of the flesh [*per carnem*].[22]

Because there is only one acting subject in Christ who is both God and man, it is rightly said that God assumed our sin, suffered on the cross, and died. As Hilary puts it, "God dies by means of the flesh." It is this truth, which is the scandal of the cross, that philosophy or worldly wisdom fails to grasp.

Hilary continues with an extended discussion of the particulars of Christ's saving work. Jesus Christ, in whom the fullness of the Godhead dwells bodily, took flesh that we might receive of his fullness by being reborn through faith unto eternal life. Elsewhere in the treatise Hilary puts it this way: "The Son of God is crucified, but on the cross God conquers human death. Christ, the Son of God, dies, but all flesh is made alive in Christ. The Son of God is in hell and man is brought back to heaven."[23] Our adoption into Christ and our salvation in him is made possible because God became man, assuming our lowliness, our weakness, and our sin so that we might assume his eternity, in part now by faith, in full in the world to come. Hilary summarizes Christ's saving work by paraphrasing Colossians 2. He writes, "he brought us to life with himself, forgiving our sins and canceling the handwriting of the law of sin, which, because of the former ordinances, was opposed to us, abolishing it and nailing it to the cross, stripping himself of the flesh by the law of death, exposing the powers to mockery, and triumphing over them in himself."[24] For Christ's saving work to be accomplished, he had to be *verum Deum et verum hominem,* as stressed above. Hilary emphatically writes, "Hold fast, therefore, to Christ the man, whom God has raised from the dead! Hold fast to Christ the God, accomplishing our salvation when he shall die!"[25]

Hilary insists that we must understand and confess that the God who raised Christ from the dead is the same God who worked as Christ in the flesh and the one whom we say also died for us. Although our language constrains us to speak in such a way that we confess that Christ died in the flesh as man and that Christ was raised by God from the dead, such that we ascribe death to the man and the resurrection to the power of God, we must not forget that Christ, true God and man, is one (person), not two. These two natures, insists Hilary, do not imply two acting subjects that are somehow distinct from each other and work independently of one another. As such, we must never divide Christ, who is one, when discussing the actions proper to one nature. Hilary writes,

> Do you understand that the flesh that has been put off and he who puts off the flesh are not distinct from one another? He triumphs in his own person [*in semetipso*]—that is to say in that flesh which he himself put off. Do you realize that it is in this manner that he is proclaimed as God and man, such that the death is attributed to the man, and the resurrection of the flesh to God, but not in such a manner that he who died is one and he through whom the dead one is raised is another? The flesh put off is the dead Christ and again he who raises Christ from the dead is the same Christ who himself puts off the flesh. See the nature of God in the power of the resurrection and recognize the dispensation of man in the death. Although each action is done in accordance with its proper nature, bear in mind that it is one Christ Jesus [*unum Christum Iesum*] who is present in each of them.[26]

Because Christ is one person, the actions formally attributed to one nature are rightly communicated to the other by virtue of their union in this one person. As such, God suffers and dies for us just as the man

Jesus raises the dead and forgives sins. A further point being made by Hilary is that no difference exists between saying that the Father raised Christ from the dead and Christ proclaiming, "I lay down my life that I may take it up again" (John 10:17–18). Just as we confess that there is one God in three persons, not three gods, so too we acknowledge that there is one power and one wisdom, not three powers or three wisdoms.[27] Hilary explains, "It is not to be understood as a contradiction when the Apostle proclaims Christ the power of God and the wisdom of God, and attributes all the magnificence of his work to the glory of the Father, since whatever Christ does, the power and wisdom of God does, and whatever the power and wisdom of God does, without any doubt God does, whose wisdom and power Christ is." Christ possesses this power and wisdom not by adoption but because he possesses "a nature that does not differ from that of God the Father."[28]

Christ's saving work was accomplished because he was true God and true man in one person. He possessed the weakness of man in his true and complete human nature and he possessed the power of God in his true and complete divine nature. As the Apostle writes, "For though he was crucified through weakness, yet he lives through the power of God" (2 Cor 13:4). Again the Apostle writes, "For the death that he died, he died to sin once for all, but the life that he lives, he lives unto God. Thus do you consider yourselves also as dead to sin, but alive to God in Christ Jesus" (Rom 6:10–11). Hilary comments, "He attributed death to sin, that is, to our body, but life to God whose nature it is that he lives. We ought, therefore, to die to our body that we may live to God in Christ Jesus, who, assuming our body of sin, lives now wholly for God, uniting the nature he shared with us into a participation of the divine immortality."[29] Through our adoption into Christ, we too will live wholly for God, realizing the true and complete humanity he possesses which is in perfect union with God—a union we were always intended to share.

The Suffering of Christ

By attending to Hilary's discussion of the incarnation and the two natures in Christ in book 9, we are able to navigate more successfully his discussion of Christ's suffering without pain. When we turn to book 10 of *De Trinitate,* we encounter the discussion that has troubled so many later commentators and invited the conclusion that Hilary's statements appear to be *contra fidem* or nakedly docetic.

Hilary characteristically begins his discussion by outlining the faulty theological method of his opponents. Their distorted view of Christ results from their refusal to submit to the words of Scripture.[30] They prefer, instead, to follow their own perverted will, a will that rejects the truth of Scripture by accepting whatever seems pleasing to it at the moment. As Hilary puts it, these opponents defend as true whatever they desire rather than desiring what is true.[31] By neglecting the truth of Scripture and proclaiming as true only what agrees with their limited understanding, these opponents proclaim a "fatal doctrine," either asserting that Jesus is "not God" or "speaking of two gods differing in their divinity."[32]

At this point, Hilary summarizes what he has argued throughout *De Trinitate*. The Son is not a God of a nature different from God the Father, nor are Father and Son merely names designating the same being at different times. The Father and Son are eternally distinct from one another yet indistinguishable in power and substance such that they are not two gods. The Son is eternally and ineffably generated from the Father in a manner that transcends all human understanding. Finally, in these latter days, the Son, by the power of the Holy Spirit, was born from the Virgin Mary, emptying himself of the form of God and receiving the form of a slave.[33] Here, we arrive at the issue that will occupy Hilary for the rest of book 10: if Jesus, as true man and true God, possesses the nature of an impassible God, how do you account for his suffering?[34] As we will see, Hilary's opponents promote a false understanding of Christ in order to avoid the seemingly contradictory conclusion that the impassible God suffered and died.

The question of God's suffering and the presence of pain in that suffering is for Hilary a question about the type of body and soul possessed by Christ. He writes, "Let us see what kind of body the man Christ possessed, so that the pain should remain in the suspended, bound, and pierced flesh."[35] We see immediately that for Hilary the issue is not, strictly speaking, whether Christ, the incarnate Son of God, suffered, but whether he experienced pain in that suffering.[36] There is no question that God suffered and died by means of the flesh he assumed. As described above, Hilary does not hesitate to assert that the Impassible suffered (*inpassibilis patitur*) and the Living died (*vivens moritur*). To argue that Christ did not truly suffer and die would suggest that his humanity was not real and would lead to the error of the Docetists. Hilary is aware that such a view argues that Christ had only a "phantom" (*fantasma*) body, and he emphatically denounces it.[37]

Although suffering is not an issue for Hilary, the question of pain is another matter. Hilary firmly rejects the notion that Christ felt pain when he suffered. For Hilary pain is felt by the soul, not the flesh. It is the nature of bodies, argues Hilary, that by their association with the soul they are animated. As such, "when punctured or torn bodies suffer pain, the feeling of the pain is received through the sensation of the soul that has been poured into them."[38] If the union with the soul is severed, the body experiences no pain. The question is naturally asked, "Did Christ experience pain?" If he did, he must not be God because pain involves change or corruption and God is incorruptible and impassible. On the other hand, if he did not experience pain, then, it seems to follow that he did not possess a human soul and his humanity is incomplete. Hilary writes,

> If it were true that the man Jesus Christ began his life as our body and soul begin, and if he were not God, the ruling principle [*princeps*] of his own body and soul, when he was fashioned in the likeness of man and found in the form of man and born, then, yes, he would have felt the pain of our body since he would have been conceived as we are and possessed a body animated at conception by a soul like our own.[39]

Hilary rejects both alternatives and clearly asserts that Christ is God and possesses a human soul. He also introduces a distinction between a "weak soul" (*animae infirmis*) and, presumably, a strong or true or complete soul.[40] A person feels the pain inflicted on the body because he possesses a soul weakened by sin. To assert that Jesus felt pain would be to attribute a "weak soul" to him. The only way Christ could have a weak soul, which is a soul belonging to a person conceived and born "naturally," that is, a soul born with sin,[41] is if the man Jesus existed before the Word assumed him. If he did, then he had a body and soul prior to his union with the Word. This argument would lead Hilary to two conclusions that he is unwilling to draw. First, that there was a time when the man Jesus existed before being assumed by the Word and, therefore, that there are two acting subjects in Jesus Christ, one human and one divine. To exist as man before being assumed by the Word means that the man became God rather than God becoming man. Although such a divisive Christology could easily account for suffering and pain, it would destroy the unity of Christ, undermine the incarnation, and ultimately evacuate any soteriological value to Christ's redeeming work. Second, even if this were the case, Hilary is not willing to concede that the adopted man would have necessarily felt pain. That is to say, it is possible for someone born naturally with a weak soul to suffer in the body without feeling the pain of that suffering. As we will see, this is an important point for Hilary that will be crucial in his understanding of Christ's body and soul. Hilary continues,

> But if through his own effort he assumed flesh from the Virgin and if he himself also joined a soul to the body conceived through himself, then the nature of his suffering must be in keeping with the nature of his body and soul. For when he emptied himself of the form of God and received the form of a slave, and when the Son of God was born as the Son of Man, without sacrificing anything of himself and his own power, then God the Word brought about the perfect living man.[42]

For Hilary "every soul is the work of God" and created directly by God for each person.[43] As such, flesh begets flesh but the soul is from God. Therefore, at every human conception, God imparts a soul that animates the flesh and makes a human being.[44] In the case of Jesus, he was conceived by the Holy Spirit, born of the Virgin Mary, and was the perfect living man. This "spiritual conception" (*spiritalis conceptionis*), as Hilary calls it, means that the human soul was ineffably united to the Word in such a way as to animate Jesus Christ, true God and true man.[45]

Hilary explains, "just as in the nature appointed for us by God, the source of our origin, man is born with a body and soul, so too Jesus Christ, by his own power, is God and man with flesh [*carnis*] and soul [*animae*], possessing in himself both truly and completely what man is and truly and completely what God is."[46] In the case of all humans, our bodies are animated when God bestows a soul upon us at conception. In the case of Jesus, the Word animates the flesh not by becoming its animating principle to the exclusion of a human soul but by uniting with that human soul in a mysterious and nontemporal manner.[47]

At this point, Hilary articulates his position against the backdrop of one of the Christologies advanced by his opponents. By drawing this contrast, Hilary reveals to us what is at stake for him in this discussion and why he feels compelled to assert what he does about suffering and pain. He writes, "They do not wish the only-begotten God, who in the beginning was God the Word with God [*apud Deum*], to be a self-existent God [*substantiuum Deum*], but merely the utterance of a voice, so that what a word is to those who speak, so too this Son is to God the Father."[48] By paraphrasing the beginning of St. John's prologue, emphasizing that the Word was *apud Deum,* and using the phrase "utterance of a voice," Hilary is characterizing these opponents as promoting the christological position of Photinus of Sirmium.[49] Hilary comments,

> They subtly wish to insinuate that it was not the Word of God subsisting and remaining in the form of God who was born as Christ the man. Rather, since the cause of the man's life was of human origin rather than the mystery of a spiritual conception [*spiritalis conceptionis*], he was not God the Word who made himself man by birth from the Virgin, but as the spirit of prophecy was in the prophets, so the Word of God was in Jesus.[50]

Their position asserts that Jesus existed as a true living man, animated by a human soul, prior in time to his union with the Word. Such a position assumes that there are two acting subjects or subjects of predication in Jesus Christ, and, moreover, that he is God not by birth but by adoption. On the contrary, the proper way of understanding the mystery of Christ's spiritual conception, explains Hilary, is that "He was born not that he might be first one and then another, but that it might be understood that the one who was God before he was man is the same one who has now assumed a human nature and is both God and man."[51] Hilary rejects the adoptionist position by arguing that the true union of the Word with humanity does not allow for two centers of consciousness or acting subjects united together to form Jesus Christ, true God and true man, but rather allows only one. To suggest otherwise promotes a divisive Christology that either compromises Christ's divinity or humanity or asserts a *tertium quid*. As such, when we say that Christ was in the form of God and the form of a slave, we mean that while he is truly God and truly man he is also "one and the same" (*unum tamen eumdemque*). Hilary asserts,

> Therefore, after Jesus Christ was born, suffered, died, and was buried, he also rose again. In these various mysteries, he is not able to be divided from himself such that he is not Christ—since there is no other Christ than the one who in the form of God received the form of a slave, nor is the one who died different from the one who was born, nor is the one who rose again different from the one who died, nor is the one in heaven different from the one who rose again, nor finally is the one in heaven different from the one who previously descended from heaven.[52]

Hilary is quite clear that in Christ Jesus there is one acting subject in two natures. The assumed man is not another person from the person of the Word but is one and the same, *unum eumdemque*. Moreover, the Word is the ultimate subject of all predication, and therefore it is correct to say that God truly suffered and died on the cross, or the *inpassibilis patitur* and the *vivens moritur*.[53]

At this point in book 10, Hilary takes up the question of how Christ is said to suffer without compromising his divinity. As seen above, Hilary has all the resources necessary to locate that suffering in Christ's humanity and to attribute the full range of emotions associated with human suffering to Christ's human soul. Moreover, by virtue of the union between divinity and humanity, as expounded by Hilary, he would be able to attribute this suffering and pain to God through the *communicatio idiomatum*. But although he will continue to attribute suffering and death to God through the *communicatio,* he will not, because of his theological anthropology, which is guided by a Stoic moral psychology, attribute fear or pain to Christ's soul. Hilary insists on a distinction between suffering and pain that ultimately rests upon his earlier distinction between a soul weakened by sin and a strong or complete soul free from sin. Jesus Christ, the only-begotten God, who is the Son of Man and the Son of God, was struck, wounded, and experienced the violence of the passion, but such suffering "did not occasion the pain of the passion."[54] According to Hilary,

> The Lord Jesus Christ truly suffers when he is struck, suspended, crucified, and dies. But the suffering that assails the body, although a true suffering, does not manifest the nature of suffering [*naturam passionis*]. Although the suffering rages with the purpose of delivering punishment, the power of the body [*virtus corporis*] receives the force of the pain against itself without feeling pain.[55]

To this point, Hilary seems to be saying only that outside the *communicatio idiomatum* the divinity of Christ does not experience the pain or corruption of his suffering. According to the *communicatio,* God suffered, but that should not be understood to mean that the substance or essence of God is corruptible and passible.[56] Hilary, however, intends to say more than this:

> It is true that the body of the Lord would have been capable of feeling pain as our natures do, if our body possessed such a nature as treads upon the waves and walks on the waters without sinking as it walks or forcing the waters apart by the pressure of its footsteps, or if it could pass through solid structures and not be hindered by the obstacle of a closed house. But if such is the nature only of the Lord's body, so that by his own power, his soul is borne over the water, treads upon the waves, and passes through walls, why do we judge the flesh conceived by the Spirit according to the nature of the human body [conceived naturally]? That flesh, that is, that Bread, is from heaven, and that man is from God. He certainly possessed a body to suffer, and he did suffer, but he did not possess

> a nature that could be touched by pain. For that body possessed a nature unique and peculiar to itself; a body that was transfigured in heavenly glory on the mountain, drove away fevers by its touch, and restored eyesight by its spittle.[57]

We begin to see what is involved in possessing a strong or complete soul free from all sin. As is indicated in the scriptural narrative, Christ's body was transfigured or sanctified or divinized to such an extent that it could walk on water and drive away fevers by its touch.[58] Therefore, asserts Hilary, that body truly suffered but did not possess a "nature" that could feel pain. To borrow a phrase from Maximus Confessor, Hilary seems to suggest that Christ truly suffered but did so divinely.[59] This divine suffering does not manifest the experience of pain because Christ possesses a perfect human nature, not a sinful human nature.

The indebtedness of Hilary's theological anthropology to a Stoic moral psychology has long been observed.[60] As indicated above, Hilary does not embrace a bipartite or tripartite division of the soul, as many of his Platonic contemporaries did. Hilary's commitment to a unified soul has important implications for his Christology. According to Stoic epistemology and ethics, the soul encounters impressions or desires in its engagement with the world, and these impressions impact or alter the soul depending on the state of the agent's moral progress.[61] To use Hilary's terms, a "weak" soul responds to an impression with the action that appears necessary based on the content of the impression. A "strong" soul, on the other hand, considers the content of the impression and the reality it intends to represent before dismissing it as false or assenting to it as true. As such, the "weak" soul is moved by the impression itself, and the "strong" soul is moved by its deliberation of the impression as true or false.[62] Since this assent is given by a unified soul, there is no conflict between rational and irrational parts such that the irrational could triumph over the rational by being misled by a false impression.[63] Since the impression and the assent belong to the same faculty, the individual who properly exercises reason will always avoid error. Or, as Hilary would put it, the person with a strong soul will always avoid sin.

The assent of the soul to an impression is an expression of belief that is characterized as either an "opinion" that is false or true, or "knowledge" that is always true and is the characteristic of the Stoic sage. Moreover, for the Stoic, virtue alone is good and evil alone is bad. All other things are considered "indifferent" because they are neither beneficial nor harmful.[64] The problem with most people, however, is that they falsely assign value to things that are indifferent. As such, health, wealth, and comfort are judged as good, and disease, poverty, and pain are judged as evil. Life is ordered around the attainment of false goods and the avoidance of false evils. These false beliefs are characterized as "emotions."[65] The four main species of emotion are desire, fear, pleasure, and pain. In terms of Hilary's Christology, the emotions of fear and pain are particularly relevant. Fear is the opinion that some future thing is evil and should be avoided. Pain is the opinion that some present thing is evil and we should be sad about it.[66] As such, regret and mourning are both a subspecies of pain. Here we see that the real issue for the Stoic is the emotional value attached to pain. Since pain is neither a virtue nor a vice, no such emotional value should be given it by the soul. When this happens, the soul is involved in the suffering and pain of the body because it has succumbed to a false impression and false belief. Since assigning the value of good or evil to an indifferent thing is false, the Stoic sage will never have these emotions.[67]

Hilary's Christology is guided by this Stoic anthropology and moral psychology.[68] Christ's human soul, by virtue of its spiritual conception, is endowed from birth with a strong soul, which is to say a soul without sin, and therefore immune to the false beliefs expressed by the emotions of desire, fear, pleasure, and pain.[69] Since the union between the Word and the humanity happens according to the person, the man Jesus never existed with a body and soul prior to his spiritual conception. For Hilary, such a conception, unique to Christ alone, does not mean that Jesus is without a human soul but rather that the human soul is so infused with the power of the Word that it is sanctified or divinized to the point that it experiences no corruption or pain. Put another way, the humanity of Christ is appropriated by the Word in such a way that it is entirely without sin and is therefore the most true and complete example of humanity ever known. Understood in this way, Christ's humanity underscores a fundamental soteriological point for Hilary. The union between the divinity and humanity in Christ expresses the intimacy with God that is the goal and principle by which all humans seek union with God. As Hilary explains,

> It was not necessary for him, through whom man was made, to become man, but it was necessary for us that God take flesh and dwell among us, that is, by the assumption of one flesh he made all flesh his home. His humility is our nobility, his shame our honor. As such, God assumed flesh that we, in turn, would be restored from the flesh to God.[70]

Through such a union we become most truly human as we are freed from the disordering effects of our sin, effects which only diminish our true humaneness and humanity and lead us to regard indifferent things as true or false. Christ's humanity, then, is not less human because he suffers without pain; rather, according to Hilary's anthropology and moral psychology, he is more truly human because his soul is properly and perfectly ordered toward that which is true and good.

The Suffering of the Martyrs

For Hilary, the sanctification or divinization of Christ's soul is the goal of all humanity and is partially seen in the suffering and courage of the martyrs. Hilary explains,

> Since the consciousness of an animated body derives life from its association with the soul diffused throughout it, and the soul mingled with the body gives life to it in order to experience the pain inflicted upon it, whenever the soul in the blessed zeal of its heavenly faith and hope looks down upon the beginning of the body's earthly origin, the body forms a unique consciousness and spirit for itself toward pain, so that it no longer feels the suffering that it suffers.[71]

Again, the soul is what allows the body to experience pain. Because of Christ's spiritual conception, which for Hilary seems to be a way of designating the hypostatic union, the human soul, which is ordinarily the center of consciousness or acting subject for a human being, mingles with the power of God in such a way that there is only one person in Jesus Christ, the eternal Son of God. Such a special union means that although suffering and pain rage against the body of Christ on the cross and the person of Christ receives that suffering, he does so impassibly. Although this sounds contradictory, Hilary insists it is not. As he explains, "even earthly bodies are unaware of fear and pain where there should certainly be pain and fear."[72] We see this with Shadrach, Meshach, and Abednego in the fiery furnace, with Daniel in the lions' den, and with the apostles who rejoice to suffer in the name of Christ. In each case, these individuals overcome the natural fear and pain experienced by their bodies through the blessed zeal of their faith and hope. By anticipating their complete and perfect union with God in glory and their crown of righteousness, the fear and pain of the martyrs is overcome by an emboldened and joyous soul:

> With hymns the martyrs offer their necks to the executioners to be cut off and with canticles they ascend the pile of burning logs raised for them. As they are doing this, the consciousness of their faith removes from their bodies the fear of a natural weakness and changes those very bodies in such a manner that they are no longer aware of the pain they feel. As such, the resolve [*firmitas*] of their bodies is strengthened by the purpose of the soul, and the animated body endures only that toward which it is moved by the zeal of its soul. Therefore the body, emboldened by the soul, does not feel the suffering that the soul disregards because of its desire for glory.[73]

For Hilary, Christ possesses a humanity truer and more consonant with God's creative intentions. His humanity is unlike ours in that it is free from all sin and therefore a truer example of humanity than our humanity, which is disordered and fragmented by sin. The union with the Word infuses the humanity with such power that it is perfectly sanctified or divinized. It is this perfection that the martyrs anticipate with the consciousness of their faith, a faith that emboldens their soul and strengthens their bodies to endure the suffering of their martyrdoms without fear of death and the pain of suffering.[74] Put another way, their faith rightly interprets fear and pain as emotions with indifferent value. The martyr's fear is overcome with joy as the soul now sees death as another name for eternal life.[75] The pain inflicted on the martyr's body does not touch the soul because the soul is united to the Truth and confesses with the apostle, "It is no longer I who live but Christ who lives in me" (Gal 2:20). If the martyrs, who were conceived with a sinful nature, do not fear their impending death or experience the pain of their suffering because of the zeal and anticipation of their faith, then surely, argues Hilary, Christ, who is born without sin and who bestows the gift of salvation through his cross and suffering, neither fears the cross nor succumbs to the pain of his suffering. Hilary concludes,

> Therefore, the only-begotten God suffered all the infirmities of our passions that pressed upon him but he suffered according to the power of his nature . . . . It follows that he suffered the infirmities of our bodies in his own body, but took upon himself the passions of our body according to the power of his own body. And to this part of our faith the word of the prophet testifies when he says, "He bears our sins and suffers for us. And we looked upon him in his sorrows, in his blows, and in his hardship. But he was wounded for our iniquities and he was made weak because of our sins" (Isa 53:4–5).
>
> Therefore the opinion of human judgment is false when it supposes that he felt pain because he suffered. To be sure, he "bore our sins," that is to say, he assumed our body of sin, but he was himself without sin. For indeed, he was sent "in the likeness of sinful flesh" (Rom 8:3), truly bearing sin in the flesh, but those sins were ours. And he suffered pain for us, but he did not suffer pain as we experience it because "he was found in the appearance of man" (Phil 2:7), possessing for himself a body subject to pain, but not possessing a nature subject to pain. Although "found in the appearance of man," his origin was not that of a natural birth but rather he was born by a conception of the Holy Spirit.[76]

Just as it is correct to say, according to Scripture, that Christ bears our sins, we also acknowledge that he himself does not commit sin. So too, argues Hilary, according to Scripture, Christ truly suffered and possessed a true body subject to pain, but, because he is God and because a true union exists between the Word and the man such that there is one person in two natures, Christ did not succumb to the pain of that suffering.

Hilary's Conclusion

After his lengthy discussion of Christ's two natures and the manner in which Christ suffered without pain, Hilary ends book 10 of *De Trinitate* by exposing the weaknesses of the various Christologies advanced by his opponents. Here we encounter the historical challenge faced by Hilary in articulating his Christology. If he were to assert that Christ suffered *with* pain, he would, in his estimation, be forced to embrace one of the divisive Christologies articulated by his opponents.

Hilary identifies two false Christologies that undermine the faith of the church and our salvation in Christ. The first group argues that God the Word was "completely absorbed into the soul of the body" and "performed the duty of the soul in vivifying the body."[77] Although this christological position becomes explicit in the writings of Apollinarius of Laodicea, it is most likely known to Hilary from "Arian" circles. Hilary's criticism of this Christology is that it ultimately undermines Jesus' identity as true God and true man. The second group of opponents rejected by Hilary argues that the Word of God "dwelt in him [i.e., the man Jesus] as the Spirit had dwelt in the Prophets."[78] This adoptionist Christology, which we encountered above, is associated with Photinus of Sirmium, who argues that "Jesus Christ is not Christ before he was born from Mary."[79] Rather, the Word "extends" itself and dwells in the man Jesus, who, according to Photinus, does possess a human soul.

The faith of the church, argues Hilary, "does not separate Jesus Christ so that Jesus himself is not Christ. Moreover, it neither distinguishes the Son of Man from the Son of God, lest, perhaps, the Son of God is not also rightly judged as the Son of Man, nor does it absorb the Son of God into the Son of Man." As argued above, these divisive Christologies, in seeking to protect the impassibility and immutability of

God, diminish either Christ's divinity or humanity and inevitably lead to a *tertium quid*. Hilary rejects such Christologies as heresies:

> [The faith of the church] neither separates Christ by a threefold faith . . . so that Jesus Christ is cut up into Word, soul, and body, nor again does it absorb God the Word into the soul and body. In him is the whole God the Word and in him is the whole man Christ. We cleave to this one thing in the mystery of our confession: never to believe that Christ is anything other than Jesus, nor to preach that Jesus is anything other than Christ.[80]

Jesus Christ is truly man and truly God in one person. To suggest otherwise is to deny the salvation won for us by Christ. The divisive Christologies of the heretics sever, divide, and separate Christ. They believe that Christ crucified is one person and the wisdom of God another person. They believe that the Son of Man is one person and the Son of God another person.[81] A proper and orthodox Christology does not divide Christ but regards the one who reigns in heaven as the same one who dies on the cross for our salvation.[82]

Hilary ends his discussion in *De Trinitate* as he began it, with comments on theological method and the faith of the church. We must bear in mind, he urges, the limitations of our minds to grasp and our words to express the mystery of Christ's incarnation and passion. Moreover, we must recognize that a discussion of the two natures in Christ and their union and the manner in which Christ suffered and died on the cross, although necessitating abstract language, deals with the central teaching of the church, our salvation in Christ Jesus. Hilary's pastoral concern emerges at this very point. Salvation consists not in subtle distinctions or persuasive speech but in confessing that Jesus is Lord and knowing that he died in order that we might live in him. Hilary explains,

> What madness it is to represent falsely the nature and character of Jesus Christ, when salvation consists only in knowing that he alone is Lord! . . . God does not call us to the blessed life through difficult questions, nor does he create confusion for us by the various uses of

> persuasive speech. For us eternal life is certain and easy: believe that Jesus was raised from the dead by God and confess that he himself is the Lord. Therefore, let no one falsely use what we have discussed in our ignorance as an opportunity for impiety. We must know that Jesus Christ died for us that we might live in him.[83]

Had Hilary not entertained a discussion on the nature of Christ's suffering or the relationship between experiencing pain and feeling pain, his Christology would never have raised suspicions in the fifth century, the thirteenth century, or today. At the same time, when we read Hilary's comments on Christ's suffering in the context of his discussion of the incarnation and human soul in Christ and when we observe his indebtedness to a Stoic moral psychology, it is apparent that he is neither "nakedly Docetic" nor does he sail close to the cliffs of Docetism. Although Hilary never develops a technical christological vocabulary and never fully exploits his insights on Christ's human soul to account for the range of emotions experienced by Christ on the cross, his consistent articulation of two natures in one acting subject, his commitment to the presence of a human soul in Christ, and, finally, his insistence that God truly suffered and died in the flesh for our salvation marks his Christology as an important contribution to fourth-century patristic thought and a decisive step toward the theological formulations embraced a hundred years later at Chalcedon.

Notes

My interest and fascination with Hilary of Poitiers was first kindled at Notre Dame in Brian Daley's doctoral seminar on fourth-century trinitarian theology. I will always be indebted to Brian for his gentle mentoring, his friendship, and for showing me how to handle with care and sensitivity the theological, historical, and pastoral issues involved in the writings of the church fathers. It is a pleasure to offer this essay on Hilary's Christology in honor of my friend and mentor.

1. Claudianus Mamertus, *De Statu Animae* (PL 53.752B).
2. Bonaventure, *Commentaria in Quatuor Libros Sententiarum,* in *S. Bonaventurae Opera Omnia,* studio et cura PP. Collegii a S. Bonaventura, 11 vols. (Grottaferrata: Collegium S. Bonaventurae ad Claras Aquas, 1882–1902), 3.16

dubium 1, 3:359 (hereafter, *Sent.*). Cited in Kevin Madigan, "On the High-Medieval Reception of Hilary of Poitiers's Anti-'Arian' Opinion: A Case Study of Discontinuity in Christian Thought," *Journal of Religion* 78:2 (1998): 215, 221–22.

3. Bonaventure, *Sent.* 3.16.1.1 responsio, p. 346: "Non solum evacuat fidem Christi et Christi Evangelium, sed etiam evacuat redemptionem nostram et dicit, Christum non esse Christum." Text cited in Madigan, "On the High-Medieval Reception," 222.

4. Bonaventure suggests that William of Paris had seen this letter. Cf. Albert the Great, *Commentarii in IV Sententarium,* in *B. Alberti Magni Opera Omnia,* ed. É. Borgnet (Paris: Vivès, 1890–95), 3.15.G.10 solutio, p. 287; Thomas Aquinas, *Scriptum super Sententiis Magistri Petri Lombard,* ed. P. Mandonnet and R. P. Moos (Paris, 1929–33), vol. 3, p. 505, n. 1; Bonaventure, *Sent.* 3.16.1.1 ad primum, p. 346. For a discussion of these sources, cf. Madigan, "On the High-Medieval Reception," 223, nn. 40–41.

5. Martin Chemnitz, *Oratio de Lectione Patrum sive Doctorum Ecclesiasticorum (1554)* (Frankfurt and Wittenberg, 1653), p. 4a; and Martin Chemnitz, *De Duabus Naturis in Christo* (Frankfurt and Wittenberg, 1653), cap. III, p. 15b.

6. For a survey of the nineteenth-century views, cf. R. Favre, "La communication des idioms dans les oeuvres de Saint Hilaire de Poitiers," *Gregorianum* 17 (1936): 510–12; and G. Giamberardini, "De Incarnatione Verbi secundum S. Hilarium Pictaviensem," *Divus Thomas* 51 (1948): 3–13. For a brief comment on the place of Bonaventure's rumor in the history of scholarship on Hilary's Christology, cf. Favre, "La communication," 512–13.

7. E. W. Watson, "Introduction," *NPNF,* 2nd series, vol. 9, lxxvii. The quote is from Theodore Förster, "Zur Theologie des Hilarius," *Theologische Studien und Kritiken* 61 (1888): 662.

8. C. F. A. Borchardt, *Hilary of Poitiers' Role in the Arian Struggle,* Kerkhistorische Studien, vol. 12 (The Hague: Martinus Nijoff, 1966), 130, emphasis mine. For varying degrees of assessment on this Docetic strain in Hilary's thought, cf. also Jean Doignon, *Hilaire de Poitiers avant l'exil* (Paris: Études Augustiniennes, 1971), 274–79; J. N. D. Kelly, *Early Christian Doctrines* (London: A. & C. Black, 1958), 335; M. M. Thomas, *The Christology of Hilary of Poitiers* (unpublished thesis presented to Union Theological Seminary, New York, 1964), 190–94.

9. Pierre Smulders devotes only a few pages to this issue and concludes that Hilary was susceptible to Apollinarianism, not Docetism. Cf. Pierre Smulders, *La doctrine trinitaire de S. Hilaire de Poitiers,* Analecta Gregoriana, vol. 32 (Rome: Gregorian University, 1944), 203–6. Similarly cf. Alois Grillmeier, *Christ in the Christian Tradition,* vol. 1, *From the Apostolic Age to Chalcedon (451),* trans. J. S. Bowden (New York: Sheed and Ward, 1965), 396–97.

10. Paul Burns, *The Christology in Hilary of Poitiers' Commentary on Matthew,* Studia Ephemeridis Augustinianum, vol. 16 (Rome: Institutum Patristicum Augustinianum, 1981), 88–89, emphasis mine. Cf. also Favre, "La communication," 481–514. Favre demonstrates this psychological understanding in Hilary's *Commentary on Matthew, De Trinitate,* and *Tractates on the Psalms.*

11. Mark Weedman, "Martyrdom and Docetism in Hilary's *De Trinitate,*" *Augustinian Studies* 30 (1999): 40. Cf. also Mark Weedman, *The Trinitarian Theology of Hilary of Poitiers* (Leiden: Brill, 2007).

12. R. P. C. Hanson, *The Search for the Christian Doctrine of God: The Arian Controversy 318–381* (Edinburgh: T. & T. Clark, 1988), 501.

13. It should be noted that although Claudianus Mamertus and Bonaventure agreed that this was the inevitable conclusion of what Hilary *seems* to be arguing, they did not draw the conclusions that Hanson does.

14. Hanson, *Search,* 501–2.

15. Hanson's critique of Hilary's Christology goes so far as to assert that he only gives the appearance of teaching a two-natures Christology. Cf. Hanson, *Search,* 493.

16. Hilary of Poitiers, *De Trin.* IX.1–2. The Latin text for *De Trin.* is taken from SC 443 (books 1–3), 448 (books 4–8), and 462 (books 9–12). Citations of the text correspond to book, chapter, and line numbers in these volumes. Unless noted otherwise, translations are my own.

17. The Fathers sought to counter many of the heretical readings of Scripture by appealing to the context, place, or logic of a particular text within the larger narrative of salvation history or God's progressive revelation to us about the Son. By reading Scripture within such a context, they were enabled to interpret individual texts as all pointing to salvation in Christ.

18. On the use of *spiritus* in Hilary, cf. "Introduction," SC 443, 36–37 and SC 462, 42, n. 4.

19. *De Trin.* IX.3.6–24; cf. Pierre Smulders, *La doctrine trinitaire,* 284.

20. *De Trin.* V.18.21–25.

21. Cf. *De Trin.* V.18.1–6.

22. *De Trin.* IX.7.11–24.

23. *De Trin.* III.15.7–10.

24. *De Trin.* IX.10.11–15.

25. *De Trin.* IX.10.27–29.

26. *De Trin.* IX.11.17–28.

27. For Hilary's discussion of the phrase "personarum distinctio," cf. *De Trin.* IV.21–24.

28. *De Trin.* IX.12.14–22.

29. *De Trin.* IX.13.9–15.

30. On Hilary's theological method, cf. Carl Beckwith, "A Theological Reading of Hilary of Poitiers' 'Autobiographical' Narrative in *De Trinitate* I.1–19," *Scottish Journal of Theology* 59 (2006): 249–62.

31. *De Trin.* X.1.

32. *De Trin.* X.3.8–11.

33. *De Trin.* X.6–7.

34. *De Trin.* X.9.

35. *De Trin.* X.13.3–5.

36. For a similar discussion, cf. Hilary of Poitiers, *De Synodis* 38 and 49.

37. *De Trin.* X.41.17–19. Cf. Hilary's comments on the Eucharist at *De Trin.* VIII.14.

38. *De Trin.* X.14.7–9.

39. *De Trin.* X.15.1–6.

40. *De Trin.* X.14.20–22.

41. *De Trin.* X.20.

42. *De Trin.* X.15.6–13. On the role of the Son in the incarnation for Hilary, cf. SC 462, p. 194, n. 1.

43. *De Trin.* X.20.9.

44. On the question of the soul's origin, Tertullian had been a traducianist (*De Anima* 19), but in the fourth century Lactantius had insisted on the soul's origin as deriving from God's direct creation (*De Opificio Deo* 19). Augustine is famously divided on the question (*De libero arbitrio* 3.20.56–57; *Retractiones* [*Contra Academicos*] 1.1.3; and *De anima et eius origine*).

45. For the phrase, *spiritalis conceptionis,* cf. *De Trin.* X.21.7 and X.35.15.

46. *De Trin.* X.19.5–10

47. For Hilary's explicit rejection that the Word replaces the human soul in Christ, cf. *De Trin.* X.50–52.

48. *De Trin.* X.21.1–4.

49. Cf. *De Trin.* II.4.5–10: "Thus, Ebion [Photinus], assuming a beginning entirely from Mary, produces not a man from God, but God from man. The Virgin would not have received the pre-existing *Word* that *was in the beginning with God and was God,* but would have brought forth flesh through the Word. He [Photinus] says that the nature of the only-begotten God did not exist before in the Word, but was [only] a sound uttered by a voice." Hilary uses the beginning of the prologue to St. John's Gospel in his *Commentarium in Matthaeum, De Fide,* and *De Synodis* to refute the teachings he associates with Photinus of Sirmium. For a further discussion of Hilary and Photinus and the distinction between *apud Deum* and *in Deo,* see Carl L. Beckwith, "Photinian Opponents in Hilary of Poitiers' *Commentarium in Matthaeum,*" *Journal of Ecclesiastical History* 58:4 (2007): 611–27.

50. *De Trin.* X.21.4–10.

51. *De Trin.* X.22.16–18.

52. *De Trin.* X.22.36–43. Cf. also *De Trin.* X.61–62, where Hilary rejects those who wish to divide the one Christ into Word, soul, and body and assign his different experiences to the appropriate nature, and emphatically states that "the same one" who reigns in heaven dies on the cross and the one who dies is the same as the one who reigns.

53. It should be noted that despite the true union of the Word and the flesh, the Word still remains the Lord of heaven and earth and is present everywhere. Cf. *De Trin.* X.16.

54. *De Trin.* X.23.

55. *De Trin.* X.23.14–19.

56. *De Trin.* X.59–60.

57. *De Trin.* X.23.19–33.

58. Grillmeier characterizes Hilary's Christology as a "transfiguration-theology." Cf. Grillmeier, *Christ in Christian Tradition,* 1:397.

59. Maximus Confessor, *Ambigua* 113b (PG 91.1056AB). A similar position is found, of course, in Cyril of Alexandria. Cf. Warren J. Smith, "Suffering Impassibly: Christ's Passion in Cyril of Alexandria's Soteriology," *Pro Ecclesia* 11:4 (2002): 463–83.

60. Although not the first study to identify Stoic elements in Hilary's Christology, the most significant is Favre, "La communication," 481–514. For more recent works, cf. Doignon, *Hilaire de Poitiers avant l'exil,* 375; Burns, *Christology,* 89; Weedman, "Martyrdom and Docetism," 26–33.

61. The following description of Stoicism follows Tad Brennan, "Stoic Moral Psychology," in *The Cambridge Companion to the Stoics,* ed. Brad Inwood (Cambridge: Cambridge University Press, 2003), 257–94, and Dirk Baltzly, "Stoicism," in *The Stanford Encyclopedia of Philosophy* (Winter 2004 Edition), ed. Edward N. Zalta, URL = http://plato.stanford.edu/archives/win2004/entries/stoicism/.

62. Brennan, "Stoic Moral Psychology," 260–63. The terms "strong" or "weak" soul are from Hilary, not Brennan.

63. Baltzly, "Stoicism," section "3. Physical Theory."

64. For a fuller explanation of these terms, cf. Brennan, "Stoic Moral Psychology," 263.

65. Ibid., 264.

66. Ibid., 270, for these definitions of fear and pain.

67. Ibid., 270.

68. Again, this observation has long been established in Hilary scholarship. Cf. Favre, "La communication," 481–514; Doignon, *Hilaire de Poitiers avant l'exil,* 375; Burns, *Christology,* 89; Weedman, "Martyrdom and Docetism," 26–33.

69. For a similar christological position, cf. Clement of Alexandria, *Stromateis* 6.9. For Hilary's similarity to Athenagoras and Tertullian, cf. Weedman, "Martyrdom and Docetism," 31–33.

70. *De Trin.* II.25.14–18.

71. *De Trin.* X.44.6–12.

72. *De Trin.* X.44.15–16.

73. *De Trin.* X.46.3–12.

74. Hilary's understanding of the martyrs is widespread in both Christian and Jewish circles. For example, in the *Martyrdom of Polycarp* (12.1), the fear of Polycarp's impending death is replaced by joy (χαρᾶς), and in the *Martyrdom of Perpetua and Felicitas* (18.1), Perpetua trembled with joy (*gaudio*), not fear (*timore*). Cf. the rabbinic martyrdom of Akiva, whose sufferings were met with joy. For Polycarp, cf. Michael W. Holmes, ed., *The Apostolic Fathers: Greek Texts and English Translations* (Grand Rapids: Baker Books, 1999), 234; for Perpetua, cf. H. Musurillo, ed., *The Acts of the Christian Martyrs* (Oxford: Clarendon Press, 1972), 127; and for Akiva, cf. Robert Selzer, *Jewish People, Jewish Thought: The Jewish Experience in History* (New York: Macmillan, 1980), 303–4. For examples from other Christian martyrdoms, cf. Weedman, "Martyrdom and Docetism," 33–35.

75. Cf. *De Trin.* I.14.3–4.

76. *De Trin.* X.47.1–24. Hilary proceeds to quote 2 Cor 5:20–21.

77. *De Trin.* X.50.3–6.

78. *De Trin.* X.50.7–8.

79. *De Trin.* X.50.9–10.

80. *De Trin.* X.52.

81. *De Trin.* X.65.

82. *De Trin.* X.65.36–43.

83. *De Trin.* X.70.21–34.

5

Gregory of Nazianzus on the Unity of Christ

Christopher A. Beeley

> What we needed was a God made flesh and put to death, so that we might live.
>
> —St Gregory of Nazianzus, *Or.* 45.28

One of the many fruits of Brian Daley's career as a patristic scholar has been his demonstration that Cappadocian Christology is much richer than the received categories of interpretation have admitted. In two recent articles and in his 2002 D'Arcy Lectures in Oxford, Daley has shown that Gregory of Nyssa offers a consistent and powerful "Christology of transformation."[1] Despite his reputation for being puzzling and unsatisfactory according to the canons of fifth-century controversy, Gregory of Nyssa represents Christ as being so thoroughly divinized in his humanity—to the point that he is no longer even human, in the "fleshly" sense, after the resurrection[2]—that all human beings can find their own transformation in his. For similar reasons, the Christology of Gregory of Nazianzus—on whom Daley has also authored several studies[3]—is in need of reassessment as well. Scholars have long recognized that Gregory's *Letters* to Cledonius (*Ep*. 101–2) and to Nectarius (*Ep*. 202) are major christological treatises that significantly influenced later developments; his famous *Theological Orations* (*Or*. 27–31) have long been regarded as classic expressions of Trinitarian orthodoxy.[4] Yet, as with Gregory of Nyssa, Gregory Nazianzen's doctrine of Christ remains encumbered by anachronistic views that largely overlook his own rather substantial interests.

To mention just two points of confusion: Gregory of Nazianzus's Christology—like that of many pre-scholastic writers—has suffered the fate of being artificially separated from his doctrine of the Trinity, despite the fact that his work very strongly resists such a division. Even though Gregory's doctrine of Christ takes shape primarily in Constantinople from 379 to 381 in opposition to homoian and anhomoian positions, scholars have typically focused on his late *Ep*. 101–2 and 202, from A.D. 382 to 383, at the expense of his more substantial, earlier work. A second, related matter is that Gregory's Christology tends to be characterized primarily as anti-Apollinarian. For many years the standard handbooks have depicted Cappadocian Christology as essentially an orthodox response to the Apollinarian problem.[5] Yet this is a rather odd judgment, if we consider that Gregory hardly mentions Apollinarius until the end of his career; and it is questionable whether even at this late date he thinks Apollinarius's is the worst christological error on the contemporary scene, compared with the alternatives presented by Eunomius of Cyzicus and Diodore of Tarsus. The resulting neglect of Gregory's central concerns is both unfortunate and ironic, considering his seminal place in later Christian tradition and the great esteem in which he was held by later theologians such as Cyril of Alexandria and Maximus Confessor.

Central to the scholarly confusion is the question of whether Gregory's Christology is basically unitive or dualist. According to the received interpretation, Gregory holds a primarily dualist understanding of Christ's identity. J. N. D. Kelly notes approvingly that for Gregory, Christ is "twofold" (διπλοῦς, *Or*. 38.13), though without implying that there are two sons.[6] Alois Grillmeier focuses on Gregory's two-nature language, and goes so far as to conclude that "[Gregory's] own Christological formula . . . sounds very 'Antiochene.'"[7] One can find similar assessments in more recent scholarship as well.[8] On this reading, Gregory is a kind of proto-Chalcedonian—or even a representative Antiochene—stressing the distinction between the divine and human natures of Christ against imagined proto-Eutychians, who wrongly confuse them or collapse them into one another. While there are certain passages that might lend themselves to a dualist reading—several of which we will consider below—my contention is that the received view has it rather backwards and overlooks many of Gregory's deeper concerns. In order to demonstrate the fundamentally unitive character of Gregory's Christology, I focus here on the specific question of whether biblical references to Christ ultimately refer to one or two subjects.[9]

One Acting Subject

Before we consider the more technical aspects of the problem, we should first observe the most typical way in which Gregory speaks of Christ. Throughout his corpus, Gregory often refers simply to "Christ" being and doing a wide variety of things, both apart from and in the incarnation. A passage in his first oration sets the pattern:

> Let us become like Christ, since Christ became like us. Let us become gods for his sake, since he for ours became human. He assumed the worse, so that he might give away the better. He became poor, so that we through his poverty might become rich. He took the form of a servant, so that we might receive back our freedom. He descended, so that we might be exalted. He was tempted, so that we might conquer. He was dishonored, so that he might glorify us. He died, so that he might save us. He ascended, so that he might draw us to himself, who were lying low in the fall of sin. Let us give all, let us offer all to him who gave himself as a ransom and an exchange for us. (*Or.* 1.5)

Here it is simply "Christ" who exists before the incarnation, becomes human to save us, and continues to calls us as the risen Lord, with no explicit differentiation between the eternal Son of God and the human Jesus of Nazareth, or between Christ's divine and human natures. While fervent devotion to Christ is of course to be expected from a Christian bishop, and Gregory is for the most part reflecting the language of the New Testament and the Nicene Creed, there is more here than meets the eye. In 362, at the beginning of his career, Gregory is aware of the christological controversies that have racked the church since the 320s, and he is concerned in all of his work to articulate an orthodox doctrine of Christ. His simple predication of various statements to the one Christ is both meaningful and deliberate, and there are numerous other passages in the pre-Constantinopolitan orations (from 362 to 379) which bear the same stamp. It is "Jesus," Gregory says, who both created us and became human for us (*Or*. 14.2). When the Old Testament saints knew God through the Logos which was presented to their minds, their faith was "in Christ" (*Or*. 15.1). "Christ" created the great heritage of the church, and he also inherits it (*Or*. 4.67). And so Gregory considers a wide range of titles, from "God" to "human being," all to be "the titles and powers of Christ" (*Or*. 2.98).[10]

It is noteworthy that as Gregory's involvement in these controversies deepens, he does not come to regard this simpler kind of reference as an inferior or no longer sufficient way of speaking; in fact, such statements are more prevalent during and after his time in Constantinople, when he dealt with sophisticated opponents in increasingly technical ways. In an early oration in the capital, for example, it is "Christ" who does miracles in the Old and New Testaments (*Or*. 24.10).[11] In the hottest moments of trinitarian debate during the summer of 380, Gregory speaks of "Christ's bodily dwelling" on earth (*Or*. 41.5). And in the fifth *Theological Oration,* he writes that all things have been created "through Christ," even though the exegetical context of John 1:3 would make it more natural to say "through the Logos" (*Or*. 31.12). While the *Theological Orations* otherwise lack such references,[12] since Gregory is responding to Eunomian and Pneumatomachian objections with consistently high precision, the pattern continues soon afterward. He opens one of his most important orations on Christ by declaring that "Jesus" humbled himself and became human to save us from the "unsettled and bitter waves of life" (*Or*. 37.1). Even more strikingly, he adds that Jesus travels from place to place, though he is uncontained by any place—"the timeless, the bodiless, the uncircumscript, the same who was and is . . . . He was in the beginning with God and was God" (John 1:3)—all predicated of "Jesus" rather than the eternal Word, again despite an exegetical incentive to do so (*Or*. 37.2).[13]

Perhaps the most striking instance comes in the triptych of sermons that Gregory delivered in the Church of the Holy Apostles for Christmas/Epiphany 380/81 (*Or*. 38–40)—a set of texts as doctrinally significant as the more famous *Theological Orations*. As the new archbishop, Gregory presided over the Epiphany baptisms and delivered the mystagogical catechesis in the presence of the new emperor, possibly the conquered Gothic chieftain Athanaric, and Gregory's former theological rivals. He opens the series in a stream of liturgical praise:

> Christ is born—glorify him! Christ is come from heaven—rise up to meet him! Christ is on earth—be exalted! "Sing to the Lord, all the earth!" (Ps 95:1 LXX) And to say them both together: "Let the heavens rejoice and the earth be glad" (Ps 95:11 LXX) because the heavenly one now dwells on earth. Christ is in the flesh—rejoice with trembling and joy! (*Or*. 38.1)[14]

More explicitly than usual, Gregory again refers both heavenly and earthly statements to Christ. The ultimate cause of Christian praise and joy, he declares, is that the one Christ has come from heaven to earth for our salvation: thus begins this important set of festal homilies. The second and third homilies begin similarly: "Again my Jesus . . . the true light who enlightens every person who comes into the world (John 1:9)" and who restores the light that he originally gave us from above at the beginning of creation (*Or*. 39.1); and "my Christ" created us, became incarnate, was baptized, and rose from the dead for us, honoring all three types of human birth in his own person (παρ' ἑαυτοῦ, *Or*. 40.2). Gregory hardly repeats this practice in the body of the sermons,[15] but the more technical forms of argument found there serve to represent and make sense of the simpler confessional statements with which he began.

The pattern can also be found in Gregory's last three orations, delivered in Cappadocia in 382 and 383,[16] thus spanning his entire career.

Yet of course Gregory has plenty more to say about Christ's identity, and he mounts an advanced, technical Christology in several places. Although he rarely explains his theological method in such detail, the debates in Constantinople led him to give an explicit definition of his practice of christological exegesis. Gregory's clearest statement of christological method thus comes not in his late epistles, but in the heart of the *Theological Orations,* delivered in July–August 380. In the Constantinopolitan period Gregory typically combines his various opponents under the most extreme position of the heterousian theologian Eunomius of Cyzicus, whom he believes represents the fundamental logic of the rest. In the third and fourth *Theological Orations* (*Or*. 29–30) he responds to the Eunomians' objections to the full divinity of the Son. After answering a series of logical objections in *Or*. 29.3–16 and before turning to biblical objections in *Or*. 30.1–16,[17] Gregory gives a brief statement of his own doctrine of Christ based on Scripture and a descriptive account of his method of christological exegesis in *Or*. 29.17–20—one of the most important christological passages in his corpus. He offers the following rule of biblical interpretation and christological reference:

> Apply the loftier passages to his Divinity, to the nature that is superior to passivities and the body, and apply the lowlier passages to the composite one (ὁ σύνθετος), to him who for your sake emptied himself and became flesh and, to say it no worse, was made human, and afterwards was also exalted. (*Or*. 29.18)

The key to interpreting the various things that are said about Christ, Gregory says, is to understand that the more exalted and the humbler statements refer to the same Son of God, though in different ways. In order to answer Eunomian arguments against the full divinity of Christ, Gregory distinguishes purely divine statements about Christ from those which describe him in his incarnate state. Grander titles like "God," "Word" (John 1:1), and "Christ the power of God and the wisdom of God" (1 Cor 1:24) refer to Christ's identity as the divine Son of God in his eternal relationship with the Father, which Gregory signifies here with the shorthand term "his Divinity."[18] On the other hand, lowlier expressions like "slave," "he hungered," and "he wept" (Phil 2:7; Matt 4:2; John 11:35)—and above all his cross and death—refer to the Son of God who has assumed human existence in the person of Jesus and is now "composite." Thus when Wisdom—now generally assumed to be the Son—says in Prov 8:22, "The Lord *created* me as a beginning of his ways," this is not a statement about the Son in his pre-incarnate condition, as if to say without qualification that the Word of the Father is a creature. Rather, the Son as Wisdom is proleptically making a statement about his future incarnation, or composite state, in which he becomes also a creature of God, the human being Jesus. By referring the lesser sayings to the Son in his incarnate form, Gregory is able to counter the claim that such texts prove that the Son is in himself a creature and therefore not fully divine.

At the same time—and central to our purposes here—when Gregory distinguishes between unqualified and qualified references to Christ, he is saying that both kinds of statements refer to *the same Son of God*. While the lofty sayings refer to the Son without qualification, the lowly ones refer to the same Son with the qualification that he is now the incarnate, human Lord. In other words, Gregory's rule of interpretation is as much a definition of the unity and unchanging identity of the Son of God in his eternal and incarnate states as it is a distinction between those states—a point which is central to his doctrine of Christ as a whole. Yet, as we have noted, Gregory has been variously interpreted on just this question of whether there is a fundamental unity or a fundamental duality in Christ. In this passage he has been taken to be advocating a strong distinction between Christ's divine and human attributes, with biblical statements being referred to two distinct subjects. An influential example occurs in what was until recently the standard English translation of the *Theological Orations,* by Browne and Swallow. The phrase in question reads: "the composite condition of him who for your sakes made himself of no reputation."[19] According to this reading, lowly statements refer to the composite (incarnate) condition *of* the Son, that is, to Christ's humanity as distinct from his divinity, rather than referring to the Son himself in human form. Thus Gregory is seen as advancing a scheme of double predication which divides the statements between distinct final referents. However, the Greek text does not support this reading. The parallel dative construction τῷ συνθέτω καὶ τῷ διὰ σὲ κενωθέντι makes it clear that ὁ σύνθετος means "the one who is composite" (in parallel with "the one who emptied himself"), namely, the Son of God who is incarnate, rather than "the composite condition" of the Son of God.[20] The correct reading is supported by the second instance in the *Theological Orations* where Gregory gives his hermeneutical rule. Here, the "lowlier and more human" expressions refer to "the New Adam, God made passible in order to defeat sin" (*Or*. 30.1), that is, to the eternal Son of God in his human form as the New Adam. Gregory is therefore not saying that the lofty sayings refer to the Son's divinity and the lowly sayings to his humanity; nor is he distinguishing between Christ's pre-incarnate and incarnate states, as if the lofty expressions referred to him before the incarnation and the lowly ones referred to him in the incarnation. Rather, statements that refer to Christ's divinity apply always, both before and during the incarnation, as can be clearly seen in the New Testament, where they are often spoken of or by the human Jesus. To read Gregory's hermeneutical rule in a dualist fashion, assuming predication to two different subjects or two distinct phases of Christ's career, misses his meaning entirely. At this central point of his career, when he is pressed to give an account of his christological method, Gregory both assumes and advances a doctrine of the unity and unchanging identity of the Son of God in his eternal and his incarnate states.

So deeply embedded is the unity of Christ in Gregory's thought that it leads him to push the Eunomians beyond what appears to be their actual position. In his extant works Eunomius argues against the full divinity of Christ on the basis of texts that refer to the *pre*-incarnate Son—so that the Son of God is already a creature, apart from the incarnation—and there is no indication that he ever appealed to Jesus' lowly, human status per se. It is Gregory who presses the Eunomians to that point. After listing several texts that Eunomius has cited,[21] Gregory then adds further sayings that refer not to the Son's pre-incarnate condition, but specifically to his lowly, human status:

> If you want, list also "slave" and "obedient," "he gave," "he learned" (Phil 2:7, 8; Jn 18:9; Hb 5:8) . . . . Or add sayings that are even lowlier than these, like the fact that he slept, was hungry, got tired, wept, was in agony, was subjected (Mt 8:24; 4:2; Jn 4:6; 11:35; Lk 22:44; 1 Cor 15:28)—maybe you even reproach him for his cross and death! (*Or.* 29.18)

Gregory is suggesting that if texts like Proverbs 8:22 indicate the Son's created status, how much more do his hunger, tears, and death on the cross. The hidden premise is that both kinds of statement refer to the same subject, a point that Gregory tacitly assumes and Eunomius seems to have held as well.[22] If Christ was composed of two different subjects, then the humble passages that Gregory raises could simply be attributed to the human Jesus as distinct from the pre-incarnate or eternal Son, and they would not stand as proof against his divinity at all. But, significantly, Gregory does not do this. He extends the Eunomian position to include *all* biblical statements about Christ's creaturely status—pre-incarnate and incarnate—to which he counters that the lowly, crucified Christ "is for us true God and on the same level with the Father" (*Or*. 29.18). To be sure, Gregory is also making the second point that such texts refer to the Son in a different way—in the incarnation, or "economically" (29.18)—but the whole point of his method of predication is to confess that the crucified Lord *is* the eternal Son of God. Nowhere in this passage does he avoid the Eunomian objection by separating human from divine referents. In fact, as the next section shows, his argument runs in the opposite direction: the very one whom the Eunomians scorn is none other than the merciful and humble Lord who was crucified for our salvation (*Or*. 29.19). In this important passage, Gregory advances the unity of Christ as a single subject of reference both in the way he sets up the problem and in the christological method that he goes on to define.

As a climactic conclusion to his argument, Gregory illustrates the singularity of Christ in one of his most beautiful passages. With great rhetorical skill and liturgical sensibility, he recites a litany of seemingly contrary acts of the one Christ, paired in matching antitheses:

> He was begotten [ἐγεννήθη], yet he was also born [γεγέννητο][23] of a woman . . . . He was wrapped in swaddling bands, but he took off the swaddling bands of the grave by rising again . . . . He was exiled into Egypt, but he banished the Egyptian idols . . . . He was baptized as a human being, but he remitted sins as God . . . . He hungered, but he fed thousands. . . . He thirsted, but he cried out, "If anyone is thirsty, let him come to me and drink." . . . He prays, but he hears prayer. He weeps, but he makes weeping to cease. He asks where Lazarus was laid, for he was a human being; but he raises Lazarus, for he was God . . . . As a sheep he is led to the slaughter, but he is the shepherd of Israel . . . . He lays down his life, but he has power to take it up again . . . . He dies, but he gives life, and by death destroys death. He is buried, but he rises again. (*Or.* 29.19–20)[24]

Together with each of Christ's divine qualities or actions—some extra-incarnate, some incarnate—Gregory pairs a corresponding action that he accomplishes as a human being, so that it is the same Son of God who does them all. As he comments, the Son does some things "as God," things which only God can do (whether or not in human form), such as rising from the dead, forgiving sins, and destroying death; while others he does "as a human being," such as praying, being hungry, and dying—things which all of us do apart from God's saving work, and which characterize the condition that the Son came to heal and save.

The hermeneutical rule that Gregory gives in *Or.* 29.18 provides a rubric for his overall understanding of Christ's identity. In the following section he gives a brief but telling account of Christ, still addressed to the Eunomians:

> The one whom you now scorn was once above you [ὑπὲρ σέ]. The one who is now human was once incomposite [ἀσύνθετος]. What he was, he continued to be; what he was not, he assumed. In the beginning he existed without cause [ἀναιτίως], for what is the cause of God? But later on he was born for a cause [δι᾽ αἰτίαν]—namely that you might be saved, who insult him and despise his Divinity because he took upon himself your thickness,[25] associating with

> flesh through the intermediary of a [human] mind, and being made a human being who is God on earth [γενόμενος ἄνθρωπος ὁ κάτω θεός],[26] since [human existence] was blended with God and he was born as a single entity [ἓις], because the One who is more powerful prevailed [over his assumed humanity], so that we might be made divine to the same extent that he was made human. (*Or.* 29.19)

As Frederick Norris has observed—and similar to Brian Daley's analysis of Gregory of Nyssa's Christology—Gregory Nazianzen's understanding of Christ is defined primarily within the broader framework of the economy of salvation as a whole.[27] At a particular point in time, Gregory argues, the divine Son of God, who was previously incomposite (ἀσύνθετος) and not mingled with his creation, took upon himself our created, human existence—a form of existence radically different from his own—and became composite (σύνθετος, *Or.* 29.18) in order to save us. While remaining the divine Son of God ("what he was, he continued to be") he has now also become a human creature ("what he was not, he assumed"). Moreover, because the eternal being of the Son is that of the Creator God, his divine nature predominates over his new, creaturely form and gives primary identity to it. Even though God and human existence are ontologically distinct, the difference between them is so great that the incarnate Christ is not two distinct things, but a single entity (ἓις) as before, only now in a composite state. Gregory does not imagine Christ as a God-man existing in a kind of personal duality or ontological balance; this is not what he means by composition or synthesis. Rather, he understands Christ to be the Son of God in the most fundamental sense, even in the incarnation. For this reason he often speaks of "Christ" as the subject of the Son's divine acts, as we saw above: not because Christ's flesh existed before the incarnation, as the Apollinarians were accused of holding;[28] nor because the Spirit eternally anoints the Son, making him Christ even in his divinity, as Gregory of Nyssa held;[29] but because Christ is himself the Son of God made human. On account of his transtemporal identity, which for Gregory of Nazianzus goes well beyond a mere *communicatio idiomatum*—according to which the names and attributes of Christ's divinity and humanity are merely predicated of the other term but do not reflect an actual ontological state, such as the Antiochenes held—everything that the Son does Christ does, and vice versa.

In the major orations from 379 on, Gregory defines Christ's identity within the same unitive, economic framework, making the Son the ultimate referent of Christ's divine and human acts.[30] The opening sections of *Oration* 37, from late 380, are an important example:

> The one who is uncontained moves from place to place—he who is timeless, bodiless, uncircumscript, who was and is, who was both above time and came under time, who was invisible and is seen. He was in the beginning and was with God and was God (Jn 1:1) . . . . What he was he set aside; what he was not he assumed. Not that he became two things, but he deigned to be made one thing out of two [οὐ δύο γενόμενος, ἀλλ' ἓν ἐκ τῶν δύο γενέσθαι ἀνασχόμενος]. For both are God, that which assumed and that which was assumed, the two natures meeting in one thing [δύο φύσεις εἰς ἓν συνδραμούσαι]. But not two sons: let us not give a false account of the blending [ἡ σύγκρασις]. (*Or.* 37.2)[31]

With apologies for the difficulty of expressing such thoughts—"Pardon my speech: I am speaking of the greatest things with a limited instrument!"—Gregory labors to explain that the limited, human Savior is the visible form of the invisible God, who has himself taken on our life in a single, compound entity. The opening sections of *Oration* 37 remind us again that Gregory often expresses his Christology in the simpler terms that we first examined.[32] The same holds true in the great Epiphany sermons, where he begins with simple language—"Christ is born . . . Christ from heaven . . . Christ on earth" (*Or.* 38.1)—and then goes on to give a more refined exposition of the same basic idea. The fullest statement comes in *Oration* 38.13 (= 45.9), which is then echoed more briefly in *Orations* 39–40: the incomprehensible and invisible Word of God himself "came to his own image and took on himself flesh for the sake of our flesh and mingled himself with an intelligent soul for my soul's sake, purifying like by like, and in all ways except sin was made human." As Gregory explains, in terms similar to *Or.* 37.2 above, this means that the one born of Mary is "God together with what he assumed, one thing made out of two opposites [ἓν ἐκ δύο τῶν ἐναντίων], flesh and Spirit, of which the latter deifies and the former is deified." As in *Or.* 29.19, then, Gregory defines Christ as the eternal Word of God who has taken on a complete human form, "mingling" himself with our condition so intimately that his divine nature unifies and most fundamentally characterizes Jesus' identity, even in its human element, so as to make him truly "one thing" (ἕν).[33] This unitive, narrative christological framework pervades Gregory's corpus and remains fundamental to his doctrine throughout his career. In the late christological epistles, for example, he argues that initially (πρότερον) God the Son existed entirely separate from the temporal economy of salvation (μόνον καὶ προαιώνιον), but that finally (ἐπὶ τέλει) he became also a human being (*Ep.* 101.13–14). Again, the Son of God is eternally begotten of the Father, "and after this" (καὶ μετὰ τοῦτο) was born of the Virgin Mary (*Ep.* 102.4). In all of these passages the crucified Jesus is understood primarily as the Son of God, making the apostolic confessions "Jesus Christ the Son of God" (Mark 1:1) and "Christ is Lord" (1 Cor 12:2) true and accurate—even if counterintuitive—statements of his identity.

More prevalent than the technical definitions given in *Or.* 29.19 and 37.4, however, are the numerous passages where Gregory simply speaks of God, or the Son of God, as the one who underwent the human experiences of Christ. In his first major christological statement in Constantinople, Gregory insists on the confession that *God* was born and died and rose for us, and he severely criticizes those who avoid such vivid language (*Or.* 22.13). Likewise, in his poem against Apollinarius, written in 382/83, he argues that it is essential that "God was conceived and born" (*Carm.* 1.1.10.22) and that

> God came to an end as man, to honor me,
> so that by the very things he took on, he might restore,
> and destroy sin's accusation utterly,
> and, by dying, slaughter the slaughterer.
>
> (*Carm.* 1.1.10.6–9)[34]

For Gregory (as for all the orthodox Fathers), the focus and climax of Christ's saving work is his death on the cross. He frequently speaks of God—a single subject—dying on the cross for our salvation. "We needed a God made flesh and put to death, so that we might live," he writes in his final Easter oration in Cappadocia, and so "God is crucified" (*Or*. 45.28–29).[35] Gregory is so intent on proclaiming God's direct involvement in Christ's human life and death that he even uses language that some believed threatens to contradict the fundamental distinction between God and created beings, terms that Gregory of Nyssa also uses,[36] and which would later become suspect for their Apollinarian associations. The impassible Son of God, Gregory says, is "mingled" (μίγνυται) with human suffering and the immortal one with human corruptibility. So real is the Son's assumption of fallen human existence in the incarnation that when the Devil attacks Jesus, he unwittingly meets with God, and death is defeated by death (*Or*. 39.13).

The soteriological significance of Christ's divine identity is clearest at the greatest point of his suffering, as he cries from the cross, "My God, my God, look upon me, why have you forsaken me?" (Ps 21:1 LXX; cf. Matt 27:46). For Gregory, Jesus' cry of dereliction does not indicate that God has abandoned him, in which case there would certainly be two subjects involved: Christ has not been abandoned either by the Father or by his own divinity—as if God were afraid of suffering! Rather, Jesus' ultimate desolation conveys just how authentically the Son has assumed and represented (τυποῦν) our fallen condition, "making our thoughtlessness and waywardness *his own*" (*Or*. 30.5). Jesus' cry of abandonment, in other words, does not reflect the *absence* of God in his suffering, but rather reflects God's inclusion of our abandonment within his saving embrace and his healing *presence* in the midst of the suffering and death that our sin has brought about. Christ's suffering shows just how great God's love for us is, because in him *God* has died in order to forgive our sins (*Or*. 33.14). In Gregory's view, it is not enough for God to associate himself with human existence without actually becoming human: the Son himself must assume and undergo human suffering and death in order to purify like by like (*Ep*. 101.51). Gregory therefore defines Christ as "God made passible for our sake against sin" (*Or*. 30.1),[37] and—keenly aware of the paradox involved—

he declares that we are "saved by the sufferings of the impassible one" (τὰ τοῦ ἀπαθοῦς πάθεις, *Or.* 30.5).[38] Thus for Gregory the awesome nature of the Christian faith is quite literally "to see God crucified" (*Or.* 43.64). He emphasizes the point in the final sections of his last oration: "We needed an incarnate God, a God put to death, so that we might live; and we were put to death with him" (*Or.* 45.28). Because it was *God* who died on the cross—the Son of God made human just for this purpose—then his death can be the death of all fallen humanity, and we can be purified and made a new creation by his divine life.[39]

Two Acting Subjects?

As I noted above, one finds a rather different picture of Gregory's Christology in most current studies. Scholars have almost universally overlooked the unity and singularity of Christ in Gregory's work on the basis of a handful of texts in which he seems to be saying just the opposite. In the fourth *Theological Oration* Gregory appears to argue that, in order to avoid christological error, the human Jesus, or Christ's humanity, must be conceived as a subject of existence distinct from the eternal Son of God. Although in certain passages he follows the pattern of single-subject predication outlined in *Or.* 29.18 and 30.1, in others he practices a kind of double predication, referring certain things to Christ's humanity in a way that appears to be independent of his divinity. Some of these passages resolve themselves into the single-subject paradigm,[40] such as *Or.* 30.2, where Gregory considers the interpretation of Proverbs 8:22 and provides yet another instance of his hermeneutical rule. Gregory comments that whatever has to do with Christ's being caused, such as the term "created," must refer to his humanity (ἡ ἀνθρωπότης), whereas whatever is simple and uncaused refers to his Divinity (ἡ θεότης). The question is whether Gregory means Christ's human nature per se, as a subject of existence other than the Son of God, or whether he means the Son of God in his human form, as in *Or.* 29.18 and 30.1. At the end of the section he plainly indicates the latter, saying that Wisdom (the divine subject) is called these things in different respects.[41]

Yet there are other passages that do not resolve themselves so neatly into the unitive scheme.[42] In *Or.* 30.16, for example, Gregory argues that statements about Christ's human acts—such as keeping God's commandments (John 15:10; cf. 10:18; 12:49), learning obedience through suffering (Heb 5:8), and the agony of his passion (Heb 5:7; Luke 22:44)—refer to "the passible element, *not* the immutable nature that is far above passion."[43] Rather than referring the lowly passages to the Son of God in his human form, as in *Or.* 29.18 and 30.1, Gregory's point here seems to be that they do not refer to God at all, but rather to Jesus' humanity as *distinct* from his divinity, thus positively resisting single-subject predication. In other, related passages he explicitly describes Christ as being dual or double. In his reply to Eunomian arguments from John 14:28 and 20:17—"the Father is greater than I" and "I am ascending to my Father and your Father, to my God and your God"—Gregory explains that while the Father is Father of the Word, God is not the God of the Word, "because he was two-fold [διπλοῦς]." What misleads heretics, he says, is a failure to appreciate just this duality, and to realize that even though Christ's divine and human titles are "yoked together on account of the mixture [ἡ σύγκρασις]," nevertheless "the natures are distinguished and the names are separated in our thoughts . . . . Even though the combination of [God and human existence] is a single entity, he is such not in his [divine] nature [alone], but in the union of the two" (*Or.* 30.8).[44] As above, Gregory appears to be saying that the key to understanding Christ's identity is to distinguish his two natures from one another as distinct referents and subjects of existence.[45] In light of such passages, one might indeed be led to agree with Grillmeier that Gregory's Christology is "very Antiochene."

The challenge that these passages pose runs to the heart of Gregory's soteriology. In his view, God created human beings into a process of "divinization" (θέωσις), a dynamic condition of eschatological growth into the likeness of God and toward the union of the soul with the Trinity.[46] However, in the sin of Adam we fell into a condition of sin and death, from which we are unable to save ourselves. In order to reestablish our divinization, God therefore sent his only Son to become human and to suffer death on the cross. But for Gregory, Christ is not merely the instrumental cause of the divinization of others: he is himself the first instance and the paradigm of our salvation—the New Adam and the archetype of a renewed human race—because he is "God on earth" (*Or*. 29.19). Gregory argues that sin and death could be defeated and the process of divinization restarted only if God took on our condition and healed it from within. Christ is the constitutive principle of salvation precisely because he is most fundamentally the Son of God, who has assumed our fallen condition *as his own*. The unity of Christ as a single entity (ἕν, εἷς)—with his human existence given the fullest possible articulation *within* his divine identity—is therefore the central tenet of Gregory's soteriology and his Christology. As a signification of Christ's saving work, we should expect that all of Christ's human acts belong to the Son of God in his human form, or to his "economy" (*Or*. 29.18), just as his divine acts (before or in the incarnation) refer to the Son without economic qualification. The passages that seem to distinguish Jesus' humanity from his divinity, as distinct referents and subjects of existence, must therefore be seen as threatening Gregory's soteriology at its very core, so that it could no longer be said that in Christ *God* suffered, died, and rose from the dead for our salvation.

There are several points to be made in response to this problem. First, we must observe that the single-subject paradigm is the most prevalent mode of christological reflection in Gregory's work. Single-subject constructions far outweigh dual ones, in both frequency and importance, in major and minor orations as well as in the dogmatic poems. Secondly, it is significant that the greatest concentration of apparently dualist exegesis comes in the fourth *Theological Oration*—a fact which urges us to look more closely at the oration as a whole. We have already examined the introduction to *Oration* 30 above (*Or*. 29.17–21); we must now turn to the conclusion. At the end of the oration, Gregory returns to the subject with which he began in *Or*. 29.17, recapitulating his christological argument in a lengthy meditation on the names of God and Christ (*Or*. 30.17–21). He first discusses the Son's lofty names—those which belong to him "both above us and for us," and then turns to his lowly names—those which are "uniquely ours and which belong to what he assumed from us." This second phrase might again suggest the dualist model: that the lowly names belong to Christ's humanity as opposed to the eternal Son; here, however, Gregory reemphasizes the unity of Christ's human existence with his divine sonship. Christ is called "human being," he says, to signify that the incomprehensible One is comprehended "through his body," and that he sanctifies humanity "through himself": in each case the eternal Son is the subject of Christ's actions. Gregory also signals the unitive model by returning to his typical practice of using the term "nature" to refer primarily to the divine being, which primarily defines Christ's identity. In the commentary that follows, Christ's divine identity subsumes and defines his incarnate, human status. While he is a complete human being—body, soul, and mind—Christ has united human existence to himself so fully that he is, in the truest sense, "God made visible to intellectual perception" (θεὸς ὁρώμενος, διὰ τὸ νοούμενον). And he is called "Christ" for the same reason: because in becoming human the divine Son anoints his humanity through his complete presence as the anointer (παρουσίᾳ δὲ ὅλου τοῦ χρίοντος), as opposed to the anointing of prophets and kings, which takes place merely by divine action (ἐνεργείᾳ)—and which, we may add, occurs between two distinct entities. Finally, Gregory urges his readers to "walk through" all the titles of the Son, both the lofty and the lowly, in a godly way (θεϊκῶς). Even as we identify with Christ's assumed, human qualities because they are our own (συμπαθῶς), by faith we come to see that these too belong to God (θεϊκῶς again), and in so doing we "ascend from below and become God, because he came down from above for our sake" (*Or*. 30.21). In this dogmatic and spiritual tour de force, *Oration* 30 climactically resolves into the economic paradigm with which it began, framing the entire piece in a single-subject doctrine of Christ.

The general pattern of Gregory's corpus and the main argument of *Or*. 29.17–30.21 strongly suggest that the apparently dualistic passages be reconsidered within the economic paradigm. Either they must be susceptible to an economic interpretation, or they are deeply inconsistent with Gregory's larger christological project. To return to *Or*. 30.16—the strongest such passage—we find that Gregory need not be saying that Jesus' human and divine acts refer to two different subjects of existence. He is more likely saying that Christ's human acts refer to "*his* passible element, not *his* immutable nature that is far above passion":[47] that the lowly passages refer to the human existence, or the human form, that the Son has assumed, while still being the Son of God in that assumption, rather than to his own, divine nature per se, apart from the incarnation. Likewise, statements that Christ is "two-fold" (διπλοῦς, *Or.* 30.8, 38.13) need not mean anything other than what Gregory argues in *Or.* 29.18: that in the economy the Son is now "composite" (σύνθετος), and thus can be said to be and do human things on account of the human form that he has assumed. As it turns out, each of the apparently dualist texts can be thus interpreted within the economic paradigm.

What appears to be happening in *Oration* 30, with slight residual effects afterward, is the result of Gregory's attempt to make his case for the unitive, economic paradigm as strongly as possible. As he addresses Eunomian exegesis—and by extension all subordinationist opposition to the Son's full divinity—he finds it necessary to add the qualification that, although they are *God's* human actions, they must not be understood as God's actions apart from the incarnation. As important as it is that in Christ the Son of God died a human death, it is equally important not to suggest that he died a *divine* death as well—that in the fullness of his being God died on the cross and therefore has ceased to be God; otherwise, the Eunomian position would have very much to recommend it indeed. In this regard, the single-subject, economic paradigm is not only capable of accommodating such qualifications, but it necessarily includes them, either explicitly or implicitly—whether they be fulsome accounts of Jesus' humanity or statements that he possesses two elements or natures—without subverting the central claim that Christ's identity is determined primarily by his divinity. Given that the contested passages fit perfectly well within Gregory's unitive, economic structure, it would appear, then, that the confusion stems not from the potential contradiction of certain texts, but rather from a presupposed christological dualism on the part of the interpreter. If one has a full, economic understanding of Christ's unity, as Gregory does, then it makes perfect sense to speak of certain things as belonging to Christ's humanity as distinct from his divinity, so long as one assumes that the ultimate subject of Christ's human actions is the eternal Son of God; and it is unnecessary—indeed it would be tiresome—to spell this out every time. Gregory's Christology is therefore dualist only if one assumes that the unitive, economic paradigm is not in force, which means that on closer examination the dualist reading very much begs the question. Finally, we may speculate that the prevalence of the dualist view stems in part from scholars' relying too heavily on *Oration* 30 and studying the *Theological Orations* in isolation—or possibly only with the christological epistles—rather than interpreting them within the larger context of Gregory's corpus.

Conclusion

For reasons central to his understanding of salvation and the Christian life, Gregory of Nazianzus consistently and deliberately maintains a unitive Christology. Christ's identity as the divine Son of God who has become human as a single subject of existence is the central tenet of Gregory's doctrine of Christ and the essential expression of his soteriology. His common practice of referring both lofty and lowly sayings simply to "Christ" is a coherent reflection of this unitive scheme. Because the incarnate, human Lord is in his fundamental identity the eternal Son of God, it is not only permissible to say that Christ created us as well as redeemed us, but by keeping the focus on the incarnate Christ as the one in whom Christians know God in the power of the Holy Spirit, it is in a sense more faithful to do so. Moreover, the unitive doctrine examined here helps us to see that Gregory is the main source of the deepest principles of Cyril of Alexandria's Christology,[48] and, through others such as Maximus Confessor, a large measure of subsequent christological orthodoxy. Gregory's doctrine is not fundamentally Antiochene, anti-Apollinarian,[49] or in any other sense dualistic, as has been alleged; and rather than compromising the integrity of Christ's human existence, it gives a compelling, traditional account of its real meaning.

Notes

1. Brian E. Daley, S.J., "Divine Transcendence and Human Transformation: Gregory of Nyssa's Anti-Apollinarian Christology," in *Studia Patristica,* ed. Elizabeth A. Livingstone, vol. 32 (Leuven: Peeters, 1997), 87–95, repr. *Modern Theology* 18 (2002): 497–506; and Daley, "'Heavenly Man' and 'Eternal Christ':

Apollinarius and Gregory of Nyssa on the Personal Identity of the Savior," *Journal of Early Christian Studies* 10 (2002): 469–88.

2. Gregory of Nyssa, *Antirrh.* (*GNO* 3.1.222). Daley, "'Heavenly Man' and 'Eternal Christ,'" 474, n. 20.

3. Brian E. Daley, S.J., "NAPS Presidential Address. Building the New City: The Cappadocian Fathers and the Rhetoric of Philanthropy," *Journal of Early Christian Studies* 7 (1999): 431–61; "The Cappadocian Fathers and the Option for the Poor," in *The Option for the Poor in Christian Theology,* ed. Daniel G. Groody (Notre Dame, Ind.: University of Notre Dame Press, 2007), 77–88; "Saint Gregory of Nazianzus as Pastor and Theologian," in *Loving God with Our Minds: The Pastor as Theologian: Essays in Honor of Wallace M. Allston,* ed. Michael Welker and Cynthia A. Jarvis (Grand Rapids: Eerdmans, 2004), 106–19; and *Gregory of Nazianzus,* The Early Church Fathers (London: Routledge, 2006), an introduction to Gregory's life and work with a selection of new translations.

4. References to Gregory's texts are as follows: *Or*. 1–3, 6–12, 20–43, and *Ep*. 101–2 and 202 are to the SC editions; *Or*. 4–5, 13–19, and 44–45 are to PG. (For *Or*. 1–3, SC vol. 247; 6–12, vol. 405; 20–22, vol. 270; 24–26, vol. 284; 27–31, vol. 250; 32–37, vol. 318; 38–41, vol. 358; 42–43, vol. 384; for *Ep*. 101–2, 202, vol. 208. For *Or*. 4–5, 13–19, PG 35; for *Or.* 44–45, PG 36.) Passages from Gregory's orations are listed in chronological order, following McGuckin's revised dating: John A. McGuckin, *St Gregory of Nazianzus: An Intellectual Biography* (Crestwood, N.Y.: St. Vladimir's Seminary Press, 2001), vii–xi and passim.

5. Most famously, J. N. D. Kelly's *Early Christian Doctrines,* rev. ed. (San Francisco: HarperSanFrancisco, 1978), 295–301, here 297; and Alois Grillmeier, *Christ in Christian Tradition,* vol. 1, *From the Apostolic Age to Chalcedon (451),* trans. John Bowden (London: Mowbrays, 1965), 278–91; rev. ed. (1975), 367–77; new German ed., *Jesus der Christus im Glauben der Kirche: Von der Apostolischen Zeit bis zum Konzil von Chalcedon* (Freiburg: Herder, 1979), 435–47, a shorter account that omits some of the points made here.

6. Kelly, *Early Christian Doctrines,* 297.

7. Grillmeier, *Christ in Christian Tradition* (1975 ed.), 369.

8. E.g., Donald Winslow, *The Dynamics of Salvation: A Study in Gregory of Nazianzus,* Patristic Monograph Series 7 (Cambridge, Mass.: Philadelphia Patristic Foundation, 1979), 83–84; Kenneth Paul Wesche, "The Union of God and Man in Jesus Christ in the Thought of Gregory of Nazianzus," *St. Vladimir's Theological Quarterly* 28 (1984): 83–98; Claudio Moreschini, SC vol. 358 (1990), 53f.; Peter Bouteneff, "St Gregory Nazianzen and Two-Nature Christology," *St. Vladimir's Theological Quarterly* 38 (1994), 255–70; Frederick Norris, "Christ/Christology" and "Gregory of Nazianzus," in *Encyclopedia of Early Christianity,* 2nd ed., ed. Everett Ferguson, assoc. eds. Michael P. McHugh and Frederick W. Norris (New York: Garland, 1998), 242–51, 491–95.

Previous studies of Gregory's Christology include Norris's 1971 Yale dissertation, "Gregory Nazianzen's Doctrine of Jesus Christ." See also his commentary *Faith Gives Fullness to Reasoning: The Five Theological Orations of Gregory Nazianzen,* intro. and commentary by Frederick Norris, trans. Lionel Wickham and Frederick Williams (Leiden: Brill, 1991); and John A. McGuckin, "'Perceiving Light from Light in Light' (*Oration* 31.3): The Trinitarian Theology of St Gregory the Theologian," *Greek Orthodox Theological Review* 39.1 (1994): 7–32, and "The Vision of God in St. Gregory Nazianzen," *Studia Patristica* 32 (Leuven: Peeters, 1997), 145–52.

9. For a comprehensive treatment of Gregory's Christology, see Christopher A. Beeley, *Gregory of Nazianzus on the Trinity and the Knowledge of God: In Your Light We Shall See Light,* Oxford Studies in Historical Theology (New York: Oxford University Press, 2008), chap. 2.

10. See also *Or.* 4.19, 37; 5.36; 7.23; 14.4, 15; 8.14; 12.4; 17.12; 19.12–13.

11. From this period see also *Or.* 32.5, 18.

12. As does *Or.* 42, for similar reasons.

13. The pattern continues throughout the oration. See esp. *Or.* 37.3, 7–8. During this period, see also *Or.* 24.2; 32.33; 33.9; 41.4; 26.6.

14. Trans. Daley adapt.

15. One exception being *Or.* 39.12.

16. *Or.* 43.61, 64; 44.2, 7; and 45.1, another festal homily which opens in the same way as *Or.* 38–40.

17. I will examine Gregory's concluding treatment of the divine names in *Or.* 30.17–21 below.

18. Gregory gives a longer list of such passages in *Or.* 29.17.

19. Trans. Charles Gordon Browne and James Edward Swallow, *NPNF,* 2nd series, vol. 7, 307–8; reprinted in *Christology of the Later Fathers,* ed. Edward R. Hardy, Library of Christian Classics, vol. 3 (Philadelphia: Westminster, 1954), 173.

20. Lionel Wickham's more recent translation avoids this error: "predicate the lowlier [expressions] of the compound, of him who because of you was emptied . . . ." (St. Gregory of Nazianzus, *On God and Christ: The Five Theological Orations and Two Letters to Cledonius,* trans. Frederick Williams and Lionel Wickham [Crestwood, N.Y.: St. Vladimir's Press, 2002], 86). Cf. also Bouteneff, "St Gregory Nazianzen and Two-Nature Christology," 260.

21. John 20:17; John 14:28; Prov 8:22; Acts 2:36; John 10:36.

22. Richard Paul Vaggione, *Eunomius of Cyzicus and the Nicene Revolution,* Oxford Early Christian Studies (Oxford: Oxford University Press, 2000), 109.

23. The majority manuscript reading. Paul Gallay prefers the *lectio difficilior* form ἐγεγέννητο. SC vol. 250, 218.

24. Gregory's fondness for this construction can be seen in his adaptation of it at least twice more, in *Or.* 38.16 and *Carm.* 1.1.2.62–75.

25. I.e., the thick corporeality of human existence.

26. The translations of this phrase in *NPNF* by Browne and Swallow, "his inferior nature, the humanity, became God," is again misleading in a dualist direction, suggesting that Christ's humanity somehow existed independently and *then* was divinized. Gallay's French translation reflects the same problem: "l'homme d'ici-bas est devenu Dieu" (SC vol. 250, 219). Nothing could be further from Gregory's mind. Wickham's translation, "being made that God on earth, which is Man," while avoiding this error, unwittingly suggests that humanity in general is divine.

27. Norris, "Gregory Nazianzen's Doctrine of Christ," 167. Daley observes that Gregory of Nyssa's Christology is also defined within a narrative structure, in "'Heavenly Man' and 'Eternal Christ,'" 480.

28. Gregory Nazianzen, *Ep*. 101.16; Gregory of Nyssa, *Antirrh*. 166 (*GNO* 3.1).

29. *Antirrh*. 220–22 (*GNO* 3.1). Daley, "'Heavenly Man' and 'Eternal Christ,'" 480.

30. A helpful, though ultimately different, analysis of Gregory's "economic paradigm" can be found in Norris, "Gregory Nazianzen's Doctrine of Jesus Christ," 167–201.

31. Trans. Browne and Swallow adapt.

32. Cf. *Or*. 37.1 and 2.

33. Gregory uses both masculine and neuter pronouns to express Christ's unity: *Or*. 29.19, γέγονεν εἷς; *Ep*. 101.21, τὰ γὰρ ἀμφότερα ἕν. For other advanced formulations, see *Or*. 38.13–15 (= 45.9, 26–27); 39.12–13, 17; 40.6, 33, 45; 43.38, 61, 64; 44.4; 45.2, 13, 22, 28–29.

34. Trans. Peter Gilbert, *On God and Man: The Theological Poetry of St Gregory of Nazianzus* (Crestwood, N.Y.: St. Vladimir's Seminary Press, 2001), 81.

35. See also *Or*. 43.64; 45.19; *Carm*. 1.1.6.77; 1.2.14.91; 1.2.34.190; 2.1.11.1603; 2.1.13.35; 2.1.60.9.

36. Gregory of Nyssa, *Eun*. III.1, 3, 4 (*GNO* II/2: 19, 119, 123, 130, 131, 139, 158); *Antirrh*. (*GNO* III/1: 161, 201, 217, 225); *Cat or*. (*GNO* III/4:48, 79); *Ep*. 3.15. Daley, "Divine Transcendence," 497–98, n. 2; "Identity of the Savior," 471, n. 7. It has not yet been determined whether Gregory of Nyssa followed Gregory Nazianzen in this regard, whether they drew from similar sources, or both.

37. See also *Or*. 17.12; 30.1; 26.12; 39.13; 44.4.

38. See also *Or*. 45.13: Christ is the victim who is in his first nature unsacrificeable.

39. See also *Or*. 18.28; 21.24; 26.12; 44.4; 45.13; 45.22, 30.

40. The most helpful discussion of the problem thus far is Norris, "Gregory Nazianzen's Doctrine of Jesus Christ," 172–76 and ff.

41. Other passages that resolve themselves in this way are *Or*. 30.9, 10, 13, 21.

42. *Or*. 30.2, 5, 8, 12, 15, 16, 21; 38.15 (= 45.27); 43.69; 45.25.

43. τὸ πάσχον . . . , οὐ τὴν ἄτρεπτον φύσιν καὶ τοῦ πάσχειν ὑψηλοτέραν.

44. Εἰ γὰρ καὶ τὸ συναμφότερον ἕν, ἀλλ᾽ οὐ τῇ φύσει, τῇ δὲ συνόδῳ τούτων. Similar passages can be found at *Or*. 30.5, 12.

45. See also *Or*. 38.15: "He was sent, but as a human being; for he was twofold [διπλοῦς]." However, unlike *Or*. 30.8, this passage resolves more clearly into the single-subject paradigm.

46. On Gregory's doctrine of *theosis,* cf. Norris, "Gregory Nazianzen's Doctrine of Jesus Christ," 58–62, 129–48, and Winslow, *Dynamics of Salvation*. In Gregory's text, see esp. *Or*. 38.9–16; 39.7–8; 40.5–8.

47. See above, n. 43.

48. On which see Christopher A. Beeley, "Cyril of Alexandria and Gregory of Nazianzus: Tradition and Complexity in Patristic Christology," *Journal of Early Christian Studies,* forthcoming.

49. Gregory's opposition to Apollinarius over the presence of a human mind in Christ is peripheral compared to the issues we have been considering here. See Beeley, *Gregory of Nazianzus on the Trinity,* chap. 2.

6

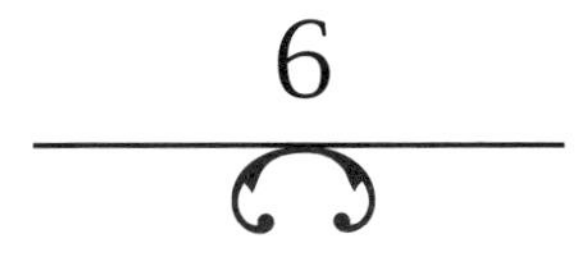

Two Early Nicenes

Eustathius of Antioch and Marcellus of Ancyra

Kelley McCarthy Spoerl

The controversy set off by Arius of Alexandria in the second decade of the fourth century continues to generate important scholarship. While Athanasius of Alexandria has received the lion's share of attention, in recent years attention has also shifted to other supporters and opponents of Arius, notably, Marcellus of Ancyra, an opponent of Arius, and Eusebius of Caesarea, at least at one time a supporter of the Alexandria presbyter. Moreover, scholarship on these figures has demonstrated that the conflicts between supporters and opponents of Arius before and during the Council of Nicea in 325 continued to play out in the decades that followed, significantly shaping developments in trinitarian theology and Christology as the century progressed.

José Declerck's magisterial new edition makes it possible to consider in detail another early opponent of Arius: Eustathius of Antioch.[1] In this essay I provide an overview of Eustathius's career in the pre- and post-Nicene period and a survey of his trinitarian and christological views. I then compare Eustathius's views with those of Marcellus of Ancyra, the understanding of whose theology has advanced tremendously in recent years through the publication of several important editions and monographs. A comparative examination of the thought of these two figures proves useful for two reasons: (1) it illuminates the kinship between thinkers who belonged to an identifiable early pro-Nicene coalition, as well as their notable differences, revealing that this coalition was by no means monolithic; (2) by establishing the similarities between the thought of Eustathius and Marcellus in both trinitarian and christological areas, as well as their shared enmity with Eusebius of Caesarea, it provides context for the emergence later in the century of significant heresy from within the same pro-Nicene coalition, notably in the thought of Apollinarius of Laodicea.

Eustathius's Life and Career

Details about Eustathius's life and career are scanty and inconsistent. According to Jerome's *De viris inlustribus,* he was a Pamphilian from the city of Side;[2] Athanasius[3] and Theodoret[4] say that he was a confessor, presumably during the Diocletian persecutions from 303 to 313. Theodoret says that by the time of the outbreak of controversy over the teachings of Arius in Alexandria, Eustathius was bishop of Beroea (modern-day Aleppo) in Syria; he received a warning letter from Alexander of Alexandria about Arius's teaching.[5] At some point after the death of Philogonius, bishop of Antioch (ca. 323), Eustathius was translated to that city.[6] He then participated in the Antiochene synod that took place in late 324 or early 325, wherein Eusebius of Caesarea, Theodotus of Laodicea, and Narcissus of Neronias were placed under provisional ban until the ecumenical synod that summer.[7] As we now know, the great council that eventually took place at Nicea was originally going to meet in Marcellus's see of Ancyra.[8] Marcellus does not seem to have been present at the synod of Antioch at which Eustathius was present. However, Logan speculates that it was Marcellus who suggested the line of questioning over the existence of one or two οὐσίαι in the Christian godhead that Ossius took with Eusebius of Caesarea in an effort to smoke out his Arian sympathies.[9] Even before Nicea, Eustathius made evident his anti-Arian sympathies and his hostility to Eusebius of Caesarea, and he was part of an informal alliance against the Arian threat that included Ossius of Cordoba, Alexander of Alexandria, and Marcellus of Ancyra. Furthermore, Athanasius credits Eustathius with driving out of the diocese during his tenure a number of allies of Arius.[10] Eustathius participated at the council of Nicea, and took the anti-Arian line that Ossius of Cordoba, Alexander of Alexandria (with the young Athanasius in his train), and Marcellus of Ancyra shared.[11] Between late 325 and the autumn of 327, Eustathius also engaged in a pamphlet war with Eusebius of Caesarea, whose dishonesty about his confession of faith at Nicea Eustathius denounces.[12]

The conflict came to a head at the provincial synod of the diocese of Coele-Syria in the fall of 327, when Eustathius was deposed. The causes for Eustathius's deposition vary: doctrinal reasons (Sabellianism),[13] a breach of clerical discipline (Theodoret's story of a woman slapping Eustathius with an ill-timed paternity suit),[14] and a treasonous violation of imperial etiquette (making disparaging remarks about Constantine's mother Helena).[15] Two reports about this event are of particular interest. First, Socrates claims that he has the report that Eustathius was deposed for Sabellianism from George of Laodicea in his encomium of Eusebius of Emesa, an author of later anti-Marcellan treatises.[16] Secondly, Theodoret says that in cooperation with Theodotus of Laodicea, Eusebius of Caesarea, initiator of the literary tradition of treatises *contra Marcellum,* led the charge against Eustathius at the synod.[17]

Paulinus of Tyre, one of the early partisans of Arius (with Eusebius of Caesarea),[18] whose orthodoxy Marcellus of Ancyra criticizes,[19] took over for six months as bishop of Antioch but then died.[20] Eusebius of Caesarea was suggested as a possible replacement after Paulinus's death, but, mindful of the Nicene ban on the translation of bishops, he refused the appointment. Later, Flacillus, dedicatee of Eusebius's *Ecclesiastical Theology,* the Caesarean bishop's most complete refutation of the theology of Marcellus of Ancyra, took over the see.[21]

Eustathius's fate after his deposition is uncertain. His deposition brought with it exile from the empire. Theodoret[22] says that he went to a city of Illyricum in Thrace, while Jerome states that he went to Trajanopolis.[23] Philostorgius reports that he was sent into exile εἰς τὴν

῾Εσπέραν "into the west."[24] The date of Eustathius's death is equally unclear. Socrates speaks of his appearance in Constantinople in 363 and renewed banishment to Bizya, another city of Thrace.[25] Theodoret says that Eustathius died before the election of Meletius to the see of Antioch, which would place his death before 361.[26] R. P. C. Hanson, however, speculates that that it is unlikely Eustathius could have survived that late into the fourth century and concludes that Eustathius must have died in exile before 337.[27] In the wake of Eustathius's deposition, his followers seceded from the community under his successors, and the Antiochene church remained divided into the fifth century.[28]

From the survey of evidence above, it is clear that Eustathius had a well-attested feud with Eusebius of Caesarea, anti-Marcellan polemicist par excellence, both before and after Nicea, and that Eusebius was instrumental in eventually bringing Eustathius down, replacing him with the dedicatee of his most comprehensive anti-Marcellan work. Eustathius seems to have been regarded thereafter as a *bête noir* in the anti-Marcellan tradition.[29] At the same time that Eustathius was battling with Eusebius, he was on the same side of the debates as Marcellus before, during, and after Nicea. While the exact nature of their relations is unclear, Sara Parvis speculates that Eustathius's deposition at the hands of Eusebius and Paulinus of Tyre outraged Marcellus.[30] It is a fact that Marcellus himself was deposed in 336 by a similar-minded coalition of bishops with Eusebius of Caesarea at its head, whose treatise *Contra Marcellum* constituted Exhibit A for the prosecution.[31]

Eustathius's Trinitarian Theology—Survey and Comparison with Marcellus

A survey of the extant fragments deemed authentic and the short treatise against Origen's exegesis of the Witch of Endor episode in 1 Samuel amply supports ancient reports of Eustathius's opposition to the theology of Arius and the bishop of Antioch's pro-Nicene convictions. A number of statements in the fragments even echo passages in the Nicene creed. Eustathius asserts that the second person of the Trinity is "true God" or "genuine Son of God."[32] He is not, as Arius notoriously contended, created out of nothing, but is begotten φύσικως from the Father.[33] As God begotten from the Father, all things were created through him.[34] The fragments also contain some references to the Nicene anathemas. In Fr. 19, Eustathius insinuates that Christ, having been born from the unchangeable divine nature, is unchangeable in his divine spirit.[35] In Fr. 88, Eustathius asserts that there is only one ὑπόστασις of divinity, as the Nicene anathema asserts.[36] What is lacking in Eustathius is any reference to the controversial Nicene watchword ὁμοούσιον, though Eustathius does make one reference to the undefiled οὐσία at Fr. 78[37] and the divine *substantia* in Fr. 95.[38] Elsewhere, in Fr. 21, Eustathius asserts the singularity of the godhead (θεότης).[39] In some passages, Eustathius speaks about the divine nature[40] and asserts that the second person of the Trinity is "Son of God by nature."[41] In Fr. 50, quoting Colossians 2:9, Eustathius asserts that as Son of God, the second person is the "fullness of the godhead" and as such is perfect (τέλειος).[42]

Interestingly, since it was one of Arius's more notorious slogans, there is no direct evidence that Eustathius addressed the claim that "there was a time when [the Word/Son] was not." He simply says in Fr. 65 that the Word and God was "from the first" (ἀνέκαθεν) with the Father, the "beginning" attributed to him in Proverbs 8:22 referring to his human birth from the Virgin Mary.[43] Another reference to the Word's activity ἀνέκαθεν appears at Fr. 72, where Eustathius states that as Wisdom and Word, the second person has the power of rule ἀνέκαθεν, rather than the human Jesus whom the Word assumed, who received it after his death and resurrection, as Peter proclaims in Acts 2:36.[44] Fr. 82 alludes to another issue contested in the early Arian controversy. Eustathius says that the Word of God, "being God who was begotten from him [the Father]," does not have an extrinsic or newly acquired (ἐπίκτητος) glory, though the "man of Christ," that is, the man whom the Word assumes, does.[45] Eustathius thereby asserts that the second person enjoys glory in his preexistent state, which one would assume was on par with that of his Father.

Eustathius's titles for the second person of the Trinity vary. Aside from asserting that the second person is "true God," Eustathius frequently refers to him as the "Word and God."[46] But he also refers to him as "Son" and "Son of God,"[47] and in one case as "most divine Son" (ὁ θειότατος υἱός).[48] It is clear from a number of fragments that Eustathius applies the title "Son" to the preexistent second person of the Trinity, thereby indicating that the Son's begetting takes place in his pre-incarnate existence.[49] Indeed he says at Fr. 96 that the title "Son" belongs "properly" (*decibiliter*) to the God who dwells in the crucified man Jesus.[50] A kindred term for "Son," distinctive of Eustathius's usage, is "child" (παῖς) of God, as in *De Engastrimytho* 23, where Eustathius asserts that only God and ὁ θειότατος αὐτοῦ παῖς had the authority to reclaim souls from hell.[51] In a statement that puts him in diametric opposition to Marcellus, Eustathius in two fragments speaks of the preexistent Son of God as an image: in Fr. 68 as image of the Father,[52] and in Fr. 95 as image of the divine substance.[53]

De Engastrimytho, while mostly exegetical in nature, contains one passage where Eustathius makes some interesting remarks about the relationship between the Father and Son. I have described my overview here as focused on Eustathius's "trinitarian" theology, but like many theologians in the first half of the fourth century, Eustathius confines his reflections to the shared divinity of the Father and Son, giving scant attention to the Holy Spirit.[54] Consequently, there are no self-conscious references to "the Trinity" in the extant works of Eustathius. There is one reference to the "dyad" of Father and Son in *De Engast.* 24, where Eustathius gives an exegesis of Deuteronomy 13:1–3, concluding that "[Moses] showing here the Dyad of the Father and of the only-begotten Son, named one the Lord who tests, and the other besides this is the "beloved" Lord and God, so that from the Dyad, he might reveal the one godhead and the true divine begetting."[55] In this passage Eustathius tries to balance the claims of divine unity with those of divine distinction that the "trinitarian problem" requires.[56] He wants to assert that there is one godhead (thereby preserving Christian monotheism), while at the same time acknowledging the personal distinctions of Father and Son that result from a true θεογονία.

Without giving a comparable survey of Marcellus's trinitarian theology, we can make the following observations about the similarities and differences between his trinitarian thought and that of Eustathius.

In keeping with his anti-Arian and pro-Nicene sympathies, Marcellus is emphatic that there is only one God.[57] He states that the Word is Lord and God,[58] that the Word is one and the same with God,[59] and that the Word belongs to the unity or oneness of God.[60] As Eustathius did, Marcellus asserts the existence of one ὑπόστασις in the Christian godhead.[61] Marcellus coordinates this with an assertion that there is one πρόσωπον in the godhead; the evidence for a comparable statement in Eustathius is less explicit, though it might lend itself to a similar conclusion.[62] Marcellus, like Eustathius and the Nicene Creed, asserts that all things are made through the Word,[63] whom he also calls Wisdom, as Eustathius does at his Fr. 72.[64] Like Eustathius, Marcellus does not devote attention to the Nicene ὁμοούσιον, though he is scandalized by the notion of multiple οὐσίαι in the godhead, a view he attributes in the pre-Nicene period especially to Eusebius of Caesarea.[65] On a couple of points we see especially close parallels between the teaching of Marcellus and Eustathius. In his Frs. 76–80, Marcellus states that the Word has his own glory in his pre-incarnate existence, which glory is then granted to the man whom the Word assumed in the incarnation.[66] And regarding the Arian prooftext Proverbs 8:22, Marcellus, like Eustathius, attributes the description of "creation" to the human flesh that the Word assumed, asserting, also like Eustathius, that "the ways" created for humanity by the incarnation include instructions regarding justice.[67] Lastly, Eustathius and Marcellus share anti-Origenist views. The entire commentary on the Witch of Endor has an anti-Origenist thrust, mostly against Origen's allegorical exegesis.[68] Marcellus criticizes Origen's trinitarian theology in his Frs. 19–22.[69]

Comparison of the extant fragments of both thinkers reveals some significant divergences between the trinitarian theologies of the two bishops. On the basis of what survives, one might say that, at least superficially, Marcellus is more self-consciously trinitarian than Eustathius, in that he gives some attention, however obscure, to the Holy Spirit in addition to the Father and Son,[70] and he speaks about the "Triad" as well as the "Dyad."[71] Marcellus also frequently uses the term "monad" for the Christian godhead, which does not occur in Eustathius.[72] Marcellus is more explicit and emphatic about the second person's eternity than Eustathius is.[73] What most notably sets Eustathius and Marcellus apart is their consideration of the second person's preexistent generation and the titles he bears as a result. I noted earlier that Eustathius often uses the title "Word and God" for the second person in his pre-incarnate state. But he also uses the title "Son" for the pre-incarnate second person, which one might expect since he insists upon a "true divine birth" and the Son's preexistent begetting, not creation. When one looks at the fragments of Marcellus, the evidence is contradictory, which has generated much scholarship on these questions: Does Marcellus use the title "Son" for the preexistent Word? Does Marcellus speak of a pre-incarnate begetting of the Word/Son?[74] Opponents held that Marcellus denied both claims, along with rejecting the three ὑποστάσεις, which in their view would result from a "real" generation. In some fragments Marcellus insists that the title "Word" is the "first" name of the pre-incarnate Christ.[75] Likewise, there are fragments that seem to restrict the title "Son" to the incarnate Word.[76] But then there are also statements that the Word is "God's true Son"[77] and references to the Son in contexts that predate the incarnation.[78] One observes the same ambiguity with Marcellus's use of "begetting" language. Marcellus uses the vague language of "coming forth" for the emergence of the Word[79] and in some fragments seems to reject outright the notion of a preexistent generation or birth of the Word.[80] But he also makes statements such as the following:

> Therefore, to have said that "He was begotten before the age" seems to me a correct statement: that which has come forth from the Father who sent it forth becomes an offspring. But the [latter] statement was no longer correctly or piously understood by him [Asterius]. For to say that he who has come forth from Him is not the Word but simply "only Son" and that this is the true manner of his begetting has often given those who hear of it the impression of a human appearance.[81]

Here we glimpse the reason for Marcellus's ambivalence about the use of language about sonship and begetting for the preexistent Word:

he is afraid that it will import anthropomorphism into Christian ideas of deity.[82] But given the language of Scripture and liturgy in which all sides of the Arian controversy were invested, it is unavoidable, and so it is clear that Marcellus *will* use such language—but only if it is carefully qualified, and in his case, usually with the language of the Word and his "coming forth."[83] Given that his preferred language lends itself much less readily to a recognition of the Word's personal distinctiveness, it is understandable why his opponents drew the conclusions they did. Again, Eustathius does not seem to share Marcellus's ambivalence about this language,[84] which suggests that he had a fuller notion of the distinctions between Father and Son.

This conjecture may receive further confirmation from the fact that while Marcellus and Eustathius agree that the incarnate Word is an image of God, they completely disagree about whether the preexistent Word is an image of the divine. As noted above, Eustathius asserts that the Son is both image of the Father and image of the divine substance.[85] Marcellus discusses this proposition extensively in his Frs. 51–56, arguing that an image must be corporeal and perceptible, that through which the invisible becomes comprehensible.[86] Later, in Frs. 113–14, he criticizes Asterius for just the claim Eustathius makes in his Fr. 95, that the Word is an "unchanged image of [the Father's] substance": "Therefore, if he is image of [the Father's] οὐσία, then he can no longer be οὐσία itself. . . . For the image is not of itself, but is [image of] something [else]."[87] Marcellus argues here that if the preexistent Word is image of God, he cannot be God himself—the very "Arian" position he is trying to refute.

The similarities between the trinitarian ideas of Eustathius and Marcellus were enough, in their time, to have the two bishops placed in the same "Sabellian" camp and fall victim to the same theological opponents. Nevertheless, their theologies are not identical. In view of his dialectical statements about unity and duality in the godhead, his unqualified use of the language of sonship and begetting, and his insistence on Christ's status as preexistent image of God, I contend that Eustathius was clearer on the personal distinctions in the Christian God and less emphatically unitarian than the bishop of Ancyra.[88]

Eustathius's Christological Teaching: Survey and Comparison with Marcellus

When Eustathius describes the incarnation, he most often speaks of it as involving the divine Word's "bearing" or "assuming" a man.[89] He therefore refers to the "god-bearing man."[90] He frequently uses the idiosyncratic expression "the man of Christ."[91] He also speaks of the mode of incarnation in terms of analogies with fastening,[92] clothing,[93] or a mixture.[94] While the man whom the Word assumes is constructed of many parts,[95] he is still perfect (τέλειος), just as the indwelling Son of God is perfect.[96] Hence the assumed humanity comprises both a completely normal body capable of the normal physiological processes, especially digestion,[97] and a human soul capable of the normal psychological experiences, including the emotions of fear and grief, especially evident in the agony in Gethsemane.[98] The soul, in fact, is necessary in order for the experiences of the body, such as hunger and pain, to be perceptible.[99] But the inclusion of both body and soul in the humanity of Christ is also essential to Christ's salvific mission, according to Eustathius. The latter describes this generally in Fr. 99—"for the sake of the salvation of men, he attached a man to the Word and God"[100]—but he is more specific elsewhere. In Fr. 50, Eustathius insists that in order to save the whole human being, body and soul, God the Word must assume a human soul as well as a body: "Not partially healing and having left behind uncared for the more honorable part of this [the human temple], but dispensing the care of the whole, he assumed the whole of what belongs to us."[101] This stress on the role of the human soul in effecting salvation then becomes a key part of Eustathius's biblical exegesis, notably his claim that it was Christ's soul that brought that of the repentant thief to heaven on the day of his crucifixion and entombment.[102]

When making this claim about the necessity of the human soul in the incarnate Savior, Eustathius looks back to the past as well as to the present. Denial of the existence of a human soul in Christ, he says, is just another form of the Docetism that Marcion espoused in the second century;[103] Eustathius argues implicitly that denying the existence of a human soul in Christ compromises his real humanity and thus the authenticity of the incarnation just as much as the denial of a human body in him. But the more contemporary reference to this error applies to the Arians, who, Eustathius says, deny the human soul in Christ so as to attribute Christ's experiences of weakness and vulnerability to the indwelling Word/Son, thus proving the latter's mutability.[104] While acknowledging that the Holy Spirit plays some role in effecting the incarnation[105] and strengthens the man Christ,[106] Eustathius does not think the Holy Spirit is the subject of the incarnate Christ, but rather that the "divine spirit" is, with which the human soul coexists. Eustathius thereby seems to think of the "divine spirit" as the Word/Son—though this is not absolutely clear.[107] Eustathius asserts that the human soul can coexist with the indwelling Word because it is immaculate and completely without sin,[108] just as Christ's human flesh was.[109] Between Frs. 51 and 61, Eustathius discusses whether or not human souls are unbegotten.[110] In Fr. 60 he points to the intellectual maturation of human babies as proof they are not.[111] The point of this discussion is to refute the doctrine of transmigration, which Eustathius attributes to the "Ariomaniacs."[112] Although references to the incarnate Word appear in this section in Frs. 56–57, however, Eustathius does not spell out the implications of these anthropological observations for his Christology or his eschatology.[113]

Other analogies that Eustathius uses for the assumed man include the temple,[114] the instrument,[115] the tent,[116] the form or semblance,[117] the theophany,[118] and the covering or perceptible covering.[119] With the reference to the humanity of Christ as the perceptible covering, we broach further reflections on Christ's status as image. Though Eustathius, unlike Marcellus, is willing to grant the pre-incarnate Word/Son the status of image, he is in agreement with Marcellus that the "man of Christ" is a visible image through which we perceive divinity.[120] Eustathius specifically states in Fr. 68 that just as the Son is the image of the Father, the man whom he bore is the image of the Son.[121]

It is perhaps significant, in view of what follows, that in the same fragment Eustathius asserts that "the Son is one thing, but his image is another."[122] This is a similar statement to that in Fr. 91, where Eustathius says, with regard to the notion that the "fullness of divinity" dwells in Christ, that "one thing is that which inhabits, but another is that which is inhabited."[123] This latter statement may be important because Eustathius says that the two things "naturally differ from one another,"[124] suggesting, at least indirectly, the existence of two natures in Christ. The Syriac fragment 81 says exactly this, but the text is uncertain.[125] On the other hand, in Fr. 2, Eustathius speaks of the Son's having assumed "human nature (ἀνθρωπείαν φύσιν),"[126] and statements like this, combined with Eustathius's references to the Word as God "by nature," also support Eustathius's attribution of both human and divine natures to Christ.[127]

What is unambiguous in Eustathius's extant writings is his practice of what will later be called "dividing the sayings." That is, Eustathius is careful to attribute human experiences described in the Gospels to the man Christ, and to attribute the divine actions to the indwelling Son/Word. This is most evident in Frs. 97–98, where Eustathius asserts that "they are crazy, raving, wild, and out of their minds who presume to attribute suffering to God the Word,"[128] and "neither is it right to say that the Word and God died."[129] The same sentiment appears in Fr. 125, where Eustathius reiterates the differences between the one indwelling the man Christ and the one indwelt.[130] Granted, Fr. 119 provides counterevidence for this claim; there, Eustathius says that Christ's executioners "were caught when in killing him, they nailed the divine Word to the cross."[131] Despite this discrepancy, it seems that the preponderance of the evidence suggests Eustathius's lack of support for the *communicatio idiomatum* that would obviate the need to "divide the sayings."

Finally, in addition to suggesting that Christ incorporates two natures, Eustathius also suggests in one series of Latin fragments that Christ incorporates two persons, one divine and one human. As we will see, this occurs in the context of discussing the end time, when the man Christ will rule as king—the very context in which Marcellus makes some of his most provocative christological statements. Of this time, Eustathius says: "'When the Son of Man shall sit on his glorious throne'; indeed one person (*persona*) seems to speak, but manifestly makes reference to another (*altera*). Therefore the divine spirit clearly appears to be speaking about the man."[132] Granted, it is unclear what term would have appeared in the original Greek: ὑπόστασις or πρόσωπον? Given the exegetical context of the passage, I argue that πρόσωπον is more likely.[133] This is the clearest evidence we have that Eustathius taught what might have looked to others like a "dyoprosopic" Christology, which would find further elaboration in the theologies of later Antiochene theologians such as Diodore of Tarsus, Theodore of Mopsuestia, and Nestorius of Constantinople. The fact that the passage does not survive in the original language should make us cautious. Yet combined with Eustathius's practice of "dividing the sayings" and his assertion that the indwelling Word and assumed man are two distinct things, this conclusion seems defensible.

On this point, namely, the claim that there are two things incorporated in Christ, intriguing parallels between Eustathius and Marcellus appear. Before turning to them, we should note some basic similarities and differences between the Christologies of the two bishops. Like Eustathius, Marcellus describes the incarnation as the assumption of a man.[134] He speaks of the incarnation as involving the union of the man with the Word[135] or the joining of the man to the Word.[136] In keeping with his exegesis of Proverbs 8:22, which he shares with Eustathius, Marcellus states that the man is created in himself (the Word) and thereby is the "firstborn of all creation."[137] On the other hand, Marcellus equally and even more frequently speaks of the incarnation as the assumption or taking of the flesh,[138] as being born in the flesh,[139] as union with flesh,[140] or as the assumption of a body.[141] Along these lines, Marcellus also speaks of the economy according to the flesh,[142] though in one instance he will link this to "the man," as in Fr. 72, where he says, "we know to refer the economy according to the flesh to the man. . . ."[143] In one instance, Marcellus speaks of the incarnation as involving the addition of the flesh to the Savior (ἡ κατὰ σάρκα προσθήκη), which gives the impression of diversity in the single godhead or monad, whereas "if one were only to consider the spirit, the Word would naturally appear to be one and the same with God."[144] Given that Eustathius also identifies the divine element in the incarnate Word as "the divine spirit," this is a point of agreement between Marcellus and Eustathius, though Eustathius is eager to stress the fellowship between the divine spirit and the human soul in Christ; Marcellus does not discuss the latter explicitly.

As noted above, whether he speaks of it as the man or as the flesh, Marcellus, with Eustathius, insists that the humanity of Christ is the image of the invisible God: "it is clear from the start that before the assumption of our body, the Word in and of Himself was not 'image of the invisible God' (Col 1:14). For it is fitting for the image to be seen, so that through the image what has hitherto been invisible might be seen."[145] The latter statement, with its revealing reference to the incarnation as the assumption of our body (τοῦ ἡμετέρου σώματος), leads us to some observations about Marcellus's view of the purpose of the incarnation. Marcellus attributes numerous benefits to humankind resulting from the incarnation. Through the incarnation, the flesh acquires healing through communion with the Word,[146] the race of the god-fearing is called into adoption,[147] the Devil is conquered,[148] and man acquires kingship and status as Lord and God,[149] as well as glory[150] and immortality.[151] Distinctive about Marcellus's exposition of these benefits is that when he says they accrue to humankind through the assumption of the man, the "man" often has not only an individual reference to the humanity of Christ, but also a corporate reference to all humans descending from Adam.[152] Fr. 80 illustrates this best:

> And he deemed the man who fell through disobedience worthy to be joined through the Virgin to his own Word. For what other sort of glory among men could be greater than this glory? Having said, "I have glorified you," [the Father] continues, saying "And I will glorify [you] again," (John 12:28) so that because of his abundant lovingkindness in the second glory after the resurrection of the flesh, he might make immortal the man who was previously mortal . . . .[153]

The reference to the Johannine text makes clear the blurring between the individual humanity of Christ and the generic humanity of the redeemed. Another fragment indicates that such blurring could give the impression of adoptionism. In Fr. 111, Marcellus states: "And because of this, [he] does not call himself Son of God, but everywhere he says that he is Son of Man, so that through such a confession, he might enable the man to become Son of God by adoption (θέσει)[154] through his communion with him . . . ."[155] Of note for our purposes here is how the pointed use of the titles "Son of God" and "Son of Man" in Fr. 111 could suggest a "dyoprosopic" Christology in the thought of Marcellus, wherein Christ is comprised of the divine πρόσωπον (which need not presume the hypostatic independence of the Word) fused to the human πρόσωπον of the man Jesus. As noted earlier, Marcellus does not endorse an independent πρόσωπον or ὑπόστασις for the Word apart from the Father. But the idea that the humanity of Christ could incorporate a ὑπόστασις distinct from that of the undifferentiated godhead appears in Fr. 85, where Marcellus suggests that Asterius argues for a second hypostasis of the Word *on the basis of the human flesh that the Word of God assumed*.[156] While the terminology that the two bishops use is different, I argue that Marcellus and Eustathius both attribute a distinctiveness to the humanity of Christ, whether on the level of ὑπόστασις or πρόσωπον, that might well give rise to accusations of teaching "two sons."

Compounding this impression in Marcellus is his suggestion that the humanity of the incarnate Christ is separable from the divinity, and may well become so in the final times. This claim occurs in those fragments that preserve Marcellus's exegesis of 1 Corinthians 15, where he speculates about what will happen to the incarnate Word after the conclusion of salvation history.[157] On the basis of the Pauline text, Marcellus argues that once the man Christ has subjected all things to himself, he in turn will be subjected to the Father and return as Word into the godhead. This will entail the end of Christ's kingship as man,[158] which kingship only existed after the incarnation of the Word,[159] and which began "not four hundred whole years ago."[160] Hence Marcellus concludes that "there is a certain limit and appointed time during which it is fitting for the human economy to be united with the Word."[161] What will happen to the humanity of Christ after the end of this appointed time, Marcellus is loath to specify in the absence of a clear teaching of Scripture.[162] Nevertheless, that this humanity will be separated from the Word is clear, and Marcellus justifies this on the basis of John 6:61–63, where Christ asserts, "It is the Spirit that gives life; the flesh is of no avail."[163]

These fragments find an echo in a series of fragments from Eustathius's work *Contra Arianos,*[164] in which he also speaks about the future time when the "Son of Man" will sit upon his glorious throne. Eustathius discusses here Matthew 19:28, not 1 Corinthians 15, but he, as noted earlier, uses this biblical passage to suggest that there are two different *personae* in Christ.[165] His exegesis attributes the throne more specifically to the "man of Christ" whom the Word assumes, than corporately to redeemed humanity, as in Marcellus.[166] However, one should note in the same work, shortly after this series of fragments, the cryptic statement: "Everything that has a beginning will also have an end. Everything having an end is capable of being destroyed."[167] In view of Marcellus's claim in a similar context that the incarnation will have an end, and Eustathius's insistence that the human soul is *not* unbegotten and therefore at least theoretically subject to destruction,[168] this remark is intriguing, to say the least. Of course, one would have to have a lot more context to interpret it fully.

One last point of comparison between Eustathius and Marcellus concerns Marcellus's exegesis of the Agony in the Garden from the Passion accounts of the Synoptic Gospels.[169] We should remember that Eustathius discusses this event explicitly to assert the presence of a mutable human soul in Christ as the subject of the fear the Savior endured on this occasion.[170] Marcellus discusses this to counter Asterius's claim that Christ said "I and the Father are one" (John 10:30) because of "their agreement in all things"—in other words, Asterius's positing of two ὑποστάσεις of Father and Son bonded via a moral unity. In order to refute this claim, Marcellus points to Christ's request in Gethsemane to "let this cup pass" (Matt 26:39), which, he argues, refutes the notion of moral unity between the incarnate Word and the Father.[171] Marcellus says nothing specific in this regard, but it would be natural to assume on the basis of the statement that he assumes in the incarnate Christ a human psychology capable of experiencing fear and aversion at the prospect of impending crucifixion, and a rational deliberative capacity capable of choosing to cooperate with the Passion despite these negative emotions. In short, one might well conclude that Marcellus assumes a human soul in the incarnate Word, though he never explicitly says so.[172]

Conclusion

The careers of Eustathius of Antioch and Marcellus of Ancyra were linked in the pre- and post-Nicene period. Both bishops were opposed to Arius, both supported the decisions of Nicea, and both eventually ran afoul of Eusebius of Caesarea. A comparison of their respective theologies reveals affinities: on the Trinity, both stress the single godhead shared by Father and Son and possibly the Nicene claim of a single divine ὑπόστασις;[173] both assert Christ's preexistent glory; both offer a comparable exegesis of Proverbs 8:22. But it also reveals notable differences: for example, the status of the preexistent Christ as an image of God. Thus, the early opposition ranged against Arius at Nicea and afterward was not uniform; its members sought to assert forcefully the divine unity between Father and Son but diverged in how this unity was coordinated with the distinction of the persons. Eustathius's theology appears somewhat more accommodating to the latter task than that of Marcellus. But that such divergence existed early on in the Nicene camp might have prepared the way for later attempts from within the Nicene party to balance the Nicene account of divine unity with a meaningful account of divine distinction, as occurred in the 350s, when Athanasius incorporated anti-Marcellan rhetoric in his pro-Nicene argumentation.[174]

Overall, I argue that there is greater similarity between the Christologies of Eustathius and Marcellus than between their trinitarian theologies. Both present an incarnate Word whose humanity is the subject of real physiological and psychological processes and whose distinction from the Savior's indwelling divinity is stressed. This is significant because it potentially illuminates another influence on the Christology of Apollinarius of Laodicea. My research indicates that the anti-Marcellan literary tradition initiated by Eusebius of Caesarea influenced not only Apollinarius's trinitarian theology but also his Christology.[175] The kinship between the Christologies of Marcellus and Eustathius and their shared Nicene convictions make it possible that, in the course of his anti-Marcellan researches, Apollinarius, himself a supporter of Nicea, also became acquainted with the work of Marcellus's one-time ally

Eustathius, who explicitly articulated the christological assertion that Apollinarius would one day vigorously challenge: the idea that Christ had a human soul. More work is necessary to substantiate such a claim. What is clear for now is that Declerck's monumental achievement has greatly facilitated the exploration of the thought of another key figure in the early Arian controversy. Such exploration may lend further support to the contention that this controversy provided the initial matrix for the evolution of Apollinarian thought.

Notes

1. *Eustathii Antiocheni, Patris Nicaeni, Opera Quae Supersunt Omnia,* ed. José H. Declerck, CCSG, vol. 51 (Turnhout: Brepolis Publishers, 2002) (hereafter, Declerck).

2. Jerome, *De viris inlustribus* 85 (PL 23.730B).

3. Athanasius, *Historia Arianorum* 4.1, in Hans Georg Optiz, *Athanasius Werke,* vol. 2, fasc. 1–7 (Berlin: W. de Gruyter, 1934), p. 184, and *Apologia de fuga* 3.3, also in *Werke,* vol. 2, p. 70. All sources listed under "Urkunde" numbers are from vol. 3, fasc. 12 of the same work (hereafter, Optiz).

4. Theodoret of Cyrus, *Eranistes,* ed. Gerard H. Ettlinger (Oxford: Clarendon Press, 1975), 100.6; 157.15; 231.15.

5. Theodoret, *Hist. Eccl.* 1.4.62 in Theodoret, *Kirchengeschichte,* 3rd ed., ed. Léon Parmentier and Günther Christian Hansen, GCS n.f. 5 (Berlin: Akademie Verlag, 1998), 25 (hereafter, Parmentier). Theodoret suggests that this letter was written at roughly the same time as the letter Alexander wrote to Alexander of Byzantium, which Rowan Williams dates to 321/22 in *Arius: Heresy and Tradition,* rev. ed. (Grand Rapids: Eerdmans, 2002), 58.

6. Theodoret, *Hist. Eccl.* 1.7.10 (Parmentier, 32). Cf. also Sozomen, *Hist. Eccl.* 1.2.2, in Sozomenus, *Kirchengeschichte,* ed. Joseph Bidez and Günther Christian Hansen, GCS n.f. 4 (Berlin: Akademie Verlag, 1995), 10 (hereafter, Bidez and Hansen).

7. The document appears in Optiz, Urk. 18, pp. 36–41. Cf. Declerck, ccclxxxvii, n. 5. Cf. Sara Parvis, *Marcellus of Ancyra and the Lost Years of the Arian Controversy 325–345* (Oxford: Oxford University Press, 2006), 46–47, 76–81.

8. Cf. Alastair H. B. Logan, "Marcellus of Ancyra and the Councils of A.D. 325: Antioch, Ancyra, and Nicaea," *Journal of Theological Studies,* n.s. 43 (1992): 428–46.

9. Ibid., 434–35. The line of questioning that Ossius took with Eusebius of Caesarea at Antioch is referred to in Marcellus, Fr. 116, in the edition of Markus Vinzent: *Markell von Ankyra, Die Fragmente & der Brief an Julius von Rom,* ed.

Markus Vinzent, Supp. to *Vigiliae Christianae* 39 (Leiden: Brill, 1997), 108–9. References will be to page and line numbers in this edition (hereafter, Vinzent).

10. Athanasius, *Historia Arianorum* 4.2 in Optiz, p. 185.

11. Cf. Theodoret, *Hist. Eccl.* 1.7.10 in Parmentier, 32. He says that Eustathius, by now the bishop of Antioch, offered a panegyric to the emperor Constantine at the opening ceremonies. Marcellus claims to have refuted his opponents openly at the Council of Nicea. Cf. his *Letter to Pope Julius* (Vinzent, 124.1–3).

12. Theodoret, *Hist. Eccl.* 1.8.1–5 in Parmentier, 33–34. Cf. also the critical edition of the fragment (no. 79) quoted by Theodoret in Declerck, 149–50. The pamphlet war is mentioned in Socrates, *Hist. Eccl.* 1.23.8, in *Sokrates, Kirchengeschichte,* ed. Günther Christian Hansen, GCS n.f. 1 (Berlin: Akademie Verlag, 1995), 70 (hereafter, Hansen), and Sozomen, *Hist. Eccl.* 2.18.3–4 in Bidez and Hansen, 74.

13. Socrates, *Hist. Eccl.* 1.24.1 in Hansen, 70.

14. Theodoret, *Hist. Eccl.* 1.20.4–9 in Parmentier, 70–72. Something similar is hinted at by Philostorgius, *Hist. Eccl.* 2.7, in Philostorgius, *Kirchengeschichte,* 2nd ed., ed. Joseph Bidez and Friedhelm Winkelmann (Berlin: Akademie Verlag, 1972), 19 (hereafter, Bidez and Friedhelm).

15. Athanasius, *Historia Arianorum* 4.1–2 in Opitz, pp. 184–85. The date assigned here to Eustathius's deposition is the one Sara Parvis argues for in *Marcellus,* 101–7.

16. Socrates, *Hist. Eccl.* 1.24.2–3 in Hansen, 70. The classic article by Ignace Bertin details Eusebius of Emesa's anti-Marcellan pedigree: "Cyrille de Jérusalem, Eusèbe d'Émèse et la théologie semi-arienne," *Revue des sciences philosophiques et théologiques* 52 (1968): 38–75. Cf. also Joseph T. Lienhard, *Contra Marcellum: Marcellus of Ancyra and Fourth-Century Theology* (Washington, D.C.: The Catholic University of America Press, 1999), 186–97.

17. Theodoret, *Hist. Eccl.* 1.20.4 in Parmentier, 70.

18. He is mentioned with these two men in Arius's letter to Eusebius of Nicomedia as reported in Theodoret, *Hist. Eccl.* 1.4.2 (Parmentier, 26). Cf. also Optiz, Urk. 1, section 3, p. 2. Cf. Parvis, *Marcellus,* 46–47.

19. Most notably in Fr. 121 (Vinzent, 114–15), in which Marcellus accuses Paulinus of teaching that Christ is a "second God" and a "creature."

20. Philostorgius, *Hist. Eccl.* 3.15 (Bidez and Friedhelm, 45), is the specific source for Paulinus's six-month tenure in the see. The succession, including the proposal to put Eusebius of Caesarea in the see, is also discussed in Socrates, *Hist. Eccl.* 1.24.1–8 (Hansen, 70–71), Theodoret, *Hist. Eccl.* 1.22 (Parmentier, 72), and Sozomen, *Hist. Eccl.* 2.19. Sozomen says specifically (2.19.1 in Bidez and Hansen, 74–75) that Eustathius was deposed because of his adherence to the Nicene faith and for accusing Eusebius of Caesarea, Paulinus of Tyre, and

Patrophilus of Scythopolis of Arianism—thereby showing that Eustathius as well as Marcellus saw Paulinus as an Arian sympathizer. Eusebius of Caesarea discusses the offer of translation to Antioch and his own refusal in *Life of Constantine* 3.59–62. Eusebius does not mention Eustathius, or his own role in the latter's deposition, in this account.

21. Theodoret, *Hist. Eccl.* 1.22.1 in Parmentier, 72. Theodoret says that Eulalius took over from Eustathius in the immediate aftermath of his deposition, to be followed by Euphronius and then finally by Flacillus. For the dedication of the *Ecclesiastical Theology* to Flacillus, cf. *Eusebius Werke,* vol. 4, *Gegen Marcell: Über die Kirchliche Theologie, Die Fragmente Marcells,* 3rd ed., ed. Erich Klostermann and Günther Christian Hansen (Berlin: Akademie Verlag, 1989), 60.

22. Theodoret, *Hist. Eccl.* 1.22.1 in Parmentier, 72.

23. Jerome, *De viris inlustribus* 85 (PL 23.730B).

24. Philostorgius, *Hist. Eccl.* 2.7 (Bidez and Friedhelm, 19).

25. Socrates, *Hist. Eccl.* 4.15.3 in Hansen, 244.

26. Theodoret, *Hist. Eccl.* 3.4.5 in Parmentier, 180.

27. R. P. C. Hanson, *The Search for the Christian Doctrine of God: The Arian Controversy 318–381* (Edinburgh: T. &T. Clark, 1988), 211, and Declerck, cclxxxiv–ccxc. Declerck cautiously leans to the opinion that Eustathius was dead by 337.

28. Socrates, *Hist. Eccl.* 1.24.5 in Hansen, 71, and Theodoret, *Hist. Eccl.* 1.22.2 in Parmentier, 72. The classic survey of the schism is Ferdinand Cavallera, *Le Schisme d'Antioche (IV–V siècle)* (Paris: Alphonse Picard et Fils, 1905).

29. Cf. above, n. 16.

30. Parvis, *Marcellus,* 116–18.

31. Ibid., 127–32.

32. Eustathius, Fr. 84 in Declerck, 154 (translated from the Syriac, "le vrai Dieu"). *De Engast.* 10.22.474–75 (chapter, page, line numbers) (in the phrase Θεοῦ γνήσιον υἱόν). Fragments cited below are Eustathius's until noted otherwise.

33. Fr. 19 in Declerck, 80.10–14; note the sharp antithesis with Fr. 107.169: "For if he is created, he is consequently not begotten; but if begotten, he is consequently not created . . . ."

34. Fr. 82.152.1–153.5.

35. Fr. 19.81.23–28.

36. Fr. 88.156–57. Granted, this survives only in Syriac. Also, Socrates says just the opposite, that Eustathius asserted three hypostases in the Trinity (*Hist. Eccl.* 1.23.8 in Hansen, 70). But there is no evidence in the extant materials for the latter claim.

37. Fr. 78.148.7.

38. Fr. 95.162.2.

39. Fr. 21.84.19–22: ". . . on the one hand through the one image, seeing the Dyad of both Father and Son, while on the other, in the Dyad perceiving the one godhead [τὴν μίαν θεότητα νοοῦντες]."

40. Fr. 40.112.5 (an especially clear reference to "the divine nature"); Fr. 125.186 (in Syriac); *De Engast.* 10.22.475; 17.37.881–82; 30.60.1452–55.

41. Fr. 66.138.4; Fr. 85.154.2–3; *De Engast.* 10.22.474–75.

42. Fr. 50.122.29–31.

43. Fr. 65.136.3–4. This is the first of a series of fragments (65–81) from a commentary on Prov 8:22.

44. Fr. 72.144.6–10.

45. Fr. 82.152.1–153.1.

46. Fr. 21.84.19; Fr. 32.102.3; Fr. 48.120.2; Fr. 57.127.1; Fr. 83.153.2; Fr. 98.163.1–2; *De Engast.* 17.38.905.

47. Fr. 2.65.20; Fr. 21.84.21; Fr. 50.122.30; Fr. 66.138.4; Fr. 68.139.1–2 (quoting Rom 8:29); Fr. 81(b).152 (in Syriac); interestingly, the other version of the citation has "Word of God"; Fr. 96.162.2; Fr. 116(a).178.1; *De Engast.* 10.22.475.

48. Fr. 2.65.20.

49. For example: Fr. 21.84.19–22, where Eustathius says that through the "man of Christ" we see the Word and God and "the Father and Son"; Fr. 50.122.29–33, where Eustathius says that the Son of God as the "fullness of the godhead" is perfect, having been begotten from the most perfect Father. He goes on to say that this perfect Son of God would not prepare an imperfect temple for himself (i.e., a human body without a soul). I argue that in these passages we see a clear contrast between the preexistent Son of God and the incarnate Christ, which assumes Eustathius's comfort with ascribing the title "Son" to the preexistent Word. This may also be correlated with Eustathius calling the Father "Begetter" (γεννήτωρ), which he does at Fr. 27.92.83–84.

50. Fr. 96.162.1–3: "But wishing to introduce the majesty of power, he said that even that mortified body is this Son, indeed attributing [to him] that name of sublimity, that is, which properly belongs to the God dwelling in him."

51. *De Engast.* 23.48.1131; cf. also 30.60.1452–53; Fr. 2.65.22; Fr. 19.80.14; Fr. 22.85.10–11; Fr. 27.93.103; Fr. 33.106.3; Fr. 40.112.8; Fr. 50.122.14.

52. Fr. 68.139.3–5.

53. Fr. 95.162.1–2.

54. As noted by Manlio Simonetti, *Origene, Eustazio, Gregorio di Nissa: La Maga di Endor* (Firenze: Nardini Editore/Centro Internazionale del Libro, 1989), 243–44, and also M. Spanneut, "La position théologique d'Eustathe d'Antioche," *Journal of Theological Studies,* n.s. 5 (1954): 221, n. 2.

55. *De Engast.* 24.49.1180–50.1184. Cf. Simonetti's commentary, *La Maga di Endor,* 243–44. I interpret this passage in the opposite sense from Simonetti:

where he sees it as more proof of Eusathius's "moderate monarchianism," I see it as correcting excessive stress on the unity of the godhead that would blur the personal distinctiveness of the only-begotten Son.

56. This is also the concern in the passage from Fr. 21, cited above, n. 49, as well as Fr. 88.156–57. Declerck gives this translation of the Syriac: "Les deux opèrent des (choses) admirables dans le même (temps) invisiblement. La grandeur de leur action, les Écritures divines (l') attribuent plusieurs fois à un (seul), en introduisant la dualité (à partir) de l'unicité (et) en proclamant l'unicité (à partir) de la dualité, parce qu'il y a une seule hypostase de la divinité."

57. Marcellus, Fr. 87.76.4; Fr. 92.80.22; Fr. 97.86.1–2 (in Vinzent).

58. Marcellus, Fr. 113.106.13–14.

59. Marcellus, Fr. 73.62.1–2.

60. Marcellus, Fr. 47.42.4 (the word in question is ἑνότητι); Fr. 75.66.21.

61. Cf. Marcellus, Fr. 47.42.1–4; Fr. 50.44.13–14; Frs. 85–86 (Vinzent, 74–75); Fr. 97 (Vinzent, 86–89).

62. In Marcellus, the most explicit statement appears in Fr. 92.80.13–19. In Eustathius, there are no references to the category of πρόσωπον in trinitarian contexts. All the references I have found to the term in Eustathius occur either in the context of scriptural exegesis, as in several places in the *De Engast.*; or in christological contexts, where Eustathius refers to the πρόσωπον of Christ, as in Fr. 100.165.1–6, where Eustathius talks of one *persona* speaking about another, the divine spirit speaking about the human Christ.

63. Marcellus, Fr. 16.16.7–9; Fr. 87.74.12–13; Fr. 98.88.12–13.

64. Marcellus, Fr. 88.76.11–15. Cf. Eustathius, Fr. 72.144.7–8; cf. also Fr. 71.143.9; Fr. 75.146.4; Fr. 77.148.9.

65. Marcellus, Frs. 115–17 (Vinzent, 108–11), and Fr. 120 (Vinzent, 112–13).

66. Marcellus, Frs. 76–80 in Vinzent, 68–71. Compare with Eustathius, Fr. 82.152.1–153.7.

67. Marcellus's exegesis of Prov 8:22 appears in Frs. 23–46. I cite especially Fr. 30.32.3–4: "For he [Christ] became a way of piety for us who were going to live justly, a beginning of all the ways after these." Compare with Eustathius, Fr. 128.188.1–2: "For then the man of Christ became for us a beginning of the most beautiful ways of justice." Simonetti examines the kinship between the exegesis of the two bishops in *Studi Sull' Arianesimo* (Rome: Editrice Studium, 1965), 38–48, without positing a direct relationship of dependence between the two.

68. Cf. Simonetti, *La Maga di Endor,* 19–28.

69. Marcellus, Frs. 19–22 in Vinzent, 18–23.

70. Marcellus, Frs. 47–49 in Vinzent, 42–45.

71. Marcellus, Fr. 47.42.2; Fr. 48.42.11, 17.

72. Marcellus, Fr. 47.42.1; Fr. 48.42.11; Fr. 73.62.4; Fr. 91.78.14; Fr. 92.80.13; Fr. 97.86.6. Klaus Seibt, *Die Theologie des Markell von Ankyra* (Berlin: W. de

Gruyter, 1994), 464, notes that Marcellus's use of the term (i.e., the monad extending into the triad) stems from Neopythagorean mathematical theory. My survey of the *De Engastrimytho* and the fragments has not turned up any instances of the term in Declerck's edition of Eustathius, nor in Michel Spanneut's 1948 edition *Recherches sur les écrits d'Eustathe d'Antioche* (Lille: Facultés Catholiques, 1948), 139, nor in the index provided by Wilhelmine Brockmeier, *De Sancti Eustathii episcopi Antiocheni dicendi ratione: Accedit index vocabulorum libri contra Originem scripti omnium* (Bonn: R. Noske, 1932), 117.

73. Marcellus, Fr. 3.4.18; Fr. 6.10.2; Fr. 72.60.16.

74. Cf. Vinzent's note 12 to Fr. 7, where he gives a survey of the question with all the relevant references, 132–33.

75. Marcellus, Fr. 3.4.18–6.11; Fr. 5.8.19–20: "Therefore, before He came down and was born through the Virgin, He was only Word"; Fr. 7.10.7: "For the Word 'was in the beginning' as nothing other than Word."

76. For example: Fr. 37.36.1–5, where Marcellus cites Rom 1:4 and its reference to τοῦ προορισθέντος υἱοῦ θεοῦ with reference to the fleshly economy of Christ; Frs. 74–75 (Vinzent, 62–67), where Marcellus uses the title "Son"—but in a discussion of the Agony in the Garden; Fr. 82.72.5–8, where he cites Matt 3:17 ("This is my beloved Son . . .") with reference to the "man united to the Word" (ὁ τῷ λόγῳ ἑνωθεὶς ἄνθρωπος); and Fr. 111.104.12–18, clearly in a soteriological context, speaking about the divine adoption of humankind that the incarnation makes possible.

77. Fr. 38.35.6–9, where Marcellus speaks of the mystery according to the flesh, "because of its communion with his true Son, the Word."

78. For example, Frs. 85–86.74.1–11. These concern Marcellus's discussion of Exod 3:14, God's revelation to Moses. Cf. Fr. 86.74.6–7: "If then [Asterius] says that the Father said these things to Moses while separating himself from the Son, he will not confess that the Son is God."

79. Marcellus, Fr. 66.56.3–8 with reference to the Word as τὸ προελθὸν; Fr. 75.66.18 with reference to τὸν ἐκ τοῦ πατρὸς προελθόντα λόγον; and Fr. 110.104.5 with reference to ὁ λόγος προελθὼν.

80. Fr. 36.34.11–16, where Marcellus questions Asterius's interpretation of Prov 8:23 as "He was begotten before the ages"; Fr. 57.50.7–12, where Marcellus questions Asterius's interpretation of Ps 109:3/RSV 110:3, so as to show the Word's "ancient birth/generation from above" (τήν ἀρχαίαν αὐτοῦ ἄνω γέννησιν); the context makes it clear that he does not approve of this interpretation and suggests he thinks talk of the Word's "ancient birth" is misguided; Fr. 59.52.4–12 makes it clear that Marcellus thinks the psalm verse refers to the incarnate Word's birth from the Virgin Mary; Fr. 71.60.10–14, where Marcellus rehearses John 1:1 and notes that the evangelist "makes no mention in this passage of a generation (γενέσεως) of the Word."

81. Marcellus, Fr. 66.56.3–8.

82. Cf. also Marcellus, Fr. 1.4.3–6.

83. As Marcellus does in Fr. 66 and in Fr. 69.58.11–14 with the title "Son": "For [Christ] says, 'No one knows the Father, except the Son,' that is, the Word." Cf. also Fr. 38, above, n. 77.

84. Again, note Eustathius, Fr. 96.162.1–3, where one gets the sense that the Son is the primordial name of the preexistent Christ in the way that Word is for Marcellus.

85. Eustathius, Fr. 68.139.3–5; Fr. 95.162.1–2.

86. Marcellus, Frs. 51–56 (Vinzent, 46.1–50.6).

87. Marcellus, Frs. 113–14 (Vinzent, 106.2–108.5), especially 114 (Vinzent, 108.2–5).

88. I propose this even though Eustathius does not appear to use any consistent terminology (whether πρόσωπον or ὑπόστασις) to convey this personal distinctiveness. Hence, I concur with the assessment of Spanneut, "La position théologique d'Eustathe d'Antioche," who questions the thesis of Loofs that saw the same kind of "economic" trinitarianism in Eustathius as in Marcellus. I would also nuance Lewis Ayres's brief comparison of Eustathius and Marcellus in *Nicaea and Its Legacy* (Oxford: Oxford University Press, 2004), 68–69. I question Ayres's assertion that Eustathius does not follow the Alexandrian/Athanasian pattern of using genetic metaphors to express the generation of the Word or Son. I think the evidence suggests just the opposite—that Eustathius *is* comfortable with using these metaphors, or at least *more* comfortable than Marcellus is.

89. Eustathius, Fr. 21.84.14 (ἐφόρεσε); cf. also Fr. 22.85.2; Fr. 67.139.1; to references to assuming a man, cf. Fr. 10.71.17 (ἀνέλαβεν); Fr. 11.71.2 (ἀνελάβετο); Fr. 91(a).159.11 (*adsumens*); Fr. 125.186. Fragments cited below are Eustathius's until noted otherwise.

90. Fr. 93(a).160.1; Fr. 94.161.

91. Fr. 17.78.5–79.1; Fr. 22.85.1; Fr. 48.120.1–2; Fr. 89.157.3; Frs. 110–12 (Declerck, 171–72).

92. Fr. 7.68.8 (the soul is ἐξαπτομένη to the body); Fr. 22.85.13 (ἐξάψας); Fr. 75.146.1 (περιάπτειν); Fr. 99.164.5 (*coaptavit*).

93. Fr. 10.71.17–18 (ἀμφιασάμενος).

94. Fr. 8.69.2; Fr. 22.85.1–2; Fr. 44.117.6–7; Fr. 103.167.7–8.

95. Fr. 71.143.10.

96. Fr. 50.122.29–34.

97. Cf. Fr. 4.66.1–27.

98. Cf. Fr. 6.67.1–13; cf. also Frs. 11–19 (Declerck, 71–81).

99. Frs. 9–10 (Declerck, 70–71).

100. Fr. 99.164.4–5.

101. Fr. 50.122.34–37. Cf. also Fr. 21.84.26–30; Fr. 22(a)(b).85.1–4; Fr. 28.95.21–31.

102. Fr. 22.86.19–28; Fr. 28.95.1–97.64; Fr. 32.102.1–15; Fr. 40.112.1–113.31.

103. Fr. 13.73.1–5; Fr. 19.80.1–81.32; Fr. 23.87.1–4.

104. Fr. 6.67.1–14; Fr. 19.81.21–26 ("So that, believing these sorts of things, they superstitiously proclaim the offspring of God not only half-divine, like the Greeks, but also half-human. But they do this so that, having attributed the changes of the sufferings to the divine spirit, they might convince those who are simpler more easily, that that which is changeable has not been begotten from the unchangeable nature"); Fr. 74.145.14–146.18.

105. Fr. 44.117.5–6; Fr. 50.122.26–27.

106. Fr. 48.120.1–2.

107. Cf. especially Fr. 32.102.1–3 and Fr. 50.122.20–24; cf. also Fr. 68.140.11, where Eustathius speaks of the "incorporeal spirit of Wisdom," using another christological title in a context in which the relationship between the Father and Son and the Son's status as image of the latter is discussed. In general, Eustathius speaks of the divine spirit as the divine element in Christ: cf., for example, Fr. 7.68.12–15; Fr. 10.70.1–71.5; Fr. 17.79.6–8; Fr. 19.81.23–25; Fr. 20.83.30–36; Fr. 28.97.56–64 (a reference to the "God-bearing human soul" which coexists with the divine spirit); Fr. 49.121.1–2; Fr. 76.147.1–5; Fr. 77.147.3–148.5. It is confusing that in Fr. 78.148.6–8, Eustathius speaks of the incorporeal Wisdom alongside the undefiled *substance* (οὐσία) in opposition to the corporeal "temple" (Christ's humanity) in the incarnation, suggesting that the divine spirit is divinity without personal distinctiveness. But in Fr. 100.165.1–6, Eustathius speaks of the divine spirit as the divine *persona* that speaks to the man Jesus, the human *persona*—thus suggesting that spirit could be hypostasized as Son—as opposed to the Father. In addition, Eustathius is absolutely clear in Fr. 2.65.18–24, Fr. 3.65.1–9, and Fr. 85.154.1–5 that it is the "child (παῖς) of God," the γνήσιος υἱός, and the one anointed (ὁ χρισθεὶς), as opposed to the Father himself, who becomes incarnate. Again, what we may see in this is a clear distinction in Eustathius's thinking between Father and Son—without the terminology to express it precisely.

108. Fr. 50.122.20–23.

109. Fr. 43.117.31–33.

110. Frs. 51–61 (Declerck, 123.1–130.9).

111. Fr. 60.129.1–2.

112. Eustathius condemns this doctrine explicitly as nonsense in Fr. 54 and attributes the belief to the "Ariomaniacs" at Fr. 55.

113. As Marcellus will in some of his most controversial assertions about the end of the incarnate Word's kingdom. Cf. below, n. 157.

114. Ναός or verbal cognates: Fr. 21.84.14; Fr. 50.121.7; Fr. 64.135.25; Fr. 83.153.3; Fr. 84.154; Fr. 95.162.2–3; Fr. 98.163.2; Fr. 102.167.2.

115. Ὄργανον: Fr. 1.64.16; Fr. 3.65.5 (a reference to the σωματικὸν ὄργανον); Fr. 70.142.15–16.

116. Σκηνή: Fr. 57.127.1; Fr. 66.138.2.

117. Ἀνθρωπεία εἰδέα: *De Engast*. 18.39.926–27.

118. θεοφάνεια: Fr. 22.86.19.

119. Περιβολή: Fr. 32.104.70; Fr.128.189.7.

120. Fr. 21.84.19; Fr. 80.151; Fr. 123.185.1–5.

121. Fr. 68.139.3–7: "For on the one hand the Son, bearing the divine tokens of the Father's excellence, is image of the Father, and since like are born from like, those who are born appear to be true images of [their] begetters. But on the other hand, the man whom he bore is image of the Son . . . ."

122. Fr. 68.139.2–3.

123. Fr. 91.158.1–2.

124. Fr. 91(a).158.1–3, where the critical adverb is *naturalitur.*

125. Fr. 81(a).152.

126. Fr. 2.65.18–20.

127. More evidence that Eustathius thought in terms of two natures in Christ: Fr. 64.135.25–26 (reference to the θεία φύσις); in Fr. 28.96.36 there is a reference to "the Word according to nature."

128. Fr. 97.163.3–5.

129. Fr. 98.163.1–2.

130. Fr. 125.186. Note the similarity to Fr. 91, above, n. 123.

131. Fr. 119(a).181.6–7.

132. Fr. 100.1–3.

133. Cf. Michael Slusser, "The Exegetical Roots of Trinitarian Theology," *Theological Studies* 49 (1988): 461–76. Slusser, 473, also notes Eustathius's preference for "dividing the sayings."

134. Marcellus, Fr. 75.66.17; Fr. 81.72.2; Fr. 106. 98.10. Fragments cited below are Marcellus's until noted otherwise.

135. Fr. 7.10.7–8; Fr. 82.72.5.

136. Fr. 4.8.3 (συνῆψεν).

137. Cf. Fr. 11.12.17–14.5; Fr. 15.16.2–6.

138. For example: Fr. 3.6.2; Fr. 8.12.1; Fr. 33.34.1; Fr. 83.72.9; Fr. 85.74.3; Fr. 99.90.9 (προσλαβὼν); Fr. 106.96.4; Fr. 107.100.4.

139. Fr. 42.38.9 (περὶ τῆς κατὰ σάρκα γενέσεως); Fr. 59.52.9–10; Fr. 60.52.15 (same usage as Fr. 42).

140. Fr. 28.30.11–12.

141. Fr. 53.46.10.

142. Fr. 3.6.10–11; Fr. 13.14.15–16; Fr. 26.30.3; Fr. 35.34.5–6; Fr. 37.36.2.

143. Fr. 72.60.15–16.

144. Fr. 73.62.1–4.

145. Fr. 53.46.10–48.3; cf. in general Frs. 51–56 (Vinzent, 46–51); Frs. 113–14 (Vinzent, 106–9).

146. Fr. 39.36.10–14.

147. Fr. 37.36.2–4.

148. Fr. 101.92.4–6.

149. Fr. 99.90.9–15.

150. Fr. 79.70.7–11.

151. Fr. 80.70.16–17; Fr. 106.96.4–6.

152. Lienhard, *Contra Marcellum,* 58. Seibt, *Die Theologie des Markell von Ankyra,* 386, insists against Reinhard M. Hübner that the two categories are not absolutely identical, because Marcellus in several passages does speak of a certain man assumed by the Word. Yet Seibt also speaks of an "ecclesiological" interpretation of christological scriptural passages in Marcellus. Seibt admits on 518 that this aspect of Marcellus's thought allows the independence (*Selbständingkeit*) of the man over against the Word to come into view.

153. Fr. 80.70.12–17.

154. The word technically means "constitution" or "decree" but also has the meaning of "adoption" during the early Arian controversy. Cf. G. W. H. Lampe, ed., *A Patristic Greek Lexicon,* s.v. "Θέσις."

155. Fr. 111.104.12–15.

156. Fr. 85.74.1–5: "Who then does Asterius think it is who says 'I am who am,' the Son or the Father? For he said that 'there are two ὑποστάσεις, that of the Father and that of the Son,' *looking at the human flesh that the Word of God assumed and because of it imagining that this is so,* 'separating in this way the Son of God from the Father, just as someone might separate the son of a man from his natural father.'" Emphasis mine.

157. Frs. 99–112 in Vinzent, 90–107.

158. Fr. 101.92.4–10.

159. Fr. 100.92.1–3.

160. Fr. 104.94.17–18.

161. Fr. 106.98.12–14.

162. Fr. 109.102.1–4.

163. Fr. 106.96.9–12.

164. Eustathius, Frs. 100–103 in Declerck, 165–67. For more information on the work, cf. Declerck, ccccix–ccccxi.

165. Eustathius, Fr. 100.165.1–6.

166. As noted by Seibt, *Die Theologie des Markell von Ankyra,* 519, n. 73.

167. Eustathius, Fr. 108.170.1–2.

168. Cf. above, n. 111.

169. Marcellus, Frs. 74–75 in Vinzent, 62–67.

170. Cf. above, n. 98.

171. Marcellus, Fr. 74.64.3–10.

172. It should be noted that Seibt, *Die Theologie des Markell von Ankyra,* 519, n. 73, insists that Eustathius's exegesis of John 5:30, on the same question of the harmony between the will of the incarnate Word and the Father, was explicitly directed against Marcellus's response to the question. The text Seibt refers to, however, Fr. 150 in Declerck's edition, has now been relegated to the collection of fragments labeled "spuria et dubia."

173. Again, the fact that Eustathius's statement of this in Fr. 88 survives only in Syriac should perhaps make us cautious about asserting this too emphatically.

174. Kelley McCarthy Spoerl, "Athanasius and the Anti-Marcellan Controversy," *Zeitschrift für Antikes Christentum* 10:1 (2006): 34–55.

175. Kelley McCarthy Spoerl, "Apollinarian Christology and the Anti-Marcellan Tradition," *Journal of Theological Studies,* n.s. 45 (1994): 545–68.

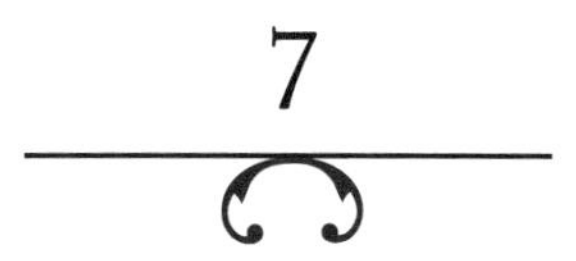

Loving Christ according to Origen and Augustine

Basil Studer, O.S.B.

When I was first invited to contribute to Brian Daley's Festschrift, I was asked to provide an overview of recent trends in the literature on the soteriology of early Christian authors.[1] While such an overview would certainly prove useful, it unfortunately lies beyond the more modest ambitions that I have set forth for this essay. I will, rather, limit myself to two theologians, Origen of Alexandria and Augustine of Hippo, both of whom, to this day, continue to receive remarkable scholarly attention. I think I am justified in selecting these two authors if only for the simple reason that, in the last few years, reference works devoted to each of these theologians have appeared. The *Dizionario Origene*[2] was published a few years ago in Italian, and more recently, the *Westminster Handbook to Origen*[3] has been offered to an English audience. For Augustine, in addition to the fascicles of the *Augustinus-Lexikon*[4] that continue to emerge, there is also the encyclopedia, *Augustine through the Ages*.[5] For my part, I have also had the opportunity to author several works on both of these theologians.[6]

The topic of Origen and Augustine's soteriologies requires, nevertheless, further restriction. If a presentation of patristic soteriology will resonate with us today, then it ought to articulate, I would contend, the personal dimension of this topic. As such, I would like to present Origen's and Augustine's views on loving Christ as integral to their respective soteriologies. It is clear that both theologians have a profound interest in the Johannine theme of God's love that preceded our love (1 John 4:8–10). But we can only speak of God's preceding love for us in its fullest sense when we also include our response, that is, our own love for God and, consequently, our love for Christ. The topic for this essay, then, is our love for Christ.

At the "Ninth Origen Conference" I delivered a paper on Origen's view of loving Christ,[7] and in my recent introduction to Augustine's *De Trinitate* I devoted the last chapter to Augustine's view of loving Christ.[8] In this essay the task remains to summarize and compare the results of both of these previous studies. Even if I cannot scale the heights that the Archbishop of Canterbury, Rowan Williams, reached in his paper on Augustine's Christology at the 2003 International Patristics Conference in Oxford,[9] I nevertheless attempt to offer in my analysis of Origen and Augustine what believers today especially wish to discover: an account of salvation that accentuates the love, and indeed the friendship, that exists between believers and Christ.

Loving Christ in Origen

"Christ is present to all who seek him."
—Origen, *Hom. Lev.* 9.14

The Theological Discipline—a Quest for the Truth

When many scholars eagerly devote themselves to Origen today, they tend to do so with the intent of studying his interpretation of Scripture and of tracing the extent to which his exegesis influenced the thinkers, preachers, and theologians of subsequent generations.[10] It used to be that Origen's *De principiis* stood at the foreground of research, and with that, a strong interest in its philosophical orientation[11] (one indication of which is the remarkable energy expended in deciphering the title *Peri archon*).[12]

De principiis was one of Origen's earliest writings, and even if we keep its fourth book in mind, in which Origen discusses at length Scripture and its interpretation, it is clear that *De principiis* does not yet reflect the robust sort of scriptural interpretation that we see elsewhere in his writings, in which he opens up to believers the deeper senses of Holy Scripture. Furthermore, many of his reflections in this work are admittedly of a philosophical nature (if one even wants to distinguish between philosophy and theology in this period), and it is certainly also the case that Origen seldom addresses Christ in this work as his "Lord and Master," as he will do in his sermons. Nevertheless, *De principiis* is a thoroughly theological project, as Origen himself announces at the beginning of the work (though the opening lines of this work are very often overlooked).[13] "All who believe and are convinced that grace and truth came by Jesus Christ," Origen begins, "derive the knowledge which calls men to lead a good and blessed life from no other source but the very words and teaching of Christ."[14] But since many who profess to believe in Christ interpret these words differently, it is imperative that these words receive an ecclesiastical interpretation, namely, an interpretation in accordance with the *regula fidei*.[15] Decisive in this introduction, however, is that it opens with faith in Christ, who is the "Way, the Truth and the Life" (John 14:6).

Perhaps the author of *De principiis* speaks even more clearly about the intent of this work at the end of the second book. In the last chapter of book 2, entitled "De repromissionibus" (Concerning the Promises), Origen offers a clear account of theological inquiry.[16] In this passage Origen describes the search for truth as an inquiry that includes the presence of Christ. He opens the chapter by referring to the person who directs *omnem industriam* to studies, "in order that he can, by inquiry into truth, learn the causes and reason of things."[17] A little later in this chapter he also describes "theology" more precisely as a "natural and appropriate longing to know God's truth and to learn the causes of things."[18] Origen asks, then, if this sort of theological inquiry will also exist in that life that is the true life, that life that is hidden with Christ in God, that is, eternal life. Now in order to satisfy fully that desire, the "love of truth" (cf. 2 Thess 2:10) that God has implanted in our minds, Origen suggests that we need to realize the *ordo vivendi* on two levels, and it is here that the presence of Christ for the theological disciple becomes evident.[19] In this earthly life, the Christian draws out the sketch of a portrait whose details will only be filled out in the eternal life. This shadowy sketch is only of value, however, if it is written on the "tablets of our heart" with the pencil of our Lord Jesus Christ.[20] From this outline of the truth and knowledge at the hands of Christ, which believers already possess in this earthly life, will emerge the beauty of a perfect picture in the eternal life. It is in that life, Origen continues, that believers will, as the apostle maintains, learn even more clearly from Christ the meaning of all things that transpire on earth—the meaning of man, of the Holy Spirit's grace to believers, the history of Israel, creation, and divine providence.[21] In heaven, in paradise, in the *locus eruditionis,* in the *auditorium,* and in the *schola animarum,* believers will be taught by Christ about everything that they saw on earth.[22] Even more, they will ascend through the heavenly spheres and learn even about these as well. To the extent that they follow Jesus who has walked through the heavens, they will attain, each according to his measure, to the vision of God.[23] For Origen, theology is therefore a search for truth, and both in this life as well as in the life to come, Christ is the teacher of this truth.

Christ, the Revelation of God

Two points must be kept in mind if we want to grasp the sense of this remarkable program. The first is that we have to be clear about the comprehensive significance of Origen's claim that Christ is the "Truth." This is a claim that he, in fact, likes to make, as in the prologue to *De principiis* where, immediately after exhorting readers to remember the words of the Lord, he writes: "I am the Truth (John 14:6)."[24] In connection with other Johannine and Pauline texts, Origen readily maintains that "to remain in Christ" means the same as to "remain in the Truth."[25] Whoever attends well to the biblical origins of the phrase "Christ, the Truth" will not be surprised that Origen understands it to mean that Christ is, above all, the revelation of God.

When Origen repeatedly and emphatically describes Christ as the "Truth," he wants to express that Christ reveals God as his and our Father.[26] This contention is repeatedly supported in Origen's writings with a reference to Matthew 11:27: "No one knows the Son except the Father and no one knows the Father, except the Son and he to whom the Son will reveal it."[27] Origen draws upon the concept of "Truth" to help explain these words of Jesus. For the first part of this verse, he notes that only the Father knows the Son, that is, the Truth, since the Father himself is the Truth.[28] But Origen will also and more customarily highlight the fact that the Son, precisely because he is also the Truth, knows the Father and therefore is also capable of revealing him.[29] As "Truth," Christ allows us traverse from the "beginnings of the law to the perfection of the gospel."[30] Nevertheless, Origen does not exclude the fact that the Truth was already among us prior to the advent of the Redeemer.[31]

What Origen contends about the "Truth," that it reveals the Father, pertains to the "Truth" that is mentioned in the opening lines of the prologue of *De principiis*. This is readily clear when we keep in mind that the first two books of the *Commentary on John,* in which Origen explores at length the revelatory action of the Logos, were written prior to *De principiis*. This assertion is also confirmed by other places in Origen's theological corpus (not only in his exegetical writings, but also in *Contra Celsum* and *De principiis*) where he speaks of "Truth" together with the other customary "aspects" (ἐπίνοιαι) of the Son—Wisdom, Logos, Life, and Justice.[32] What is particularly significant about these aspects is that Origen can connect "Truth" with "Wisdom" and "Word," a connection that makes especially clear that he has the Son as God's revelation in mind.[33] This is especially evident in a passage from *De principiis* where Origen is wrestling with the claim at the beginning of the Letter to the Hebrews that Christ is the "express image" of God's substance (Heb 1:3):

> See, then, whether the Son of God, who is called God's "Word" and "Wisdom," and who alone knows the Father and reveals him to whom he will, to those, namely, who become capable of receiving his Word and Wisdom, may not perhaps be said to express the

image of God's substance or subsistence for this reason, that he makes God understood and known; that is, when Wisdom outlines first in herself the things which she wishes to reveal to others, by means of which they are to know and understand God, then she herself may be called the "express image of God's substance" (Heb 1:3).[34]

The extent to which, for Origen, the knowledge of God is rooted in belief in Jesus Christ is perhaps most clearly expressed in his interpretation of Moses' vision in Exodus 33:21ff.[35] Origen repeatedly returns to this passage, even in *De principiis,* where, in a discussion of the invisibility of God, he explains how Moses and Christ (John 14:9) have "seen" God.[36] In another discussion of Exodus 33 in the *Commentary on the Song of Songs,* Origen wrestles with the meaning of the *foramen petrae* (cleft in the rock) and *posteriora* (back).[37] What does it mean that God put Moses in the "cleft of the rock" and, after God has passed by, Moses was allowed to see God's "back"? According to Origen, the first phrase means that in the rock, namely, Christ, there is a cleft which is open to God. The "back" of God, on the other hand, is what can only be seen at the end of time by that person who stands in the fissure of the rock, i.e. who has learnt from the revelation of Christ.[38] It is in and through Christ, the revelation of God, that believers come to know God.

Christ, the Lord and Master

In order to grasp fully the significance of Origen's claim that "Christ is the Truth" we must not only observe how Christ serves as God's revelation, but also—and this is the second point—we must discern that Origen strikes a personal note with this claim.[39] When he considers Christ the *magister eruditionis* on earth and in heaven, he means the "Truth" which looks at him and addresses him. This is already evident in those texts in which Origen speaks of Christ opening to the believing Christian the sense of Scripture.[40] Along these lines, Origen also thinks of the voice of the preacher as the voice of Christ. The apostle Paul, moreover, gives him the certainty that Christ speaks in us.[41] Origen is at his clearest in those countless passages where he takes up the Pauline theme of Christ removing the obstructing veil from those who listen to him (cf. 2 Cor 3:12–18).[42]

We also discern this personal dimension in those texts in which Origen speaks of the place, house, or dwelling where Christ is found by those who search for him.[43] We detect in such passages that someone can also serve as the Lord's companion, indeed, even be counted as his friend.[44] If someone praises Jesus, Origen preaches, and receives him, this person's strength increases.[45] This intimacy with Christ takes on heightened import in those passages where Origen presents Christ as the doctor of souls.[46] Moreover, Origen stresses the significance of the human soul of Jesus,[47] which is for him priest and mediator.[48] Precisely in this context, Christ as "Truth" signifies Christ as our Lord and Master.

Whoever attends to this personal dimension that colors Origen's discussions of Christ as "Truth" will not be surprised to learn that he repeatedly interrupts his discussion of difficult questions, especially those that arise from his labors with the Scriptures, with prayers. For example, he concludes a homily on the book of Leviticus with the request that the Lord might disclose to him and his hearers the sense of the passage that has been read in church.[49] Noticeable also is how Origen presents Joshua in the *Homilies on Joshua* and *Homilies on Judges* as the prototype of Jesus.[50] Thus it is hardly surprising that precisely in these homilies Origen turns in prayer to Christ. Take the following passage that alludes to the foot-washing scene in John's Gospel:

> Come, I pray, Lord Jesus, Son of God, take off your outer garment and pour water into the basin and wash the feet of your servants. Wash the feet of our souls, so that we can say: "I have washed my feet, so how can I dirty them again?" And when you wash our feet, we would like to remain by you and listen to you, since you are our Lord and Master."[51]

From his *Homilies on Jeremiah* comes the invitation to his hearers: "We want to pray that Jesus comes, that he reveals himself and teaches us the meaning of the passage that has been read."[52] A little later he adds: "I need an appearance [ἐπιφάνεια] of the power of Jesus, since he is Wisdom, Word and Truth, so that his arrival might illumine my face."[53] An indication of just how personal Origen understands these prayers to be is the remarkable way in which he uses "my Jesus" as a form of address.[54]

On this personal level, Origen holds to the conviction that a believer ought to love Christ who is the Truth.[55] While he does not say this expressly, the idea is nevertheless present in his writings. For example, loving Christ is implied when Origen exhorts us to search for Jesus, that is, the Logos, the Wisdom, the Righteousness, the Truth, and the Righteousness of God—all those aspects that characterize Christ—and in so doing, search for the Father as well.[56] Another example where loving Christ is implied is when Origen invites believers, like the people of Nazareth, to look up to Jesus,[57] to become his followers and become one in spirit with him.[58] Sometimes this love for Christ is explicitly stated, as when Origen exhorts his congregation to love Christ the Lord "in incorruption" (Eph 6:24), that is, to love Christ with an uncorrupted understanding or to offer an uncorrupted body to God.[59] Yet perhaps Origen is at his clearest when he offers his interpretation of Psalm 36:23 and its mention of the "steps" that are taken (*gressus*).[60] These steps signify for him the soul's continual ascent. This is an ascent, in turn, that strives for higher knowledge, and so in this context Origen takes over the request of Moses for the vision of God, though he especially speaks of striving for Christ, who is the Power of God. Upon what path should the soul take its steps to Christ? The answer, Origen says, is that the inner man must stride on a particular path, the Path, or Way, that says: "I am the Way, the Truth and the Life" (John 14:6).[61] Origen describes this Way upon which the inner man walks as a *via media* and concludes: "Whoever allows himself to be lead by God, strives for Christ and longs to remain in him."[62]

Without a doubt this open and personal encounter with Christ ought also to be seen as integral to the theological project of *De principiis*. Certainly the questions that are widely and pervasively discussed in this work concern themselves primarily, as I already mentioned above, with philosophical topics: the incorporeality and spirituality of God, providence and evil, and human freedom. Nevertheless, this fact ought not to prevent us from seeing in *De principiis* above all a loving conversation between the Christian and Christ, the Truth.[63] Even if Origen does not address Christ as "my Jesus" and also does not pray to him, nevertheless there are still intimations, here and there, that indicate to what extent the Christian life for Origen depends on discipleship of Christ.[64] In *De principiis* Christ is for Origen not only the "Truth" but also "the Way" and "the Life."

Loving Christ in Augustine

> "All the surer is our love for the face of Christ the more we recognize in his 'back' how much Christ first loved us."
>
> —Augustine, *Trin.* II 17.28[65]

Christ, the Truth

Augustine's readers know how prominent the concept of "truth" is for him. The search for the truth governed Augustine's entire existence, and the initial impulse in this direction can be traced back to his discovery of the *disciplina philosophica* during his studies in Carthage. Particularly decisive was his reading of Cicero's *Hortensius* (a text no longer extant).[66] This work awoke in him the desire to strive for that bliss that could be found in the "enjoyment of truth."[67] Taking his cues from Aristotle, the famous Roman rhetorician invited the reader to philosophy, to the love of truth. Augustine made Cicero's ideal his own—even the rhetorician ought to be a lover of truth.[68]

For Augustine, the path to "truth" is marked by philosophy even more so than was the case with Origen. Yet from the very beginning, Augustine too places "truth" in a Christian context. He understands philosophical "truth" in the light of the Christian piety that he has received from his mother:[69] for him, Christ is the "Truth."[70] The extent to which Augustine is indebted to the biblical understanding of "Truth" already appears in the fact that he continually refers to biblical, indeed, Johannine passages where *veritas* appears. He frequently refers to the saying of Jesus: "I am the Way, the Truth, and the Life" (John 14:6).[71]

He can even make use of the formula *Veritas dicit,* when citing Jesus.[72] Of even greater significance are the references to John 8:31ff.,[73] John 1:14 and 1:17,[74] and 2 Timothy 2:25.

In texts where Augustine speaks of *veritas,* something divine is usually meant—God, or expressed more philosophically, the *veritas immutabilis.*[75] In christological contexts, Augustine means by *veritas* the divinity of Christ. He distinguishes this divinity from the *via,* the humanity of Christ, which leads to his divinity, his Truth, his Life.[76] In *De Trinitate* Augustine avails himself of Pauline categories, linking *veritas* with the *forma dei* and *via* with the *forma servi.*[77]

As is the case with Origen, Augustine also speaks of the many names of Jesus.[78] While he certainly has a preference for *verbum* and *sapientia,* he can also call Christ *veritas* (and probably does so more frequently than Origen). The personal meaning of *veritas* for Augustine is expressed above all in the trinitarian theme: *aeternitas, veritas, caritas.* This is clearly articulated in the following text:

> But many who boast in the cross of Christ and do not depart from the same path, even those who do not know those things that are discussed with great subtlety, because not a single infant perishes for whom he has died, come to the same Eternity, Truth, and Love, that is, to solid, certain, and complete happiness, where everything is clear for those who remain, see, and love.[79]

In this text Augustine distinguishes the three persons not by their proper names, Father, Son, and Holy Spirit, but with the nouns *aeternitas, veritas,* and *caritas. Veritas* gives us the certainty that we can attain, with the help of *caritas,* to *felicitas,* and that *felicitas* is, in turn, rooted in *aeternitas.*[80] This trinitarian interpretation of *veritas* is also implied in those passages where Augustine, quoting Scripture, opens with "*veritas dicit*" or "*dixit.*"[81]

Our Path Is Marked by Faith in Christ

Truth and Faith

Whoever wishes to explore more deeply what Augustine meant when he called Christ "Truth" must examine more closely the relationship between *veritas* and *fides*. It is not important to know if he is talking about *veritas fidei* or the *veritas* of the Bible. Decisive here is how Augustine understands the role of Christ in the life of faith.

In his writings, and especially in his sermons, Augustine repeatedly describes the Christian life with verbs *ire, ambulare, navigari, peregrinari,* and *se extendere transire*.[82] With these images he means to depict nothing other than faith in Christ. With this faith we advance on the path that is Christ and arrive at Truth, which is Christ himself. The theme of Christian pilgrimage occupies Augustine's thoughts in his exposition on Psalm 123:

> Let us therefore so walk as if we were on the way, for the king of our country himself has made himself the way. The king of our country, the Lord Jesus Christ—there He is the Truth, but here He is the Way. Where are we going? To the Truth. By what path are we going? By faith. Where are we going? To Christ. By what path are we going? By Christ.[83]

This faith that serves as a signpost for the Christian journey encompasses the entire trinitarian *dispensatio salutis* as it is summarized in the confession of faith.[84] The source of this faith in the Son of God is, in fact, Christ. When someone approaches the Truth in faith, the divine Truth has already established in its incarnation this person's faith, so that this person's way to God has become possible through the incarnation. In order for the person confidently to traverse the path of faith to Truth, the Truth itself, God, God's Son, has taken up a man while preserving his divinity, and in that act has firmly established faith. In this way can the person reach God through the God-man. Christ, the mediator, is for this person not only the journey's end but also the way itself.[85]

Augustine goes even further in his exhortations to faith in Christ. It is clear for him that Christians ought also to deepen their faith by understanding it more profoundly. This *intellectus fidei* is based at its core on the presence of Christ. Christ helps believers attain a more comprehensive understanding of what the loving God wants. In this sense Augustine is clear: "Christus loquitur de Christo."[86] Even more, Augustine never tires of speaking of Christ as his sole teacher.[87] As *magister exterior*

Christ exhorts to faith; as *magister interior* Christ allows Christians to realize that this faith is really true.[88] Christ teaches through the Spirit whom he promised and through this Spirit's Love.[89]

Christ Rules through Faith

This conception of Christ as both the Way and the Truth clearly has its roots in Scripture, and above all, in the fourth Gospel. There is, however, another theme that Augustine develops that is equally rooted in Scripture. His encounter with the western Arians compelled him to examine in greater depth 1 Corinthians 15:24–28, where Paul spoke of the subjection of the Son to the Father at the end of time. Augustine already offered an interpretation of this passage in his early writing, *De diversis quaestionibus LXXXIII*.[90] In the first book of *De Trinitate* he returns to this Pauline text.[91]

He begins by refuting a series of interpretations of this Pauline passage.[92] First, the words of the apostle are not to be understood in the sense of a future transformation of Christ's humanity into divinity, since this divinity is not a mutable creature but rather the incorporeal and unchanging Trinity.[93] Furthermore, it is also the case that Paul did not mean by the subjection of the Son to the Father the future transformation of the creature into the substance of the creator.[94] And again, this passage certainly does not say that while the Father has, in fact, subjected all things to himself, the Son has *not* subjected all things to himself. Furthermore, Christ will not hand over the kingdom to God his Father in such a way that he, Christ, himself takes it, since he is with the Father one God.[95] Finally, one also cannot interpret the handing over of the kingdom in such a way that the Father does not have the kingdom right now.[96] After this lengthy critique of various misreadings, Augustine presents his own interpretation. Christ is now the king of all those who are just, who live by faith. As mediator between God and man, the man Christ Jesus leads men to the unveiled vision of God. "The sentence: 'when he hands over the kingdom to God the Father,' means the same as: he leads believers to the vision of the Father."[97] Augustine confirms that interpretation with other passages of Scripture, including Matthew 11:47, where the power that the Father has given to the Son is interpreted by Augustine as the revelation of the Father through the Son.[98] With such an interpretation Augustine repeats his main contention: Christ hands the kingdom over to the Father "when he, the mediator between God and man, the man Christ Jesus, leads those whom he now as king rules, those who are just and who live by faith, to the vision of God the Father."[99]

Faith Becomes Truth

In his exegesis of 1 Corinthians 15:24–28, Augustine does not describe explicitly as truth the vision of Christ in which believers will also see the Father unveiled. He does so, however, in a more philosophical passage in *De Trinitate*.[100] With an allusion to Plato—"As eternity is to that which has originated, so truth is to faith"[101]—Augustine develops his own conception of the purification of the human spirit that is required for the vision of God. We were incapable of comprehending eternal realities, he begins, because we were weighed down by our sins and mortality, and so we required purification. But we could only be purified for eternal realities by temporal realities, the useful ones that heal us and lead us, once we have recovered, to eternal things. Thus, the rational mind, once purified (*mens purgata*), is designed to contemplate eternal realities, but while it is still requiring purification (*mens purganda*), must give faith to temporal realities.[102] And what sort of purifying temporal realities ought we to believe? Here Augustine turns to the incarnation of Truth itself—the Son of God became Son of man, so that by faith in him we might be lead back to his Truth.[103] Expressed otherwise, Truth incarnate, as both eternal and temporal, serves as the bridge for us: being purified by our faith in his temporal life, of all he did for us, our faith turns to truth and our mortality turns to eternity.

> Our faith will then become truth, when we come to what we are promised as believers; but what we are promised is eternal life, and the Truth said—not the truth our faith will become in the future, but the Truth which is always Truth because it is eternity—the Truth said: "This is eternal life, that they should know you the one true God, and Jesus Christ whom you have sent" (Jn 17:3). Therefore when our faith becomes truth by seeing, our mortality will be transformed into a fixed and firm eternity.[104]

Augustine expands upon this understanding of a faith that becomes truth by paraphrasing another one of his favorite Johannine texts: "When you remain in my Word, you are truly my disciples and you will know the Truth and it will set you free" (John 8:31ff.). With these words of Jesus Augustine justifies his main thesis: "So because what has originated in him [Christ] has passed over into eternity, so too will what has originated in us pass over when faith arrives at truth."[105]

The Love for Eternal Truth

Christ is the way to Truth, is indeed the Truth himself. How central this basic conviction is for Augustine's theology becomes clear from his frequent citations of the words of Isaiah: "If you do not believe, you will not understand" (Isa 7:9b).[106] The faith that leads to truth forms above all the leitmotif of the fifteen books of *De Trinitate*. To grasp this point it is helpful to attend to the eighth book of this work, in which Augustine goes from the *res verae* (books 1–7) to the *similia veri* (books 9–15).[107] In the eighth book Augustine asks himself the important question: If we do not know the Trinity, can we really love it?[108] In the books that follow, Augustine ascends through the various analogies for the external and internal human up to the *imago sapientiae,* in order to attempt to understand approximately what the "Trinitas quae est unus Deus" is. The result of his inquiry is that such a knowledge is only possible here in this life in hope, in love, in the "stretching out to what lies ahead."[109] Put in other words, love takes place in the knowledge of the faith, in the *credendo diligere*.[110]

The love that emerges from the knowledge of the faith is rooted in a love for Jesus, and in particular, a love of his resurrection. In the second book of *De Trinitate,* Augustine develops this cardinal tenet of his trinitarian theology by referring to the theophany on Mt. Sinai.[111] There Moses requests God to show him his majesty, and God's response is that no mortal can see his "face" and live, but that he will let Moses stand on a "rock" and see his "back."[112] This verse compels Augustine to relay an interpretation of this passage customary in his day. The theophany prefigures the person of Jesus Christ, and so the "back" of Jesus is his flesh that was born from Mary, died, and was resurrected.[113] The "face," on the other hand, which no man can see and live, is described by Augustine as the immortal, divine nature of Christ, that is, the *forma* in which Christ is equal to the Father.[114] A few lines later he describes this "face" as the "open manifestation" of God's Wisdom. While no mortal can see this face, nevertheless, "this is the sight which everyone yearns to behold" who both loves God and loves his neighbor.[115]

> But while "we are away from the Lord and walking by faith and not by sight" (2 Cor 5:6), we have to behold Christ's back, that is his flesh, by this same faith; standing that is upon the solid foundation of faith, which is represented by the rock, and gazing at his flesh from the security of the lookout on the rock, namely the Catholic church,[116] of which it is said, "And upon this rock I will build my church" (Mt 16:18). All the surer is our love for the face of Christ which we long to see, the more clearly we recognize in his back how much Christ first loved us.[117]

With this emphasis upon our faith in the "back," the flesh of Christ, as integral to our love for him, it is hardly surprising that Augustine immediately turns to the resurrection of this flesh. What is its significance for the believer? Augustine answers that it is a loving faith in this flesh's resurrection that saves and justifies. This belief is what gives value to the Christian faith, and, what is more, believers also await in the certainty of hope for the resurrection of their own bodies.[118] So central is this faith in the resurrection that Augustine discusses at some length how many Jews came to believe in the Lord after his resurrection.[119] Augustine sums up his discussion of this theophany by noting that the "face" is the "supreme and supremely divine and changeless substance in which the one and only God is both Father and Son and Holy Spirit."[120] Thus, to the extent that Augustine connects the desire for the vision of this divine face with the faith in the resurrection of Christ, he basically pronounces that our love for the Trinity corresponds to our loving faith in the resurrection of Christ.[121]

In the love for the resurrected Lord, the Christian thus encounters the blessed vision of the "Trinitas quae est unus Deus." This conviction that marks Augustine's entire theological thought, in particular, his inquiry into the unity of the Father, Son, and Spirit, finds a double confirmation in his writings.[122] First, in his ascending search for the trinitarian analogies, Augustine reaches, finally, the highest image of the Trinity, the *imago sapientiae*.[123] This image consists in the believing Christian remembering, knowing, and loving God. The perfection of this highest image only transpires, however, in the resurrection to eternal life[124]—in other words, when the Christian becomes the perfect image according to which he was created, the image of the resurrected Lord.[125] Only when this person comes to resemble the glorified Jesus can he become the perfect image of the "Trinitas quae est unus Deus."[126] And second, anyone who is familiar with Augustine's writings and, in particular, attends to the openings of some of his letters must notice how often he speaks of the *dilectio Christi*.[127] It is possible that these two words had become formulaic by Augustine's day. Nevertheless, behind this expression there is the firm conviction that the Christian ought to respond in love to the love Jesus embodied, that God first loved us.

Concluding Thoughts

Throughout both Origen's and Augustine's writings, Christ appears as "the Truth." For both authors it then follows that salvation consists in a sort of knowledge. Without doubt both authors can express in other ways the perfection or renewal of spiritual creation that has been created according to the image of God.[128] Nevertheless, the interest in inner illumination predominates. This cannot come as a surprise when one takes into consideration that both authors were primarily in dialogue with intellectuals, and that they both labored to promote the knowledge of the faith in simple Christians. Their conception of salvation can be described, thus, as a Christian Gnosis or as a revelation of divine love. The intellectual orientation of their theological thinking seems, correspondingly, philosophical. But when one pays attention to how closely both Origen and Augustine follow the Johannine writings, one cannot avoid the fact that their love for the "Truth" is deeply informed by Holy Scripture. Whenever they refer to the words of Jesus,

"I am the Way, the Truth, and the Life," and other similar expressions of the Lord, they clearly indicate how much they are at home in the biblical world. They call Jesus Christ "the Son of God," and for this reason the "Truth of God" or simply the "Truth," because he reveals the Father and "explains" what he has always seen (cf. John 1:18). In his incarnation he has become the way that leads to "Truth," to the vision of his countenance against which the glory of God illumines. Moreover, both theologians leave no doubt that this "Truth" ought to be understood in a completely personal manner. Christ is the "Truth" when he looks people in the eyes and talks with them. He is the "Truth" that believers come to know in greater depth the more they strive for it and love it as it appears in Jesus, the incarnate Truth.

There are certainly noticeable differences between the ways in which Origen and Augustine speak of Christ as the Truth. Turning aside from the reflections of the bishop of Hippo about the knowledge of truth that ring more philosophical, the framework in which both theologians thinks about the Trinity is different. In Origen's pre-Nicene epoch, the distance between the Trinity and creation is less clearly expressed than in the Nicene theology of Augustine, in which the eternal identity and therefore the oneness of the three persons stand. Origen, for his part, devotes more thought to the soul of Jesus than does Augustine, whereas Augustine comes closer to the later conception of the personal unity of Christ. The bishop of Hippo puts more weight on the renewal of the sinner through grace than does the master from Alexandria, who accentuates the role of human freedom in this renewal. These and other differences in the framework of the soteriological thought of these two theologians do not, however, call into question the fundamental agreement between them. For both, Christ serves as the mediator between God and man, the way that leads to Truth. For both, the human quest for the vision of God remains unfulfilled without a faithful love for Christ. And it is precisely here that their conceptions of final salvation correspond to the expectations of people today who long for personal dialogue and loving exchange. Love for Christ is therefore what we expect most: an encounter with the one who loves us forever.

Translated by Peter W. Martens

Notes

1. Cf. Basil Studer, with collaboration by Brian Daley, *Soteriologie in der Schrift und Patristik,* Handbuch der Dogmengeschichte III/2a (Freiburg: Herder, 1978).

2. Adele Monaci Castagno, ed., *Origene: Dizionario. La cultura, il pensiero, le opere* (Rome: Città Nuova, 2000).

3. John A. McGuckin, ed., *The Westminster Handbook to Origen* (Louisville: Westminster John Knox Press, 2004).

4. Cornelius Mayer, ed., *Augustinus-Lexikon* (Basel: Schwabe, 1986–).

5. Allan D. Fitzgerald, ed., *Augustine through the Ages: An Encyclopedia* (Grand Rapids: Eerdmans, 1999).

6. Concerning Origen, my articles in the *Dizionario* on the "Incarnation" and the "Cross" both pertain directly to the doctrine of redemption (in Monaci, *Origene: Dizionario,* 102–7, 225–29); concerning Augustine, I have presented the more significant elements of his thoughts about God and Christ in my *Gratia Christi–Gratia Dei bei Augustinus von Hippo: Christozentrismus oder Theozentrismus?* (Rome: Institutum Patristicum Augustinianum, 1993); English translation, *The Grace of Christ and the Grace of God in Augustine of Hippo: Christocentrism or Theocentrism?* trans. Matthew J. O'Connell (Collegeville, Minn.: Liturgical Press, 1997).

7. Cf. Basil Studer, "Christus, die Wahrheit, bei Origenes von Alexandrien," *Origeniana Nona* (August 29–Sept 2, 2005, Pécs, Hungary), forthcoming.

8. Basil Studer, *Augustins De Trinitate: Eine Einführung* (Paderborn: Schöningh, 2005).

9. Editor's note: the essay to which Studer refers is included as chapter 8 in this volume.

10. Cf. Henri de Lubac, *Histoire et esprit: L'intelligence de l'Écriture d'après Origène* (Paris: Aubier, 1950). In addition, the friends of this author, e.g. B. F. Bolgiani, "Henri de Lubac e l'esegesi spirituale," *Annali di storia dell'esegesi* 10/2 (1993): 283–300.

11. Cf. the bibliographical study by U. Berner, *Origenes* (Darmstadt: Wissenschaftliche Buchgesellschaft, 1981), as well as the reference to F.-H. Kettler, *Der ursprüngliche Sinn der Dogmatik des Origenes* (Berlin: A. Töpelmann, 1966).

12. Cf., e.g., H. Crouzel, in SC 252,12–15.

13. Origen, *Princ.* pref. 1–10 (critical edition: *Origenes: Vier Bücher von den Prinzipien*, ed. H. Görgemanns and H. Karpp, 3rd ed. [Darmstadt: Wissenschaftliche Buchgesellschaft, 1992], 82–98, esp. 82ff.).

14. Origen, *Princ.* pref. 1: Görgemanns, *Origenes,* 82: "Omnes qui credunt et certi sund quod gratia et veritas per Iesum Christum facta est . . . scientiam

quae provcat homines ad bene beateque vivendum, non aliunde quam ab ipsis Christi verbis doctrinaque suscipiunt."

15. Cf. R. C. Baud, "Les 'Règles' de la théologie d'Origène," *Recherches de science religieuse* 55 (1967): 161–208.

16. Origen, *Princ.* II 11: Görgemanns, *Origenes,* 438–56.

17. Origen, *Princ.* II 11,1: Görgemanns, *Origenes,* 440: "quo possit inquisita veritate rerum causas rationemque cognoscere."

18. Origen, *Princ.* II 11,4: Görgemanns, *Origenes,* 446: "ita mens nostra sciendae veritatis Dei et rerum causas noscendi proprium ac naturale desiderium gerit."

19. Origen, *Princ.* I 7,3: Görgemanns, *Origenes,* 236: "captandae veritatis studio provocamur."

20. Origen, *Comm. Jo.* XIII 53,352ff., where Origen says that when Christ teaches humans directly, he has stamped into their hearts the τύποι τῆς ἀληθείας.

21. Origen, *Princ.* II 6,7: Görgemanns, *Origenes,* 370ff., where Origen says that in the heavenly theology we will grasp what stands behind the shadows of what was written in the Bible in various ways.

22. Origen, *Princ.* II 3,1: Görgemanns, *Origenes,* 300: "per eruditionem vero rationabilemque institutionem, per quam possent ad locupletiorem proficere veritatis intellectum hi, qui in praesenti iam vita in haec se studia dediderunt et mentibus purgatiores effecti, capaces iam hinc divinae sapientiae perrexerunt . . . ."

23. Cf. on the ascent through the spheres, Origen, *Comm. Jo.* XIII 40,262–70: SC 222,172–76.

24. Cf., e.g., *Hom. Ps.* 36, IV,1: SC 411,186ff. Further texts on this passage are found in *Biblia Patristica: Index des citations et allusions bibliques dans la littérature patristique*, vol. 3, *Origène* (Paris: Éditions du Centre nationale de la recherche scientifique, 1980), 340.

25. Cf. Origen, *Comm. Jo.* XX 28,245: SC 290,278, as well as *Comm. Jo.* XX 27,237: SC 290,274; XX 30,268–75: SC 290,288.

26. It is indeed true that on occasion Origen will describe Christ as the "Truth" with respect to the Father but as "Image" with respect to us. With respect to the Father, Christ resembles the Father whose Ideas he himself contains. With respect to us, Christ is an Image that opens our eyes for the Father. Normally, however, Origen calls the Son the "Truth" since he instructs people of his Father. (Cf. Origen, *Princ.* I 2,6: Görgemanns, *Origenes*, 136. In addition, SC 253,42–45, with the explanation by A. Orbe, as well as *Comm. Jo.* VI 6,38f.: SC 157,157ff., on the participation of humans in the "Truth.")

27. Cf. Origen, *Comm. Jo.* I 38,277f.: SC 120,198.

28. Origen, *Princ.* II 6,1: Görgemanns, *Origenes,* 356. In this regard, Origen can even maintain that the Father is greater than the Truth, as the Father also stands over Wisdom and the true Light (cf. Origen, *Comm. Jo.* II,151: SC 120,306, and *Cels.* VIII,15: SC 150,206ff.).

29. Cf. Origen, *Comm. Jo.* I 38,277f.: SC 120,198. In fact, Jesus leads us to the Father through all his aspects (ἐπίνοιαι)—not just the "Truth" but also "Word," "Life," "Wisdom," and so on guide us to the Father (cf. *Comm. Jo.* I 16,92: SC 120,108).

30. Origen, *Hom. Jer.* 12,13: SC 238,46.

31. Origen, *Princ.* IV 2,3: Görgemanns, *Origenes,* 706. In addition, n. 26–26a: SC 269,178f., on the partial revelation of Christ in the Old Testament.

32. Cf. Origen, *Cels.* II,64: SC 132,434; *Princ.* I 2,1–5: Görgemanns, *Origenes,* 122–32. This association of attributes is apparently dependent upon the particular biblical passage that Origen is, at any given time, commenting upon. For instance, in his *Commentary on Romans* Origen often connects "Truth" with "Righteousness" (Origen, *Comm. Rom.* I,16: Fontes Christiani 2/1, 134–42. In addition, *Hom. Luc.* 30,1 and 3: Fontes Christiani 4/2, 306 and 308; *Hom. Jer.* XIV,5: SC 238,76; XIV,16: SC 238,104, with 1 Cor 5:8).

33. Origen, *Princ.* I 2,7: Görgemanns, *Origenes,* 136ff.: the ἐπίνοιαι are located in the context of revelation: *splendor ex luce*.

34. Origen, *Princ.* I 2,8. Görgemanns, *Origenes,* 138: "Et vide ne forte, quoniam filius dei, qui est verbum eius et sapientia dicitur et qui solus novit patrem, et revelat quibus vult, id es qui capaces verbi ipsius et sapientiae fiunt, secundum hoc ipsum, quod intellegi atque agnosci facit deum, figuram substantiae vel subsistentiae eius dicatur exprimere id est cum in semet ipsa primum describit sapientia ea, quae revelare vult ceteris, ex quibus ab illis agnoscitur et intelligitur deus, et haec dicatur figura expressa substantiae dei."

35. Origen, *Hom. Jer.* 16,2f.: SC 238,134–38. Cf. *Princ.* II 4,3: Görgemanns, *Origenes,* 326ff.; *Comm. Jo.* XX 27,237–44: SC 290,274–78, where in connection with Exod 33:21 Origen says that someone must hold to the Truth who stands on the rock, Christ; *Hom. Ps.* 36, IV,1: SC 411,184ff.

36. Origen, *Princ.* II 4,3: Görgemanns, *Origenes,* 336ff.: No one has seen God (John 1:18), Origen avers, and so when Moses is said to have "seen" God, and when it says that "he who has seen the Son has seen the Father also" (John 14:9), Origen insists that what is here spoken of is not literal sight, the seeing of the eyes, but rather a figurative sight, the seeing of the mind. In this context he cites Matt 11:27, "No one knows the Son except the Father," and reminds readers that it does *not* say: "No one *sees* the Father except the Son."

37. Origen, *Comm. Cant.* IV 2,12: SC 376,704ff.

38. Origen, l.c.: "Nemo ergo videt postrema Dei, id est, quae in postremis temporibus fiunt, nisi positus in foramine petrae, scilicet cum ea Christo reve-

lante didicerit." Cf. *Hom. Jer.* XVI,2ff.: SC 238,136ff.; *Hom. Ps.* 36, IV,1: SC 411,186: "ut ea quae in novissimis temporibus implebuntur per assumptionem carnis agnoscas." In addition, cf. Irenaeus, *Haer.* IV 20,9: SC 100,654.

39. Cf. C. Reemts, *Vernunftgemässer Glaube: Die Begründung des Christentums in der Schrift des Origenes gegen Celsus* (Bonn: Borengässer, 1998), 41f.

40. See the texts quoted earlier in this chapter.

41. Origen, *Princ.* II 6,7: Görgemanns, *Origenes,* 370; *Hom. Jer.* XVII,2: SC 238,162.

42. Origen, *Princ.* IV 1,6: Görgemanns, *Origenes,* 688, with 2 Cor 3:15f.; *Hom. Lev.* 1,1: SC 286,68ff.; *Hom. Exod.* 12,4: SC 321,362ff. In addition, cf. M. Borret, in SC 321,29f., "Le visage de Moise, rayonnant de gloire et voilé," with *Hom. Exod.* 12,3: SC 321,358–62.

43. Cf. Origen, *Hom. Jer.* 12,13: SC 238,48; *Hom. Ps.* 37, II,9: 326: mansio; *Hom. Lev.*, IX,5: SC 287,94ff.: "Optamus tamen ut vel his auditis operam dedit non solum in Ecclesia audire verba Dei, sed et in domibus vestris exerceri et meditari in lege Domini die ac nocte, et ibi enim Christus est et ubique adest quaerentibus se." In addition, the introduction, "Origène contemplatif," in SC 411,30–31, with *Hom. Ps.* 38, II,12: SC 411,404.

44. Cf. *Hom. Jos.* XI,2: SC 71,284 where Origen speaks of friendship with Jesus.

45. Origen, *Hom. Jer.* XIV,10: SC 138,114.

46. Origen, *Hom. Lev.* VIII,1: SC 287,8. Cf. S. Fernández, *Cristo médico, según Origenes: La actividad médica como metáfora de la acción divina* (Rome: Institum patristicum Augustinianum, 1999).

47. Cf. M. Harl, *Origène et la fonction révélatrice du verbe incarné* (Paris: Éditions du Seuil, 1958), 116ff., 203ff., 281.

48. Cf. Origen, *Hom. Num.* IX 5,2–4; SC 415,244ff.

49. Origen, *Hom. Lev.* VI,6: SC 286,296: "Et ideo nos in his meditantes et haec die ac nocte ad memoriam revocantes ac vigilantes in ea deprecemur Dominum, ut nobis ipse horum, quae legimus, scientiam revelare dignetur et ostendere, quomodo spiritalem legem non solum in intellegentia, sed et in actibus observemus, ut et spiritalem gratiam consequi mereamur illuminati per legem Spiritus sancti, in Christo Iesu Domino nostro." Cf. *Hom Lev.* VI,4: SC 286,286.

50. Cf. Origen, *Hom. Jos.* I,3: SC 71,96: "Hic ergo ubi primum disco nomen Iesu, ibi continue etiam mysterii video sacramentum; ducit enim exercitum Iesus." Cf. J. Daniélou, *Sacramentum futuri: Études sur les origines de la typologie biblique* (Paris: Beauchesne, 1950), 201–56: "Le cycle de Josué."

51. Origen, *Hom. Judic.* VIII,5: SC 389,200ff. Cf. *Hom. Judic.* II,1: SC 389,72–76, where Origen asks the question in whom Christ lives and in whom he has died, and among other things, explains: "Sic ergo peccantibus defungitur

Christus pro eo quod nihil in iis iustitia, nihil patientia, nihil veritas et omnia illa quae Christus est operatur."

52. Origen, *Hom. Jer.* XIX,10: SC 238,216.

53. Origen, *Hom. Jer.* XIX,11: SC 238,220. Prayers are also found in the apologetic work, *Contra Celsum*: *Cels.* VII 1,7: SC 150,14, and *Cels.* VIII 1,11: SC 150,180. Cf. A. Monaci, *Origene predicatore e il suo pubblico* (Milan: F. Angeli, 1987), 74ff.

54. Cf. Origen, *Hom. Jer.* XIII,1: SC 238,54; *Hom. Lev.* XII,1: SC 287,168: "Meus autem sacerdos magnus Iesus"; *Hom. Num.* VI 3,2–7: SC 415. In addition, cf. *Comm. Jo.* V,VIII: SC 120,390, where Origen is talking about Ambrose's love for Jesus. Cf. F. Bertrand, *Mystique de Jésus chez Origéne* (Paris: Aubier, 1951), 147ff.

It should be added that Origen prays not only to Christ but also to God. Thus he can ask God, for instance, to help him defend the truth and love the Holy Scriptures as the prophet Jeremiah and apostle Paul had done before him (Origen, *Hom. Jer.* XIV,14: SC 238,98ff. Cf. *Hom. Lev.* VI,1: SC 286,268; *Hom. Jos*. IX,10: SC 71, 268; *Hom. Ps.* 36, III,8: SC 411,154: a request of God to send his Word and Wisdom; *Hom. Ps.* 37, I,6: SC 411,296; *Cels.* VIII,1,7: SC 150,180: a prayer to God through Christ who is the Truth). In his *De Oratione* and especially in his *Dialogue with Heraclides* Origen gives a clear account of the one to whom Christians ought to address their prayers (cf. esp. Origen, *Dial.* 4: SC 67,62ff. Also cf. E. von Severus, "Gebet" I, V.b, in *Reallexikkon für Antike und Christentum* 8 [1972]: 1235ff.; *Orat.* 15,1–4; GCS Origenes, II/2, 333–36, and *Cels.* V,4: SC 147,20ff.). In the *Dialogue* Origen makes the remarkable claim that prayer is not made twice, but rather once to God through God (*Dial.* 4: SC 67,62). The extent to which prayer to Christ and the Father belong together is also clear from Origen's request that believers pray with him to both Christ and to his Father (*cum Patre suo*) (cf. Origen, *Hom. Ezech.* XII,5: SC 352,396). At any rate, his insistence on the liturgical prayer directed to God is not in conflict with the personal prayer directed toward Christ. After all, as is already the case in Judaism, Christian prayer also consists in calling upon the name of God. It is oriented to the Father who is our God (cf. the openings of the apostolic letters in the New Testament). Not less personal are the prayers directed to Christ, especially those that come from the Acts of the Martyrs and can already be seen in the "Acts of the Apostles" (cf. J. Lebreton, *Histoire du dogme de la Trinitè,* vol. 2 [Paris: Beauchesne, 1928], 147–247).

55. Cf. M. I. Danieli, "Gesù," in Monaci, *Origene: Dizionario,* 192–95, esp. 194f.: "La devozione a Gesù." Among other passages cited, cf. esp. *Comm. Matt.* 10,1f.: SC 162,140–44, where Origen exhorts his hearers to enter into the house of Jesus and to become friends with him.

56. Origen, *Comm. Jo.* XXXI 31,387: SC 385,352ff. Cf. *Comm. Jo.* XIX 12,74: SC 290,92; I 16,92: SC 120,108. In the prologue to the *Commentary on the*

Song of Songs the love for Christ is not developed at all. Nevertheless, cf. *Comm. Cant.* prol. II,46ff.: SC 275,122–24: "Hunc ergo amorem loquitur praesens scriptura, quo erga Verbum Dei anima beata uritur et inflammatur . . . ." In addition, Origen cites in II,36: SC 375,116 Ignatius of Antioch, *Letter to the Romans* 7,2: "My Love is crucified."

57. Origen, *Hom. Luc.* 32,6: SC 87,390ff.

58. Origen, *Hom Lev.* XII,6: SC 287,190: "se iunxerit Domino." Cf. *Hom. Ps.* 36: SC 411,30f., as well as *Comm. Jo.* XXXII 25,326: SC 385,326, where in discussing 1 Cor 6:17 ("But anyone united to the Lord becomes one spirit with him"), Origen remarks that the union between Jesus and the Logos serves as a pattern for us.

59. Origen, *Hom. Exod.* XIII 6: SC 321,396.

60. Origen, *Hom. Ps.* 36, IV,1: SC 411,184ff.

61. Origen, l.c.: SC 411,186: "gressus interioris hominis quibus ambulare possumus per illam viam quae dicit: Ego sum via, veritas et vita."

62. Origen, l.c.: SC 411,186: "Cupiet enim qui a Deo dirigitur Christum et desiderabit permanere semper in Christo."

63. Origen, *Princ.* II 11,4f.: Görgemanns, *Origenes,* 446ff., with 2 Cor 3:3 and Phil 1:13.

64. Cf. *Princ.* IV 4,4: Görgemanns, *Origenes,* 796, where Origen discusses the imitation of Jesus, who loved justice. So too in *Princ.* II 6,3: Görgemanns, *Origenes,* 360, where Origen says that the degree of participation in the "image of the invisible God" depends upon the strength of love that the creature devotes to him, as well as upon the extent to which someone holds up the soul of Jesus, with its unique devotion to the Lord, as a model.

65. A free translation of Augustine's text. *Trin.* II 17,28: CCSL 50,119, concludes as follows: "Tanto enim certius diligimus quam videre desideramus faciem Christi quanto in posterioribus eius agnoscimus quantum nos prior dilexerit Christus."

66. Augustine, *Conf.* III 4,7f: BA 13,372–77. Also cf. M. Testard, "Cicero," in *Augustinus-Lexikon* I (1986–94), 913–30, esp. the section "Le disciple de l'Hort," 918–22.

67. On the search for God-Truth in Augustine, *Conf.* X 37,62: BA 14,254; *Conf.* X 40,65: BA 14,256–60.

68. Cf. the reception of the *Hortensius* in the *Confessions* (see n. 66 above) as well as the citation from the "Hortensius" in *Trin.* XV 19,26: CCSL 50A,557f.

69. Cf. Studer, *Gratia Christi,* 35f.

70. Of course, none of this excludes the fact that Augustine is aware of the more common usage of the noun. He opposes to *veritas, mendacium* and "error" (cf. Augustine, *Trin.* II prol. 1: CCSL 50,80; *Trin.* XIII 19,24: CCSL 50A,426, with Rom 1:18, and *Trin.* IV 3,6: CCSL 50,167, with Eph 4:25). He uses the word in the sense of "reality," i.e., of true existence (cf. the contrast between *figura* and

veritas in Augustine, *Faust.* 18,6: NBA 14/1,342, with 1 Cor 10:6. In addition, cf. *C. Jul. op. imp.* VI,36: NBA 19/1,1216: *veritas resurrectionis—veritas mortis*). He speaks also of the historical truth (cf. Augustine, *Trin.* XII 12,19: CCSL 50,373) or of true teaching (Augustine, *Trin.* III prol. 2: CCSL 50,128, with *catholica fides* and *catholica veritas*). In his later writings he firmly connects *veritas* with *beatitudo* (Augustine, *Trin.* XIV 19,26: CCSL 50A,458. In the preceding section Augustine cites frag. 17 from Cicero's *Hortensius*). Nevertheless, he also allowed the Bible to inspire his usage of the word *veritas*. It should, however, be noted that the common usage of the noun also occurs in the Latin Bible. In addition, there are expressions like *consulere veritatem* and *conspicere in luce veritatis,* where it is not clear if the *magister interior* is being presupposed. Cf. Augustine, *Trin.* XII 3,3: CCSL 50,357; XIV 6.8: CCSL 50A,31, and X,1: CCSL 50,313.

71. Cf. Augustine, *Tract. Ev. Jo.* 108,2: NBA 14/2,1456; 115,4: NBA 14/2,1522; *Enarrat. Ps.* 4:8: NBA 25,42; 39,18: NBA 25,956ff.; 56,10: NBA 26,176; 85,15: NBA 26,1268.

72. Cf. the statement that follows in this chapter, at note 82.

73. Cf. Augustine, *Tract. Ev. Jo.* 40,11; NBA 24/1,818; s. 134,1,1ff.: NBA 31/1,230ff.; etc.

74. Cf. Augustine, *Trin.* XIII 19,24: CCSL 50A,416; *Faust.* 19,7: NBA 14/1,354–58.

75. Cf. Augustine, *Trin.* I 2,4: CCSL 50,32; III 3,8: CCSL 50,133.

76. Cf. Augustine, *Enarrat. Ps.* 123,2: NBA 28,62: *ibi veritas, hic via*.

77. Cf. Augustine, *Trin.* I 12,24: CCSL 50,62ff.

78. Cf. Augustine, *Fid. symb.* 2,3: NBA 6/1,256ff.: *multa vocabula*.

79. Trans. Roland Teske, *Letters 156–210* (in *The Works of Saint Augustine: Translation for the 21st Century*, II/3 [Brooklyn, N.Y.: New City Press, 1990–). "Multi in cruce christi gloriantes et ab eadem uia non recedentes, etiam qui ista, quae subtilissime disseruntur, ignorant, quia non perit unus pusillus, pro quibus mortuus est, ad eandem perueniant aeternitatem, ueritatem, caritatem, id est ad stabilem, certam plenam que felicitatem, ubi manentibus, uidentibus, amantibus sint cuncta perspicua." Cf. Augustine, *Ep.* 169,1,4: NBA 22,788. In addition, cf. *Trin.* IV prol. 1: CCSL 50,160; *Trin.* XIV 14,20: CCSL 50A,448f.

80. The deepest description of the triad *aeternitas, veritas,* and *caritas* is perhaps found in his interpretation of a trinitarian text of Hilary. The Father is *aeternitas* so far as he is without origin. The Son is "species" (beauty) as the perfect image and form of the Father. The Holy Spirit is the "use" so far as he is the gift, the sweet link between Father and Son (Augustine, *Trin.* VI 10,11: CCSL 50,240, with Hilary, *Trin.* II 1,1: SC 434,276. Cf. Studer, *Augustins De Trinitate,* 189–95). Augustine, in this passage, does not call the Son *veritas,* though the title of *imago* indicates supreme conformity with the Father. The true Word is, as he says in another text of *De Trinitate,* like the Father in all respects, the perfectly coherent

expression of the Father who pronounces it (cf. Augustine, *Trin.* XV 11,20: CCSL 50,489, and *Trin.* XV 15,24: CCSL 50A,498).

81. Cf., e.g., Augustine, *Ep.* 155,414: NBA 22.574; Sermon 114A,5: NBA 30/2,472; *Trin.* XIV 14,19: CCSL 50A,447; XIV 19,25: CCSL 50A,457. Cf. also the expression *litterae veritatis* in *Trin.* XV 28,51: CCSL 50A,534.

82. On the following, cf. Studer, *Gratia Christi,* 87–92.

83. Augustine, *Enarrat. Ps.* 123,2: NBA 28,62.

84. Cf. Augustine, *Ver. rel.* 8,14: NBA 6/1,38; Sermon 113A,5: NBA 30/2,432ff.

85. Cf. Augustine, *Civ.* XI,2: NBA 5/2,68: "Per hoc enim mediator, per quod homo, per hoc et via." Augustine develops the idea of an incarnation that leads to truth in a similar manner when referring to John 1:14 and 1:17. In this idea, *gratia* relates to the incarnation while *veritas* refers to the eternal life. Cf. Augustine, *Trin.* XIII 19,24: CCSL 50A,416.

86. Cf. Basil Studer, "Christus loquitur de Christo (Augustinus)—Theologie als Begegnung mit Christus," *Schweizerische Kirchenzeitung* 171 (2003): 209–14.

87. Cf. Basil Studer, "Die Kirche als Schule des Herrn bei Augustinus von Hippo: Mysterium Caritatis," in *Stimuli: Exegese und Ihre Hermeneutik in Antike und Christentum. Festschrift für Ernst Dassmann,* ed. G. Schöllgen and C. Scholton (Munster: Aschendorff, 1996), 485–98.

88. Cf. Augustine, *Mag.* 11,38: NBA 2,784, with *Ep.* 66,1: NBA 21,542; 112,3: NBA 21,1110; 133,1: NBA 22,116.

89. Cf. Augustine, *Tract. Ev. Jo.* 96,4: NBA, on John 16:12f.: NBA 24/2,1346ff.

90. Augustine, *Div. quaest. LXXXIII* 69: NBA 6/2,194–208.

91. Augustine, *Trin.* I 8,15–10,21: CCSL 50,46–59, esp. I 8,15ff.: CCSL 50,46–52.

92. Cf. E. Schendel, *Herrschaft und Unterwerfung Christi: 1 Cor 15,24–27 in Exegese und Theologie der Väter bis zum Ausgang des 4. Jahrhunderts* (Tübingen: J. C. B. Mohr, 1971).

93. Augustine, *Trin.* I 8,15: CCSL 50,47.

94. Cf. Augustine, *Trin.* I 8,15: CCSL 50,47ff.

95. Augustine, *Trin.* I 8,16: CCSL 50,49.

96. Augustine, *Trin.* I 8,16: CCSL 50,49.

97. Augustine, *Trin.* I 8,16: CCSL 50,49.

98. Augustine, *Trin.* I 8,16–9,18: CCSL 50,49–53.

99. Augustine, *Trin.* I 8,17: CCSL 50,52: "De hac contemplatione intellego dictum: Cum tradiderit regnum deo et patri, id est cum perduxerit iustos quibus nunc ex fide viventibus regnat mediator dei et hominum homo Christus Iesus ad contemplationem dei et patris."

100. Augustine, *Trin.* IV 18,24: CCSL 50,191ff.

101. Augustine, *Trin.* IV 18,24: CCSL 50,191, alluding to Plato, Timaeus 29c ("Quantum ad id quod ortum est aeternitas valet, tantum ad fidem veritas").

102. Augustine, *Trin.* IV 18,24: 191: "Mens autem rationalis sicut purgata contemplationem debet rebus aeternis, sic purganda temporibus fidem."

103. Augustine, *Trin.* IV 18,24: 191: "Nunc ergo adhibemus fidem rebus temporaliter gestis propter nos et per ipsam mundamur ut cum ad speciem venerimus quemadmodum succedit fidei veritas, ita mortalitati succedat aeternitas."

104. Augustine, *Trin.* IV 18,24 (translation from E. Hill, *Augustine: The Trinity,* in *The Works of Saint Augustine: Translation for the 21st Century,* I/5 [Brooklyn, N.Y.: New City Press, 1991], 170).

105. Augustine, *Trin.* IV 18,24: Hill, 193: "Itaque in illo quia et id quod ortum erat transiit ad aeternitatem, transiturum est et nostrum, cum fides pervenerit ad veritatem."

106. Cf. Basil Studer, *Schola Christiana: Die Theologie zwischen Nicäa (325) und Chalzedon (451)* (Paderborn: Schöningh, 1998), 233f., with the reference to W. Geerlings, "Jesja 7,9b in Augustine," *Wissenschaft und Weisheit* 50 (1987): 5–12.

107. Cf. Studer, *Schola Christiana,* 104, and other commentaries on Augustine, *Trin.* VIII prol. 1: CCSL 50,269.

108. Cf. *Trin.* VIII 4,6: CCSL 50,274f.

109. Cf. Augustine, *Trin.* IX 1,1: CCSL 50,292f. (the theme of searching); *Trin.* XV 1,1–2,3: CCSL 50A,460ff., and esp. *Trin.* XV 27,49: CCSL 50A,531: "Non enim Christus iterum in cruce videndus est, sed nisi hoc credatur quod ita factum est atque visum est ut futurum ac videndum iam non speretur, non pervenitur ad Christum qualis sine fine videndus est."

110. Cf. Augustine, *Trin.* VIII 5,8: CCSL 50,278. In addition, *Trin.* VIII 4,6: CCSL 50,275: "Amatus ergo et quod ignoratur sed tamen creditur"; *Trin.* VIII 9,13: CCSL 50,290: "Valet ergo fides ad cognitionem et ad dilectionem dei, non tamquam omnino incogniti aut omnino non dilecti, sed quo cognoscatur manifestius et quo firmius diligatur."

111. *Trin.* II 15,25–17,32: CCSL 50,113–23, esp. 7,28–31: CCSL 50,117–22. Also cf. C. Simonelli, "La risurrezione nel De Trinitate di sant'Agostino. Presenza, formulazione, funzione," in *Studia Ephemerides 'Augustinianum'* 73 (2001): 23–29.

112. *Trin.* II 16,27–28: CCSL 50,115ff.

113. *Trin.* II 17,28: CCSL 50,117: "Non incongruenter ex persona domini nostri Iesu Christi praefiguratum solet intellegi ut posteriora eius accipiantur caro eius in qua de virgine natus est et mortuus et resurrexit, sive propter pos-

tremitatem mortalitatis posteriora dicta sint, sive quod eam prope in fine saeculi, hoc est, posterius, suscipere dignatus est."

114. *Trin.* II 17,28: CCSL 50,117: "Facies autem eius illa dei forma in qua non rapinam arbitratus esse aequalis deo patri, quod nemo utique potest videre et vivere."

115. *Trin.* II 17,28: CCSL 50,117ff.

116. *Trin.* II 17,28: CCSL 50,119: "Sed dum peregrinamur a domino et per fidem ambulamus non per speciem, posteriora Christi, hoc est carnem, per ipsam fidem videre debemus, id est in solido fidei fondamento stantes quod significat petra, et eam de tali tutissima specula intuentes, in catholica scilicet ecclesia . . . ."

117. *Trin.* II 17,28: CCSL 50,119: "Tanto enim certius diligimus quam videre desideramus facies Christi quanto in posterioribus eius agnoscimus quantum nos prior dilexerit Christus." Translation from Hill, *Augustine: The Trinity,* 118.

118. *Trin.* II 17,29: CCSL 50,119: "Quod firmissime nos credentes tamquam de petrae soliditate contuemur, unde certa spe adoptionem exspectamus redemptionem corporis nostri quia hoc in membris Christi speramus quae nos ipsi sumus quod perfectum esse in ipso capite nostro fidei sanitate cognoscimus."

119. *Trin.* II 17,30f.: CCSL 50,120–22.

120. Cf. *Trin.* II 17,32: CCSL 50,123.

121. Cf. *Trin.* II 17,28: CCSL 50,119, citation in n. 118 above.

122. Cf. *Trin.* I 3,5: CCSL 50,32.

123. Cf. *Trin.* XIV 12,15: CCSL 50A,443.

124. Cf. *Trin.* XIV 19,25: CCSL 50A,456f.

125. Cf. *Trin.* XIV 18,24: CCSL 50A,455f., with 1 Cor 15:49. Also cf. *Exp. Gal.* 38: NBA 10,2: "Formatur enim Christus in eo, qui formam accipit Christi, formam autem accipit Christi, qui adhaeret Christo dilectioni spiritali" (Commentary on Gal 4:19).

126. Cf. Simonelli, "Risurrezione," 58–63.

127. Cf., e.g., *Ep.* 191,1: NBA 23,232; *Ep.* 200,1: NBA 23,408; *Ep.* 265,1: NBA 23,932.

128. Cf. Studer, *Soteriologie in der Schrift und Patristik,* 93ff. and 160ff.

8

AUGUSTINE'S CHRISTOLOGY

Its Spirituality and Rhetoric

Rowan Douglas Williams

A Thesis

In his enormously rich monograph, *Les conversions de s. Augustin* (1950), J.-M. Le Blond observed that Augustine saw the incarnation as a *révélation de méthode spirituelle*. Augustine's deepest and most significant "conversion," he suggested, is that from *Gottesmystik* to *Christusmystik,* meaning not that the incarnate Christ somehow replaces the transcendent divine nature for Augustine as an object of contemplation, but that the sense of Christ as the path to and the form of transfiguring and participatory knowledge of the transcendent God becomes ever more pervasive, more obviously an organizing principle.[1] In what follows, I hope to trace some of the ways in which this theme works as such an organizing principle in Augustine's theology.

By the second decade of the fifth century—essentially by the time of the completion of the *De Trinitate* (*Trin.*) and *De civitate Dei* (*Civ.*)—

it is possible to see in Augustine a notably coherent christological scheme. The definitive studies of T. van Bavel and, more recently, of H. R. Drobner have established some of the important shifts in Augustine's christological vocabulary; Drobner, in particular, has also made plain the roots of so much of that vocabulary in the conventions of rhetorical analysis.[2] Among the questions raised by this is why Augustine's Christology fits so comfortably with the theology of Cyril of Alexandria in its resonant affirmations of the unity of the incarnate Word, when those in the Eastern Christian world who employed comparable methods from rhetoric ended up with a much more dualist reading of Christ's person. I want to suggest that when we have grasped with Le Blond the logic of seeing Christ as the form of the spiritual path, with all that this involves, we may understand why the "Cyrilline" structure imposes itself.

Briefly, my argument is simply that the unifying principle of Augustine's mature Christology is the understanding of Christ as *sapientia*. Wisdom, as defined in *De doctrina christiana* (*Doctr. chr.*), in *Trin.*, and elsewhere, is the contemplation of the eternal, God's delight in God; as such, it is what we hope to receive by grace, so that we acquire a share in that reflexive contemplative love which is God's very life. But that divine love as bestowing itself on creation is (as may be seen from a close reading of the later books of *Trin.*) identical with that divine action which seeks the "justice" of another's good or joy, and is therefore bound up with the divine identification with us in the incarnation. *Sapienta* is oriented to incarnation, and thus to the rhetorical paradoxes which involve the divine Word speaking not only human words, but also words of spiritual distress or apparent doubt—the constant theme of so many of the *Enarrationes in Psalmos* (*Enarrat. Ps.*). And the upshot in practical terms is, as Le Blond asserts, that "incarnation" becomes the path we must follow, *la soumission de l'espirit aux symbols temporels.*[3] The embrace of our creatureliness, and resistance to all that draws us away from the recognition of the centrality of *time* in our learning of holiness—these are the actual consequences of the act of incarnation, making sense of both the individual path of sanctity and the Church's corporate life and discipline.

Some Illustrative Texts

These themes are announced very straightforwardly in *Confessions* (*Conf.*) book 7, where Augustine offers an already very nuanced account of what it is to become wise with the *sapienta* of the divine Word, a wisdom which is not available through the speculations of the Platonists;[4] this world's "wisdom" is overtaken by the humility of the incarnation. While the wisdom of the world seeks truth by escape from the body, by techniques designed to free us from the distortions imposed by fleshly life, God's wisdom takes root in us only as we accept our bodily limitation and our spiritual frailty as things we cannot cure from within. Wisdom must become milk for infants if it is to enter our minds; it must be encountered in the flesh. The incarnation both requires and makes possible the conditions of its understanding: "non enim tenebam Dominum meum Iesum humilis humilem."[5] Grace humbles us so that we may accept the way of humility as the way to truth; only *prosternere* allows us to rise to the heights of God's wisdom. God's love brings the eternal Word into the human world, and that same love allows us to face our creatureliness and our sin in honesty, knowing that God's will is for our good. In so doing, we reflect God's *caritas* and know God's light, the *lux supra mentem* which is accessible only to love.[6] The displacement of our desire to rise by our own strength delivers us from the idolatry of the self which impedes love. Absent this process—as in the Platonic books—and growth becomes impossible. When I know that I am presently imperfect, I know I must grow in order to feed more fully on Christ who is the Truth (*cresce et manducabis*); and nothing can be built except on the foundation of humility which is Christ.[7]

Here, as in *Doctr. chr.*, the underlying point is that the abandonment required for us to receive the true knowledge of God is not, so to speak, the "spatial" abandonment of the world of material things in order to rise to a higher realm, but the abandonment of attachment to the projects and desires of the unregenerate will. The refusal to identify God with any *res* in the world, the recognition of creation itself as *signum,* with the cross of Christ as the central proof of this, is another means of saying that conversion is the willingness to keep moving in time, putting behind those desires that look for satisfaction within time (as though desire could be brought to an end, and time thus reduced to space). Growing into knowledge of the incarnate Christ means the reconstruction of desire into hope for God, the *exspectatio* which Le Blond sees as the climax of the argument of the *Confessions*. By the incarnation, God both binds us to the temporal world as always and inescapably our starting point and dispossesses us of the illusion that there is a point within that temporal world where we can settle. Every point in the temporal order becomes a point of departure, to borrow a phrase from Michel de Certeau. The leaving behind of our limited material condition is a temporal and not a spatial matter, in that it involves the journey of growth and learning in time. The *peregrinatio,* which is the basic form of discipleship, is the willingness to see every present moment as the place which a desire for God obliges me to leave, yet also as the necessary prompt or stimulus to the journey of desire, not as something simply to be negated. This is Platonism still, we may well say, but given a distinctive turn by the intensification of the particular promptings of history, focused on the crucified Christ.

To imitate the humility of the incarnate Christ is to come to occupy his position vis-à-vis God, so that his humility is indeed the doorway to knowledge of the eternal. This is the force of the language about divine *humilitas* that we find early in the *De Trinitate* (and, note, not too far distant in time from the *Confessions*). In *Trin*. 4.2.4, in the course of one of Augustine's most extended treatments of the person and work of Christ, this is spelled out very explicitly. We are unfit for the contemplation of God because of our sin. Wicked and proud as we are, we can be made capable of participating in the divine Word, being illuminated, only by means of *sanguis iusti et humilitas dei*. God stoops to become a righteous human being so that, as human but not sinful, he may intercede for us so that, created though we are, we may still contemplate God. God is what we are not by nature; but by the Word's participation in humanity, we may share the Word's divinity in being enlightened with his light (and thus, by implication, sharing his contemplative relation to the Father). In an image which Augustine goes on to develop at length, the incarnate Word "adds" to our humanity in *congruentia* or *convenientia, concinentia* or *consonantia,* "what the Greeks call *harmonia,*" an element which in its "simplicity" overcomes the discords or fractures of our "double" humanity. The merciful will of God forms a human identity in which mortal body and damnable soul are united with the single purpose of divine love so that they are made capable of seeing God and being resurrected. Of this resurrection, Christ's own is given *in sacramento et exemplo*.[8]

The incarnation here is seen as the act of divine self-offering which, so to speak, gathers up the elements of broken humanity and constitutes thereby a new humanity, integrated in virtue of the divine act which takes and holds the twofold life of human beings, body and soul, bringing them into harmony. Augustine spends a good deal of time in book 4 elaborating the mathematical appropriateness of adding a *simplum* to a *duplum;* but the theological heart of the argument is in effect an anticipation of the scholastic notion that the humanity of Christ is distinct not because of an extra element alongside the human soul and body (as if the incarnate Word were part of a threefold complex of equipollent elements) but because the soul-body compound is in this case concretely animated and individuated by a single divine agency. That is a more involved issue than can be discussed here, but, as we shall see later, it illuminates the most distinctive feature of Augustine's deployment of rhetorical idiom in this context.

It also relates to the theme opened up a little later in *Trin.* book 4 and very prominent in Augustine's preaching. In *Trin.* 4.9.12 Augustine reflects upon the prayer of Jesus in John 17, that the disciples will become one as the Father and the Son are one. Jesus, says Augustine, does not simply speak of a unity of nature (*unum*) between himself and his disciples, although the Church may say that it is *unus* with Christ, one subject, in the sense that there is one head of the Body and one Body. The focus is on the total unity between Son and Father, which is to be reflected among the disciples: this is to be not merely the natural unity between members of the human species but a harmonious *will,* a tending toward one and the same blissful heavenly end. The *unum* of the Father and the Son is a unity of substance and will; so for the Church the unity prayed for is *dilectionis societas*. This *societas* is attainable only in Christ, who binds us together in such a way that we are no longer divided by wanting radically different things. The common life becomes an image of the single focus of the trinitarian life upon its own intrinsic joy; as we are corporately directed toward this bliss, we share in God's self-relatedness. Here the major themes of the closing books of *De Trinitate* are already sketched, but they are related very directly to the understanding of the Body of Christ as the form of our renewed life under grace.

But one of the most interesting aspects of this passage is the reference to the sense in which the Church and Christ are *unus*. The argument of the passage is thereby connected to the theology of Christ as Head of the Body which pervades the *Enarrationes in Psalmos,* where it is used precisely as a tool of rhetorical criticism. Who speaks in the Psalms? Christ as Head; and as Head, he makes his own words that would otherwise shock or puzzle, words of guilt or suffering. Just as his death (as we are told at *Trin*. 4.2.4) is meritoriously effective because it is voluntarily endured, not received as punishment, so the entire range of what we might call death-directed experience in humanity is voluntarily embraced by the incarnate Word. Augustine's *de agone* offers a classical exposition of the *aproslepton atherapeuton* argument (i.e., "that which is not assumed is not healed"), and much of the *Enarrationes* can be read as an elaboration of this. In an utterance like "My God, my God, why have you forsaken me?" (Matt 27:46; Mark 15:35; Ps 22:1), we can identify the speaker not simply as a guilty and suffering human subject, but as the one who freely undertakes to make all human guilt and suffering his own. By incarnation, death, and resurrection, the Word creates a relation between himself and the human race that brings all human experience within the scope of healing and restoration. The Word animates the particular soul and body that is Jesus, and in so embracing *this* human nature becomes the animating principle of any and every human identity associated with him by baptismal incorporation and the gift of the Spirit. The speaker in the Psalms is the Christ who tells Saul in Acts 9:4 that he is persecuting *him* (the Acts text is referred to fourteen times in the *Enarrat. Ps.* as a hermeneutical principle).[9] *Enarrat. Ps*. 88.30 adds a further dimension, connecting the Head and Body theme with the earlier one of divine humility: "[Christ's] love did not allow the Head to separate himself from union with the Body" even in the exalted state following the Ascension. Thus there is no context in which Christ speaks simply as human or simply as God; he speaks as the one who by taking on humanity through his divine will and power has become Head of the Body, speaking uniquely as representative of humanity *in virtue of* his divinity. The "right" of the exalted Christ to speak for humanity rests upon the divine decision to take flesh—and not only to take the specific flesh of Jesus of Nazareth but to create *by* that flesh the historical Body that is the company of believers, so that their variegated and flawed human experience may be offered by the eternal Word and touched with his transforming presence.

It is possible, then, to say, as does Augustine in *Enarrat. Ps.* 21, that Christ speaks in our *persona*. The expression *personam sustinere* is used here, as in other places, to mean something like representing, acting in the role of someone. It is more or less the same in sense as another of Augustine's locutions, *agere personam,* and both are used by him in the works of the 390s to express aspects of the incarnation. For a related locution that does not have to do with Christology, but that also suggests a deeper level of significance, we may turn to *Trin.* 12.12.18: Adam and Eve both deserve punishment for sin, as each *personam suam portabat.* The fact, though, that Adam and Eve also represent different dimensions of human subjectivity and decision making should not lead us astray into thinking that somehow different bits of our selfhood are judged independently (as Eve would have been judged even if Adam had not sinned). Each of us is *una persona . . . unus homo* considered as an agent, a subject of desire, thought, and projection; each of us is judged as a single agent. The *persona* here is the terminus of responsibility, what finally speaks for or answers for our thoughts and desires, for the way we are. *Persona* operates on the frontier between legal, rhetorical, and what we should call psychological reference.

But we need to be alert to the complexities of this. The Word of God may be said to speak or act in our *persona* in virtue of his assumption of humanity (and there are of course several issues about how that "assumption" is best characterized, to say nothing of the varied vocabulary for it). *Agere hominem* appears in several early works (*De ordine* and *Div. quaest. LXXXIII*) as a way of describing the Word's action. But this does not mean that the *persona* of fallen humanity, the *homo* activated by the Word and for which he speaks, is some kind of independent subject associated with the Word of God. The Word's ability to sustain this *persona* is, as we have seen, grounded in the Word's eternal act and determination, the act that assumes or includes humanity in its life. Hence, prior to anything that can be said about the Word speaking our "person," is the belief that the entire earthly life of the incarnate Son is a speaking or acting in the person of divine Wisdom: *agere personam sapientiae dei.*[10] The core theological conviction emerging more and more strongly in the 390s and early 400s is that the incarnate Word constitutes a *unitas personae* in taking human nature. *Trin.* 4.20.30 speaks of the *homo* who is joined or even "mixed" with the Word so as to form such a *unitas,* and there are very many examples of this definition of the incarnate *persona* as being the Word in union with the soul and the body (which latter two normally constitute a *persona* of themselves).

It becomes clear that Augustine's *persona* is a flexible, or, better, an analogically complex term. Its basic meaning is fairly plain: identifying a *persona* is identifying who is speaking, whose role is in question in a complex of interchanges, verbal and otherwise. On that basis, *persona* questions about Christ can be answered at several different levels. The words of straightforward human suffering or fear in the Gospels are spoken in the *persona* of a fully vulnerable member of the human race; the words that must be attributed to Christ as the Word speaking in Scripture, especially in the Psalms, are spoken in the *persona* of what we might call the human condition in general, the condition of sinful people cut off from God. But the entire phenomenon that is the Word incarnate invariably speaks for the *persona* of divine Wisdom, since it is the action of divine Wisdom that creates the divine-human grammatical subject we hear speaking in Christ. *Agere hominem* in this sense depends upon *agere sapientiam,* since the utterance of human grief or pain is the result of Christ's being freely engaged, as Wisdom's embodiment, in the world of historical suffering and struggle. Thus the *persona* of Wisdom is the foundational identity with which we have to do; it is present and active in the form of the concrete historical *persona* that is a soul and body united with the divine Word; and as that historical *persona* incorporates human experience beyond its own individual limits, by setting up the relation of Head and Body in the reality of the Church, the person of divine Wisdom is free to take the role of lost humanity, *agere hominem* in the widest sense.

To engage with Augustine's use of *persona,* then, is to encounter a concept providing a fluid and many-faceted connection between exegesis, soteriology, and Christology in the stricter sense. We may say that the answer to "Who is speaking?" where Christ is concerned is always *sapientia;* yet this does not entail a divine speaker who can be identified alongside a human one. *Sapientia* is indeed and ultimately the contemplation of God by God, but it is also that which prompts and makes possible the presence of God in what is not God, in the order of creation and in the human mind. Van Bavel rightly observes that from the first, Augustine sees the incarnation as the revelation of divine reason so that our human reason may be awakened; but as his understanding of *sapientia* develops, rather more than reason comes to be involved. Wisdom is identical with *caritas,* and so it is oriented always to the other's good. The *persona* of Wisdom cannot therefore be isolated from its action as *caritas;* to say that Christ constantly acts in Wisdom's person is not to assert that he always speaks or acts as divine Word *simpliciter,* as though the humanity were both separate and insignificant. The *persona* is Wisdom-in-action, Wisdom engaging with what is not by nature God (cf. *Trin*. 4.2.4 again) so as to incorporate it into the divine life and make it capable of seeing what Wisdom sees, knowing what it knows, contemplating the absolute otherness of the creator as if it were located where eternal Wisdom is located, in the heart of the divine self-knowledge and self-love.

Hence the truth of Le Blond's observation with which this essay began: Augustine's Christology is about spiritual method. In the first instance, it is the "method" of God's own life, the method of *sapientia*. In contemplating the divine life with joy and delight, Wisdom realizes itself as love, the radically disinterested love that seeks the fruition of others in the same joy it knows; all that Augustine wrote about creation itself and in *Doctr. chr.* about the character of divine and created love must be understood in the background here. The humility of identification with the created other is the fitting expression of this, and the fitting means by which created life may become capable of divine contemplation, since it involves the "inclusion" of human experience in the life of the divine Word, by incorporation into the Body of Christ. Since our prideful self-assertion is the root of our separation from God, and the multiplicity of selfish goals and private definitions of human delight is the root of our separation from each other, only our humility opens the way to belief in the saving power of Christ and to reconciliation with God and each other.[11]

One Christ

It is possible, then, to see why the use of rhetorical categories leads Augustine to a conclusion very different from those of the Antiochenes who (as Drobner demonstrates) have what are in some ways comparable concerns. The familiar debate in the Eastern christological controversy over whether the sayings of the incarnate Word could be divided according to whether they are spoken by the Word or the human individual Jesus is circumvented by Augustine—not because he has a straightforwardly "Cyrilline" account of union *kath' hupostasin* (this is not Augustine's mental world), but because of a more carefully integrated sense of the absolute dependence of the human speech of the incarnate one upon the single act of divine Wisdom. The stress in *Trin.* book 4 on the *simplum* that is the Word's presence and activity is significant. As we have seen, it brings to the *duplum* of unredeemed humanity not simply a third element to contribute to a sum total, but an integrating unity which transforms both parts of humanity. The phraseology of *Trin.* 4.3.6 is instructive: here Augustine speaks of how the single death and single resurrection of Christ serve to overcome the twofold death to which we are condemned. The *simplum* of the Word's agency is the principle through which our natural elements are transformed, not a sort of extra subject.

Consequently, the typical Antiochene anxiety about distributing the *dicta* of Jesus cannot really arise. What substantiates or gives active presence to this particular *duplum* of soul and body is the action of the Word, without which no *human* word can be spoken by this individual, Jesus of Nazareth. He exists because the Word has elected to be incarnate, and thus what he says is said because of the eternal Word. The Word is therefore never "alongside" the human speaker. It is neatly put in *Trin.* 13.18.23: in the saints, God "reigned," *regebat,* while in Christ he "acted," *gerebat*—a very characteristic Augustinian word-chime.[12] The act that defines the speaker is always the act of *sapientia,* not a divine act engaging with the act of another subject. There is, one could say, no "drama," no dialogue of resistance and engagement and submission, between Jesus and the Word, as between the Word and other human beings. That is reserved for the relation between the single reality of the Word incarnate and God the Father. Here the natural and eternal self-surrender of the Son is enacted in the circumstances of weak flesh, both displaying and creating the possibility of obedience to the Father in all circumstances; human pride is overturned by divine humility.[13] The divine act of humility in the incarnation itself, as portrayed in *Conf.* book 7, becomes the unifying theme of the human life of Jesus. And utterances of the incarnate Word which sound inappropriate to God are thus shown to be entirely fitting to divinity since they are the product of that loving *sapientia* which is the wellspring of the incarnation.

So Augustine avoids the pitfalls of Antiochene exegesis on this question by refusing to consider the human voice of Jesus in abstraction from the divine self-determination which is the coming of the Word in the flesh. How exactly he comes to this position is far from clear, but I suspect that we should read it as very closely connected with his developing concern with exegesis in the 390s, and the resultant nuancing of his understanding of *sapientia*. Increasingly, the pattern of Christ as "reason" incarnate opens out, as the "unreasonable" in Scripture has to be systematically interpreted. There has to be a theological way of making sense of the claim that God speaks in the oddities and contingencies, the fragmented and not always edifying words of the Christian Bible; and in *Doctr. chr.* and *Conf.* a twofold hermeneutical strategy is developed, which has the consequences for Christology that we have already sketched. Scripture is a sign, that is, a communication drawing us beyond itself, requiring change and growth, the acceptance of deferred desire (including deferred comprehension); and the embrace of this unfinished and unfinishable discourse has to be recognized as what is appropriate to temporal subjects who cannot of their own efforts lift themselves out of the contingent world to eternal verities.

Reading the Bible correctly and understanding the character of God's work in the incarnation are clearly inseparable in the major works of the 390s; our humble acceptance of God's accommodation to our condition correlates with the understanding of divine humility as the unifying foundation for all God's revealing work. To paraphrase *Conf.* book 7 once again, if we cannot see that God takes our fleshly and temporal condition seriously enough to use it as his medium for communicating, we shall not take it seriously; and vice versa. *Trin.* book 4 echoes both *Conf.* 7 and considerable tracts of *Civ.* in defining the essence of religious error as the attempt to achieve reconciliation with God by means of strategies, whether ritual or meditative, to engineer a way out of the human condition; in *Trin.* 4.12.15, the three magi are presented as models of those who abandoned magic and human wisdom to adore *humilitatem domini* and learned to return to their *patria* "by another way," the way of humility taught by Christ. With a curious passing allusion to the imagery of the *Phaedrus,* by this time a trope in philosophical writing, Augustine warns against supposing that the wings of virtue can be nourished by ritual and magic; instead we are weighed down more than ever by our efforts to rise.

So Augustine's concern with humility develops during the 390s toward the mature polemic in *Trin.* and *Civ.* against pagan theurgy as well as pagan speculative metaphysics; and the incarnation has a focal place in this argument. But there is a further dimension, harder to trace with precision, that has to do with the evolving sense of what *sapientia* means. As the concept becomes more and more evidently connected with absence and dispossession in its human exercise (*Doctr. chr.* is significant in this), so when it is applied to God, its divine exercise becomes more and more linked with *caritas* and *justitia.* To enact the person of Wisdom is inevitably bound more closely with the fundamental act of self-humiliation or self-dispossession in the Word's becoming flesh. So to represent Wisdom is precisely to represent an agency that is displaced for the sake of another. The dual idiom of the Word made flesh, the *agere* of *homo* and *sapientia* inseparably, makes complete sense as a resolution of the exegetical issue.

It would be tempting but misleading to say that Augustine provides a rhetorical version of what is for the Cyrilline tradition a more obviously metaphysical schema for understanding Christology. Cyrilline theology is not simply the attempt to isolate and define an undergirding "something" in Jesus that can be described as divine; it is, no less than Augustine's language, concerned with finding what agency it is that gives unity to the components of Jesus's humanity, and displaying that unity as the act of the second person of the Trinity. Equally, Augustine is not in any sense replacing an account of metaphysical subsistents with a "functional" union between the Word and human individual (as if this were a transcription of the stale debate in New Testament criticism two generations ago about whether the New Testament ascribed ontological or functional divinity to Jesus). *Sapientia* is for Augustine a real, substantive agent—both the "locus" from which the Father can be contemplated and the specific, eternal act of loving contemplation, the person of the Word of God. But it would be fair to say that, to the extent that all Augustine's reflection on the nature of being a subject is deeply involved with reflection on language—representation, relation of word and external reality, memory as self-presence, verbal images as both prompting and expressing the complex re-routings of desire—it is not surprising that his theology of the incarnation should be, in effect, an account of how God speaks within the nexus of human relations, and that human salvation or transfiguration should be linked so often with the idea of the Word's speech taking up and taking over the varieties of confused or rebellious human speech, anchoring the tumultuous instability of what we feel and express in a solid and unbroken self-communication, the Word's self-giving to the Father. Most significantly of all, though, and most challengingly, this pattern of christological exposition insists that there can be no accurate discussion of the incarnation that is not itself incarnationally modeled—humble in its awareness of the inescapable context of material history, alert to the question of how *justitia* is realized, open to the dangerous and potentially humiliating solidarity of fallible and sinful human agents, and refusing prideful isolation. *Agere personam sapientiae* is for all believers the task of learning a new speech apt for the city of God, a *méthode spirituelle* that is both political, in the widest sense, and prayerful, continuous with the unbroken, transfiguring enactment of Wisdom that is Jesus Christ.

Notes

1. J.-M. Le Blond, *Les conversions de s. Augustin* (Paris: Aubier, 1950), 145.
2. T. J. van Bavel, *Recherches sur la christologie de saint Augustin* (Fribourg: Éditions Universitaires, 1954), and H. R. Drobner, *Person-Exegese und Christologie bei Augustinus: Zur Herkunft der Formel Una Persona* (Leiden: Brill, 1986).
3. Le Blond, *Les conversions,* 19, cf. 133–34.
4. *Conf.* 7.9.13.
5. *Conf.* 7.18.24.
6. *Conf.* 7.10.
7. *Conf.* 7.20.
8. *Trin.* 4.3.6.
9. *Enarrat. Ps.* 39.5 and 87 are particularly clear in enunciating this.
10. *De Agone* 20, 22.
11. It is a huge mistake to imagine that the *Trin.* and *Civ.* are only tangentially related: what the former has to say about common desire and about the character of justice is only one indication of the parallel nature of the two great treatises. We ought to be able to discern that *Trin.* is a treatise about politics, just as *Civ.* is a treatise about Christology. The formula of *Civ.* 11.2 in respect of Christ's work, "quo itur, Deus; qua itur, homo," reminds us that the book as a whole is a meditation on how desire is judged and reconstructed so as to release us from rivalry and violence; and that this reconstruction is effected only in the Body of Christ which exists because of the sacrifice of Christ.
12. Cf. *Ep.* 187.
13. E.g., *Trin.* 4.10.13.

9

Christology as Contemplative Practice

Understanding the Union of Natures in Augustine's *Letter* 137

Lewis Ayres

> For who knows how God assumes flesh and yet remains God, how, remaining true God, he is true man . . . . Faith alone can grasp these things, honoring in silence the Word, to whose nature no *logos* from the realm of being corresponds.[1]

It is a delight to be able to honor Fr. Brian Daley, S.J.[2] Brian has been to me an exemplary friend, mentor, and priest—all this must be said before his scholarship is even mentioned. As a scholar, Brian has been a beacon for those who believe in the significance of the study of early Christian theology in its own right and as the essential foundation of modern Christian thinking and proclamation. Brian has also modeled a style of careful investigation and charitable engagement that is an ever-important lesson for those of us prone to polemic. *Ad multos annos!*

For some years Brian has been working on a history of patristic Christology that does not treat the first few centuries primarily as "the road to Chalcedon," that is, a history which avoids focusing on how often inchoate accounts of Christ's constitution anticipate or deviate from the terminology of that later "definition." It is far more fruitful, Brian suggests, to consider how different authors talk of Christ as an integral part of describing the nature of God, revelation, salvation, and the church. To do so is to recognize that Christology is (for patristic authors, at least) also soteriology, sacramental theology, and hermeneutics. In this essay I offer a contribution to this project by considering one of the most important texts in which Augustine discusses the personal constitution of Christ.

Introduction and Context

Augustine's *Letter* 137 has received persistent scholarly attention because it marks a new precision in Augustine's christological terminology.[3] Here for the first time Augustine uses *persona* to name the metaphysical reality of Christ as a unified agent: he speaks of Christ "uniting both natures in the unity of his person."[4] At the heart of the letter Augustine also offers an analogy between the union of two natures in Christ and the union of soul and body in the human being.[5] I approach this frequently discussed text via two theses. The first is that throughout the letter Augustine attempts to encourage in his addressees a particular practice of thought and contemplation as the appropriate context for considering the constitution of Christ's person. This practice is shaped by an account of how the creation exists "within" God's presence and displays the mystery of God's ordering and governing power. At the same time, Augustine argues that such attention must exhibit the epistemological humility modeled by the incarnate Christ. My second thesis is that, against this background, Augustine offers the soul/body analogy not in order to make the union of natures more comprehensible, but to allow him to define and reflect on the incomprehensibility of the union of natures in Christ. The genius of Augustine's argument is to offer a conceptual context within which the incomprehensibility of the union may both be seen as plausible and be defined with some precision.

In order to understand the style of Augustine's focus on intellectual practices, it is important to note that *Letter* 137 is part of an exchange with some of North Africa's most influential figures. At some point before late 411, Volusianus, the addressee of the letter, was the proconsul of Africa.[6] Volusianus had written to Augustine reporting a number of questions about the doctrine of the incarnation that emerged during what appears to have been a regular philosophical discussion among Volusianus and his friends, all of whom appear to be non-Christians. Volusianus addresses Augustine as the all-knowing bishop and ex-rhetorician who should, for the sake of his own reputation, answer the questions he reports.[7] The document preserved as *Letter* 136 in Augustine's corpus is a brief note from Marcellinus, the imperial *tribunus et notarius* present in Carthage initially to act as judge at the Donatist-Catholic conference of 411. Marcellinus adds to Volusianus's questions and, more importantly, asks Augustine to compose books to confront this intellectual challenge to Christianity. While Augustine's *Letter* 137 was an immediate publicly circulated reaction, the *City of God* constituted his full response.[8] Volusianus's initial letter to Augustine also reveals that he and his friends knew at least a little about traditional Roman debates about the virtues of the various philosophical schools of antiquity, and that they treated Christian teachings as philosophically deficient superstition.[9] In this context Augustine's tactic is to offer a vision of intellectual exploration deeply rooted in late antique philosophical practice—thus making a claim on cultural capital Volusianus imagines to be his own—and yet one that finds its necessary foundation and fulfillment in Christian faith and piety.

The Liberal Arts

Augustine begins the body of his letter by criticizing those who question how the Word could have "poured" himself into the flesh of Christ (*infusus carni*) so that in the incarnation God either abandoned control of all things or somehow located that control in the body of Christ. Such questions, Augustine tells us in familiar fashion, stem from an inability to think beyond the basic conditions of material existence—spatial location and divisibility.[10] At the culmination of this argument Augustine recommends a practice of reflection on the immaterial soul and its powers of organizing and judging sense data:

> The human mind wonders at this and, because it does not grasp it, it perhaps does not believe it either. Let it first examine and wonder at itself [*se ipsam primitus scrutata miretur*]; let it, if it can, raise itself a little above the body and above those things that it is accustomed to perceive through the body. But perhaps it cannot; a certain author [Cicero] says "It is a mark of great intelligence to separate the mind from the senses and to withdraw thought from familiarity with them." Let it, then, examine those senses of the body in a somewhat different way and with greater care . . . .[11]

That Augustine would warn of the dangers of conceiving God in material terms is no surprise: that he exhorts Volusianus to consider the power of the soul, and its ability to judge sense data, should, however, attract our close attention. The particular argument deployed here is one that first appears in Augustine's early dialogues, where he attempts to demonstrate how the "liberal arts" exercise and train the mind.[12]

In his earliest works Augustine describes the various *artes liberales* as a series of steps (*gradus*) for retraining the fallen intellect.[13] The disciplines provide conceptual tools for making logical distinctions and classifications, as well as beliefs and principles that shape and sustain ways of using those distinctions and classifications. Two such beliefs lie at the heart of Augustine's account of the liberal arts: the distinction between the material and immaterial words, and the centrality of mathematical and geometrical proportion in ordering the cosmos. It is recognition of and meditation on this ordering that leads slowly toward a vision of the one divine power. At the same time, as one learns this content, one is led through exemplary practices of thought.

Augustine uses the dialogue form of the early works primarily to model for his readers practices of thought that he believes will shape appropriate attention to the soul, the cosmos, and God. Thus, for example, at *De ordine* 2.18.47 Augustine attempts to show how focusing attention on the synthesizing and unifying activity of the soul in the body (whether in the synthetic judging of sense data or in the seeking of unity with other people) may lead to a recognition of the harmonious unity of the cosmos and the importance of a life ordered according to the intrinsic measure or number of the soul.[14] Reflection on this order prepares the soul for the sight of God.[15] Similarly, at *De musica* 6.2.2–6.5.12 the "Teacher" leads the "student" through a complex process of reflection on the functions of the soul in the body. Recognition of the soul's ability to judge according to harmonic principles is propaedutic to reflection (beginning at 6.5.12) on the soul's ability to turn toward or away from God, to be rightly or wrongly ordered toward the created order.[16]

As Augustine's vision of the Christian life developed in the years following his conversion, his understanding of the possible usefulness of the various liberal arts and the practices taught within them changed. In the earliest writings, memory is sidelined in favor of the possibility of training the mind for immediate vision or intuition of wisdom: but even by ca. 390 Augustine has abandoned much of this view. By the time of the *Confessions* (397–400) Augustine has, for all practical purposes, deferred such immediate vision to the *eschaton,* thus investing the contents of the memory with an inescapable function in enabling thought of God.[17] At the same time he seems to have become increasingly clear that the *mens,* the highest part of the soul, is a mysterious unity: memory is now central to human identity.[18] This gradual development enabled a new appreciation for the paeans to the significance of memory found among some of his favorite Roman rhetorical writers, particularly Cicero.[19] The reformation of the memory through the work of grace now becomes central to the redemptive work of God.[20]

During the early 390s Augustine also developed an account of the text of Scripture as the central object of meditation for those seeking to understand themselves and their relationship to God. *De doctrina christiana* book 2 offers a clear statement of this—and has frequently been seen as the archetypal statement of a move away from the liberal arts.[21] In that book, Augustine describes some of the liberal arts as a useful propaedeutic to the work of exegesis, but he also strongly cautions against the pride that follows from placing too much store in one's knowledge of them.[22] Against this possible pride, book 2 outlines appropriate modes of humility in thinking and speaking before the divine mystery revealed in Scripture. Near the beginning of the book Augustine offers a seven-stage account of ascent to wisdom, in which knowledge that we walk in faith is the central thread.[23] At the first stage, fear of God inspires reflection (*cogitatio*) upon our mortality and possible punishment, thus inspiring holiness (*pietas*) and deference to Scripture. Augustine presents the third stage—that of knowledge and that at which the liberal arts begin to serve their propaedeutic function—as founded on awareness of our entanglement in love of this world and failure to exhibit the love that Scripture describes.[24] It is also with reference to this third stage that Augustine emphasizes how our prayer is answered by grace, that we might not despair.[25] In many ways *De doctrina* 2 is the epistemological counterpart to the contemporary but more poetic account of Scripture as the "firmament" set above us in *Confessions* 13.[26] It is, however, important to note that in both *De doctrina* and the *Confessions* the practices of thought that we find in the early works are not here condemned: Augustine only insists that they be understood in the light of the practical inescapability of faith in this life and the demands of the particular form of humility that Christ teaches and models.

We can identify three practices in particular from the latter half of the *Confessions* that persist throughout Augustine's corpus. The first is the practice of reflecting on one's soul, its nature and power, as a way of differentiating the orders of reality.[27] The second often follows closely on the first: the practice of reflecting on the difference between material existence and the immaterial in an attempt to identify and move beyond categories of time and space inadvertently predicated of spiritual or divine existence.[28] The third is reflection on the harmony of the diverse creation in the light of belief in its ordering by and dependence on the divine ordering.[29] Again, *De doctrina christiana* offers a more prosaic parallel: in *De doctrina christiana* book 1, Augustine explains that all attempt to think God, but only those who attempt to understand God through the intellect and as life itself are not mired in simple material imagery. Augustine then tells us *how* such people proceed in their thinking:

> Whatever corporeal form occurs to them, they establish that it either lives or does not live; and they esteem what lives more highly than what does not . . . . Then they proceed to examine that life, and if they find it has energy but not sense (as in the case of trees) they subordinate it to a sentient form of life . . . .[30]

These techniques are then located as useful within the purification that is also a journey to our homeland made possible by Wisdom itself becoming visible in the flesh and laying down for us an *exemplum vivendi,* an example or pattern of living.[31] Without naming the shift, Augustine has retooled the practices at the core of his vision of the liberal arts, turned them into exploratory tools that may also enable the practice and display of appropriate humility.[32]

When we see Augustine begin his answer to Volusianus by recommending a particular practice of reflection as the context within which questions about the incarnation may be answered, we must situate this recommendation within the story of Augustine's engagement with the practices of thought taught by the liberal arts. In the first place, it is Augustine's continued use of some of these practices that enables him to begin to demonstrate Christianity's philosophical respectability and make a claim on the cultural capital that gives Volusianus's challenge its force within the elite circles of Carthage. Augustine recommends an exercising of the mind that incorporates standard aspects of the liberal arts tradition located within a Plotinian framework, a mix I suggest he hopes will be recognized by at least some of Volusianus's circle as a central part of contemporary Latin philosophical tradition. Moreover, Augustine suggests this exercising of the mind via citation of the central authors of Latin tradition: it is Cicero who tells us to reflect on the mind's existence beyond the senses.[33]

In the second place, given Augustine's adaptation of the liberal arts tradition in his mature writing, we should also expect Augustine to use discussion of these practices as the foundation for recommending to

Volusianus Christian piety and humility as their condition of possibility and consummation. We have already begun to see Augustine's use of classical citation to justify his very Christian self-presentation: when Augustine tells us of the great leisure and desire needed even to approach the *profunditas* of Scripture, he alludes to Cicero's statement about the great leisure and desire that the Greeks have needed to grasp the vast fields of learning with which the orator should be equipped.[34] While this letter can be read as an accommodation to the styles of argument found in Volusianus's circle, it is also a carefully shaped piece of polemic against them.

We can see further the twist that Augustine has learnt to apply to themes from the liberal arts tradition in his growing emphasis on the difficulty that thinking the intelligible presents, and the attitude of wonder that should result from appropriate attention to it. Here, at the beginning of his answer, and after describing quickly some of the questions that arise in reflection on the soul and the senses, Augustine returns to the question "What then is the soul . . . ?" The next sentence moves immediately to this difficulty: "and we think we are told something incredible about the omnipotence of God when the Word of God . . . is said to have assumed a body . . . !"[35] Reflection on the soul leads here both to the idea of an intelligible reality unmarked by composition or spatial location, and simultaneously to wonder at the very existence of the soul. In fact, turning to the central place that Augustine accords the recognition of that which should amaze will enable us to see with much more clarity the precise contours of the practice Augustine has begun to suggest, and the full extent to which the argument in this letter depends on his Christian retooling of the liberal arts tradition.

The Power and the Mystery

At the end of his initial discussion of what one learns by reflecting on the soul, Augustine offers a summary account of the Word. He deploys an analogy, one he has offered before in his corpus and will offer again. When we speak, syllables proceed in a temporal order, the second only being possible when the first has ended. Yet a hearer hears the whole and many hearers hear the whole: one spoken word suffices for any number of hearers (within earshot). In the same manner the Word of God is omnipresent and cannot be grasped via material imagery.[36] It is, however, important to note the tone of the analogy:

> What, however, is more amazing [*mirabilius*] than what happens in our shouts and sounding words, that is, in something quickly passing? . . . Now would it not be more incredible [*potius incredibile*] if the enduring Word of God did not offer to things what a passing word of a human being offers to the ears so that, just as a human word is heard at once as a whole by each individual, the Word of God is present as a whole everywhere at once?[37]

Augustine uses the analogy to induce and model appropriate recognition of the mysterious, and thus to shift the character of our wonder at and imagination of God. Whereas his addressees have considered the incarnation to be in the category of the miraculous and have considered God within material categories, Augustine suggests that attention to the mysteriousness of the created order's existence in the immaterial enables us to imagine the omnipresence of the Word as a plausible doctrine. By such an argument Augustine does not attempt to render divine omnipresence fully comprehensible, making it analogous to innerworldly phenomena that we do comprehend. Instead he suggests a new style of attention to the mysterious presence of the sensible order in the intelligible.

In the next section Augustine pursues this strategy in more depth. He insists that we must imagine God's greatness not in terms of material conditions but in terms of power (*virtus*). The character of God's power is then shown by narrating its mysterious action in creating and sustaining all that we know. God creates specific creatures each with their own often surprising capacities: ". . . he creates from the tiniest grain of seed greatness like that of the fig tree, though from much larger seeds many much smaller plants come to be. He expands a very small pupil by the gaze that shines forth from the eyes in a moment of time and surveys almost half the sky."[38] This power, Augustine continues, accomplished the incarnation. The power that cannot be confined fertilized Mary's womb and joined itself to the soul, hence constituting the person of Christ. Augustine offers this striking summary:

> If a reason is asked for, it will not be miraculous [*hic si ratio quaeritur, non erit mirabile*]; if an example is demanded, it will not be singular. Let us grant that God can do something that we admit that we cannot search out. In such cases the whole reason for what is done lies in the power of the agent [*In talibus rebus tota ratio facti est potentia facientis*].[39]

In these dense sentences we find a summary of the lessons Augustine wishes Volusianus to learn from the *exercitatio* played out for him in the preceding paragraphs. Appropriate practices of attention to and reflection on the created order teach us that the incarnation is not *mirabilis,* that is, not extraordinary in the sense of incomprehensible by the standards of our knowledge of the cosmos. Intrinsic to these practices is an intellectual humility that not only enables recognition of that which remains beyond our epistemological grasp, but also points toward further investigation of the power of God within the created order. Practices that were originally intended to enable recognition of the informing of the sensible by the intelligible now are also intended to shape a heightened sense of the mysterious ordering and governance of the sensible by the divine power. We should, however, note that at this point Augustine's sense of the distinction between "intelligible" and "sensible" has taken on a very particular Christian flavor: the recognition of the informing of the sensible by the intelligible is always also a recognition of the necessity of faith in the face of the weakness of the "eyes of the heart."

The Mystery of Union

We are now ready to consider the paragraphs of the letter that have attracted most scholarly attention. Augustine introduces his analogy between the two natures and the body and soul with these words:

> But there are some who request an explanation of how God is joined to the human being so as to become the single person of Christ when it was necessary that it be done once, as if they themselves could explain something that happens every day, namely how the soul is joined to the body so as to form the single person of a human being. For just as the soul uses the body in the unity of the person in order that a person might exist, so God uses the man in the unity of the person in order that Christ might exist.[40]

The first sentence argues that one who had engaged in appropriate self-reflection and (hence) in appropriate reflection on the structure of creation would not request an explanation of the incarnation. Only those who think that they are able to explain the quotidian event of the union of soul and body would think it possible to explain the unique event of the incarnation. Augustine thus subtly criticizes his addressees as philosophically unsophisticated and inattentive—here they are insufficiently attentive to the nature of soul and body. The second sentence points back to the first: *nam sicut* (for just as . . .) indicates that the second is explanatory of the first. But the analogy is offered within the framework of the previous sentence's statement of the impossibility of grasping *either* the union of natures in Christ *or* the union of soul and body in a human being. Thus, the second sentence gives the grounds for Augustine's comparison in the first sentence: he can compare the attitude of his addressees to these two examples of union because they are indeed parallel—*just as* the soul uses the body so that there might be a human person, so God uses a human being so that there might be the unity of Christ's person. Augustine is saying in effect that just as the soul's union with the body is real and yet incomprehensible, so too the union of natures in Christ is real (hence the new use of *persona* to name the metaphysical reality) and yet incomprehensible.

This reading receives further confirmation when a little later Augustine writes, "the union of two incorporeal realities *ought,* nonetheless, to be believed with more ease than that of the soul and the body."[41] Even though his addressees assume the union of soul and body to be more plausible (at least insofar as they do not question its possibility), they should logically see that the union of natures in the Word is the more plausible. The point is, of course, intended rhetorically, emphasizing the incomprehensibility of the person of Christ and adding more force to the argument that the questions his addressees have asked stem from inappropriate attention to themselves, the cosmos, and God.

When Augustine speaks of the soul "using" the body, he employs a terminology that was occasionally offered in the ancient world as a way of describing the type of union involved in a human person. It is, however, noticeable that Augustine places no weight on this language here: the fact that the soul *uses* the body and the Word *uses* the human being in Christ helps to show the possibility of the analogy, but the terminology does no further work in explaining *how* these unions work.[42] Thus, Augustine sees the union of soul and body as a persistent problem that is heightened when one recognizes that a unitary person results, but he does not offer a particular model of union as a comprehensible analogy for understanding the two natures of Christ.[43] The analogy is intended to illustrate and reinforce the lesson Augustine has been offering throughout the earlier sections of the letter: the incarnation may be contemplated when one learns how to consider the creation as a revealing of the hidden and yet omnipresent creator, and when one comes to understand what may and may not be grasped by the human mind. The analogy does not resolve the paradox of the incarnation, but rather intensifies and focuses that paradox by offering precision about what may not be grasped: the mode of union of the two natures.[44]

It is important to note that while it is clear in general terms that Augustine wishes to inculcate a reflective practice founded on attention to the mysterious ordering of the cosmos by the divine, he simultaneously views this practice as enabling a certain precision in christological formulation. Such precision is based on attention to the language of faith—the language of Scripture and what may be inferred from it within the context of Augustine's exegetical practice. In the first place, Augustine is clear that we may make a number of statements about the positive character of Christ's person based on the needs of his mission. Thus we should confess that Christ's humanity included both a body and a soul and that the Word who assumed flesh was fully God. We must also assume that Christ was one agent. Augustine is also precise about what may and may not be understood about the union. We can be clear that it occurs through the divine power. But, *and also hence,* we can be sure that we cannot understand *how* it occurs: the mode of union remains beyond us. The better we understand that through the incarnation the divine power reflected as mystery in the creation takes up the "ordinary" into the "extra-ordinary,"[45] the more we will come to recognize that the union of natures cannot be understood: contemplation of its mysteriousness is contemplation of the core of the mystery of redemption itself. Thus, the developments in Augustine's Christology signaled by his use of nature and person language is also a precision about what must remain mysterious to Christians. We should, however, not stop here: an important aspect of the christological teaching of the letter would be missed if we did.

Exemplum Christi

Augustine has attempted to render the incarnation plausible to Volusianus by arguing both for a doctrine of divine omnipresence and for particular intellectual practices that will shape the mind to appreciate the relationship between Creator and creation. Only in the context of these practices can the mystery of Christ's mission and person be usefully discussed. In the latter half of the letter, Augustine makes a significant addition to his account by presenting the incarnation as structured for teaching the account of divine omnipresence that he has been suggesting. At the same time, he argues that the incarnation recommends to us the very practices that he has described, practices of thought and contemplation founded in faith and Christian *pietas*.

After offering the body/soul analogy discussed in the previous section of this essay, Augustine outlines three aspects of the Word's mission. Second in the list, but most important, Christ's *exemplum* persuades human beings that God need not be approached through intermediary powers: "God is so close to the piety of human beings that he deigned to assume a human being."[46] The humility of Christ is here presented as teaching the doctrine of divine omnipresence. Overcoming the practice of seeking the help of intermediary powers does not reveal God as a superior and more distant power: it reveals the possibility of our direct approach to the omnipresent ordering and governing divine life.[47] There is, however, also an intrinsic link between the doctrine that Christ teaches and the manner in which he teaches us to seek understanding of it. It is the willingness of the Word to become flesh that reveals the omnipresence of God; it is the same willingness that reveals to us the need for humility in our response.[48] In his reference to the *profunditas* of Scripture at the beginning of the letter, Augustine states that faith is the foundation of a life of piety: in these latter sections of the letter, Augustine describes faith as providing an "opening to the understanding" of doctrinal questions.[49] *Fides* here bears the heavy weight it does throughout Augustine's mature corpus: it refers not only to particular beliefs but also to the attitude of appropriate trust and inquiry that should shape our attention to the events narrated in Scripture. Christ offers material for humble faith and through the sending of the Spirit shows that such faith is an opening to understanding.[50] God is thus close to human *pietas* in the sense that God provides exactly what piety needs.

We may see further dimensions of this argument by turning to the first aspect of Christ's teaching that Augustine discusses. Christ confirms not only the teaching of the prophets but also the true teachings of secular writers.[51] Christ does not, however, confirm simply by repeating truths found in non-Christian traditions: through inculcating correct faith, Christ enables even the unlearned of his followers to grasp such truths. Thus belief in the immortality of the soul was originally the preserve of only a few philosophers: now the work of God through Christ and Spirit has made it (according to Augustine) a universal belief.[52] Toward the end of the letter Augustine comments on the value of the Scriptures in relation to the writings of the philosophers to make a similar point. The three divisions of philosophy—physics, ethics, and logic—are all contained in Scripture: but the style of the Scriptures is such that they are accessible to all, enabling faith in all and yet exercising appropriately the minds of all able to grasp deeper mysteries.[53] Thus Christianity's "confirmation" of the philosophers involves a reorganizing of their conceptions of philosophical practice. The church still possesses an intellectual elite comprised of those with the abilities to explore deeper mysteries, but their investigations should be conditioned by attention to the authority of Christ, who reveals the necessity of humility in any attempt to understand the omnipresent divine existence. Augustine offers a brief sketch of the church as a socially and intellectually diverse community of believers, subjecting to Christ "the most brilliant minds . . . [and converting them] to preach the way of piety and salvation."[54] If attempts to know God are completed by realization of the need for salvation (only thus can any sight of God be permanently obtained), the practices of the liberal arts are completed by their incorporation into the way of piety. The incarnate Christ draws Christians into a teaching that directly parallels and yet trumps that offered by the liberal arts: paralleling the liberal arts by initiating all into a new vision of the relationship between Creator and creation; trumping them by providing the means for the achievement of a vision that is denied the practitioner of the liberal arts in their non-Christian avatars.

The significance of faith is further reinforced when we note the third aspect of the Word's mission that Augustine mentions: that of the *adiutorium* who provides the grace of faith that is the foundation of any purification and forgiveness. This emphasis on grace complements the emphasis on faith, further adding to the relocation of the intellectual practices adapted from the liberal arts. The philosophical task is now on a continuum with the faith of illiterate Christians: the dependence of all on the gift of faith further reveals the church as the new social location for good philosophical reflection.

Conclusion

Augustine mounts a challenge to Volusianus's circle in *Letter* 137 by delineating a conception of intellectual practice that initially claims its superiority in terms internal to late-antique philosophical debate. Practices of thought and contemplation that originate in Augustine's early writing on the liberal arts are suggested as rendering plausible incarnational doctrine. And yet, these practices have been adapted so that Augustine may present them as fulfilled by Christian piety. Indeed, it is ultimately the incarnate Christ himself who serves as the model for the approach to knowledge of God that Augustine describes. At the heart of the practices Augustine recommends to Volusianus are patterns of attention to the created order. Long after the epistemological optimism of Augustine's early writings on the liberal arts has faded, he continues to present attention to the created order's mysterious revealing of the divine power as an essential part of the context within which Christian faith should be considered and explored. The remarkable sophistication of his account is seen in the transformation he effects in our reflection on the creation. In *Letter* 137 Augustine shapes what to modern eyes may seem a "reverse apologetics," in which the reasonableness of Christian doctrine is sketched not by finding a comprehensible analogy within our normal experience, but by expanding our vision of the incomprehensible until our reasoning about the created order and our vision in faith of the uncreated begin to complement each other.[55] In this new context the language of faith guides an analogical exploration of its own reflections in the creation—analogy becomes an *exercitatio mentis* for the one seeking greater understanding of the language of faith.

Against this background it becomes much clearer that Augustine's brief discussion of the union of natures in *Letter* 137 is not intended to enable our comprehension of Christ's person. Augustine is rather sketching a context within which Volusianus can recognize with precision what must remain incomprehensible about that union. Indeed, even though Augustine's account of the person of Christ is inchoate in comparison to those appearing in the wake of the christological controversies it is interesting to note that Augustine anticipates one of the central presuppositions of Chalcedonian Christologies in their fully developed forms. Solutions to the union of natures that identify with precision that which is one in Christ (other than his *persona* or *hypostasis*)—whether it is "nature" or "will"—are ultimately rejected not because Christ is primarily to be understood as two realities, but because the mode of union that results in the unity of his person depends on the action of the divine power and is by definition incomprehensible. The great and venerable work of contemplating the union of natures in Christ may and must deliver us precision in our thinking, but that precision facilitates our growing awareness of the incomprehensibility of exactly how Christ is one without confusion or change.

If *Letter* 137 reveals to us some of the initial context for the emergence of the *City of God,* it does not do so simply because questions about the relationship between Christians and the state are among the questions that Volusianus and Marcellinus pose to Augustine. *Letter* 137 demonstrates, rather, that questions about the doctrine of the incarnation are for Augustine inseparable from questions about the context within which Christian doctrine is explored and questioned. These doctrinal questions thus lead Augustine inevitably to reflect on the location of appropriate thinking within and without the *City of God*: Christology necessarily becomes hermeneutics, epistemology, and social theory if it is to be seen in its full rationality and beauty.

Notes

1. Maximus Confessor, *Ambigua* 5 (PG 91.1057A).

2. I thank Andy Gallwitz, Ian McFarland, John Rist, Thomas Weinandy, O.F.M. Cap., and James Wetzel for comments on an earlier draft of this essay. I also thank Dale Martin: the first draft was sketched over a weekend at his house in August 2000.

3. For discussions of *Ep.* 137 see T. J. Van Bavel, *Recherches sur la christologie de saint Augustin* (Fribourg: Éditions Universitaires, 1954), passim; E. Fortin, *Christianisme et culture philosophique au cinquième siècle: La querelle de l'âme humaine en Occident* (Paris: Études Augustiniennes, 1959), 111–23; J. T. Newton, *Neoplatonism and Augustine's Doctrine of the Person and Work of Christ: A Study of the Philosophical Structure Underlying Augustine's Christology* (Ph.D. Diss., Emory University, 1969), 71–110; H. R. Drobner, *Person-Exegese und Christologie bei Augustinus* (Leiden: Brill, 1986); G. Madec, *La Patrie et la voie: Le Christ dans la vie et la pensée de Saint Augustine* (Paris: Desclée, 1989), 228–34. Both Newton and Madec are dependent on Fortin.

4. *Ep.* 137.3.9 (CSEL 44.108): "in unitate personae copulans utramque naturam . . . ." For the significance of this shift in Augustine's Christology, cf. Drobner, *Person-Exegese und Christologie,* 169–72. Throughout (with occasional changes) I have used the excellent translation of Roland Teske in *The Works of Saint Augustine: A Translation for the 21st Century,* II/2, *Letters 100–155* (Hyde Park, N.Y.: New City Press, 2003).

5. *Ep.* 137.3.11 (CSEL 44.110): "nam sicut in unitate personae anima utitur corpore, ut homo sit, its in unitate personae deus utitur homine, ut Christus sit." It has been commonplace to assert that Augustine's account is Porphyrian in origin. This argument finds its origin in Fortin, *Christianisme et culture philoso-*

phique, 111–23, and H. Dörrie's *Porphyrios' Symmikta Zetema: Ihre Stellung in System und Geschichte des Neuplatonismus, nebst einem Kommentar zu den Fragmenten* (Munich: Beck, 1959). Dörrie argues that there is a specifically Porphyrian account of soul and body being united without confusion reflected in Nemesius and Priscianus Lydus (and, according to Fortin, in Augustine). J. Rist, "Pseudo-Ammonius and the Soul/Body Problem in Some Platonic Texts of Late Antiquity," *American Journal of Philology* 109 (1988): 402–15, shows that there is little evidence for this argument and teases apart the "close" parallels Fortin alleges between Augustine, Nemesius, and Priscianus.

6. Cf. *PLRE* 2:1184–85 and A. Chastagnol, "Le sénateur Volusien et la conversion d'une famille de l'aristocratie romaine au Bas-Empire," *Revue des études anciennes* 58 (1956): 240–53. We can be reasonably certain of the date before which Volusianus was *Proconsulis africae* because in late 411, Apryngius, the brother of Marcellinus, was appointed to this position.

7. *Ep.* 135.2 (CSEL 44.92): "at cum ad antistitem Augustinum venitur, legi deest quidquid contigerit ignorari." We should not assume Augustine had constant and easy access to such influential figures. We may fairly read into Augustine's response a desire to demonstrate his ability to engage in appropriate discussion with such circles. See N. McLynn, "Augustine's Roman Empire," *Augustinian Studies* 30 (1999): 29–44.

8. This particular exchange is also only part of an extended conversation that continued until Marcellinus's execution in 413. *Ep.* 138 to Marcellinus constitutes an addition to *Ep.* 137, in which Augustine addresses more directly the additional questions the *tribunus* had raised in *Ep.* 135. Marcellinus's role in the production of two of Augustine's early texts against Pelagius is also noteworthy. *Pecc. merit.* was written at the request of Marcellinus (begun in the winter of 411) and *Spir. et litt.* (412) was stimulated by further queries from him.

9. Interestingly, Volusianus's letter contains no clear reference to Platonic doctrine or tradition. In *Letter* 136, however, Marcellinus mentions the second-century North African Middle-Platonist Apuleius of Madaura as one example of a person with magical powers cited by Volusianus's friends. Augustine assumes his addressees have knowledge of traditions that envisage daemons as divine powers that are "heavenly" and "intermediate" (*potestates caelestis, potestates interpositas*). These daemons are envisaged as intermediaries between human beings and God who are approached by means of ritual practice (*Ep.* 137.3.12). While many have seen in Augustine's discussion reference to Porphyrian or Iamblichan traditions of theurgy, Augustine also has in mind Middle-Platonic daemon traditions and a variety of late antique popular religious practices.

10. *Ep.* 137.2.4.

11. *Ep.* 137.2.5 (CSEL 44.101).

12. Henri-Irénée Marrous's *Saint Augustin et la fin de la culture antique* (Paris: E. De Boccard, 1938), 187–327, is still unsurpassed as a basic guide to the

development of models for organizing the liberal arts in antiquity and Augustine's place in that tradition. Among the wealth of recent literature, I. Hadot's *Arts libéraux et philosophie dans la pensée antique* (Paris: Études Augustiniennes, 1984) is particularly notable. Virgilio Pacioni, *L'Unità Teoretica del* De Ordine *di S. Agostino* (Rome: Millenium Romae, 1996), offers, however, a better guide to the diversity of influences (including that of Varro) that may be discerned in Augustine's account of the liberal arts. Danuta R. Shanzer, "Augustine's Disciplines: *Silent diutius Musae Varronis?*" in *Augustine and the Disciplines,* ed. K. Pollman and M. Vessey (Oxford: Clarendon Press, 2005), 69–112, offers further argument for Varronian influence.

13. *Ord.* 2.12.35ff. Cf. *Sol.* 2.20.35. The latter text warns against "mistaken" construals of the *liberal arts,* thus revealing contemporary debate about how one understands their nature and purpose. Augustine follows a common pattern among late antique authors in understanding the ancient disciplines within a Neoplatonic framework: for the significance of this context, see the literature mentioned in the previous note.

14. *Ord.* 2.18.48–19.50.

15. *Ord.* 2.19.51.

16. Further good examples of these practices are provided by *Quant. an.* 22.40ff. and 31.71–73, *Immort. an.* 1.6, *Lib. arb.* 2.20–24.

17. For these developments see, first, *Ord.* 2.2.6 (ca. 386). Cf. *Quant. an.* 33.71–2 (ca. 388), *Ep.* 7.1.1 (ca. 388–91), and then *Conf.* 10.12.19–13.20.

18. See *Conf.* 10.8.15. On the gradual relocation of vision of God to the *eschaton,* cf. M. R. Barnes, "The Visible Christ and the Invisible Trinity: Mt. 5.8 in Augustine's Trinitarian Theology of 400," *Modern Theology* 19 (2003): 329–55.

19. Perhaps most famously at Cicero, *Tusc.* 1.24.57ff. For one of the most significant mature discussions of memory, see *Trin.* 11.13–14. At *Trin.* 14.4–5 Augustine discusses the continuing role of memory even in the contemplation of God.

20. Explored with particular clarity in J. Wetzel, *Augustine and the Limits of Virtue* (Cambridge: Cambridge University Press, 1992), ch. 4.

21. K. Pollman's excellent *Doctrina Christiana: Untersuchungen zu den Anfängen der christlichen Hermeneutik unter besonderer Berücksichtigung von Augustinus* De doctrina Christiana (Fribourg: Universitätsverlag Freiburg Schweiz, 1996), 192–96, offers a good example of this way of reading the matter.

22. The clearest summary statements of his position can be found at *Doctr. chr.* 2.39.58, 2.41.62. Note also his discussions of what may and may not be usefully learnt from various disciplines. The disciplines of rhetoric, dialectic, and number are discussed at *Doctr. chr.* 2.31.48–40.60 and astronomy at 2.29.46.

23. Augustine's discussion of seven stages in the soul's growth begins with *Quant. an.* 33.70–76. The account considered here finds its model in *Serm. Dom.*

1.3.10–4.12, probably written in 393. It is in the *Serm. Dom.* account that Augustine begins to focus on the relationship between knowledge and humility.

24. *Doctr. chr.* 2.9.16–10.19.

25. *Doctr. chr.* 2.10.20.

26. *Conf.* 13.15.16–18. On the discussion of Scripture here see I. Bochet, *"Le Firmament de l'écriture": L'Herméneutique Augustinienne* (Paris: Études Augustiennes, 2004), 91–116, 229–64.

27. E.g. the section of the meditation on time at *Conf.* 11.14.19 that begins with a call to the soul to consider its measurement of time. This reflection enables recognition of the ability of the mind to measure time, but then also recognition of its own distention in the world and the possibility of moving toward the stability to be found in God (11.30.40).

28. E.g., Augustine's description at *Conf.* 12.4.4ff. of his inner conversation or *cogitatio* as he attempts to understand the reality of the unformed nature of the world described at Gen 1:1. He describes in formal terms an attempt to think beyond material imagery. Considering the mutability of things leads him to recognize God as their author and hence the immutability of the divine.

29. The example given in the previous note also involves recognition of the soul's place within the created order. A further example is provided by the introduction to the famous exploration of memory at *Conf.* 10.6.9–10. The discussion of memory itself which follows can be added to the previous note as a further illustration of the soul's reflection on its own nature.

30. *Doctr. chr.* 1.8.8.17–18.

31. *Doctr. chr.* 1.10.10.22–23.

32. The examples I have given in the notes here are, of course, taken from a work addressed to an elite audience—as is *Ep.* 137. In my *Augustine and the Trinity* (Cambridge: Cambridge University Press, forthcoming, 2009) I offer a parallel reading of the *De Trinitate* which emphasizes the continuing significance of these practices in that text (in so doing I am also suggesting the importance of Marrou's insistence on the importance of dialectic in the *De Trinitate:* see his *Saint Augustin,* 315–27). In briefer and much simplified forms these practices can also be found throughout his homiletic corpus. For a very useful recent discussion of the relationship between his homiletic practice and the longer treatises, see John Cavadini, "Simplifying Augustine," in *Educating People of Faith: Exploring the History of Jewish and Christian Communities,* ed. J. Van Engen (Grand Rapids: Eerdmans, 2004), 63–84.

33. *Ep.* 137.2.5. The reference is to Cicero, *Tusc.* 1.16.38. There may well be an echo of the same text in *Conf.* 7.17.23's "abduxit cogitationem a consuetudine," where Augustine describes his initial insight into the nature of reason and immaterial truth after reading the "Platonists" (cf. O'Donnell 2.457).

34. *Ep.* 137.1.3. Cf. Cicero, *De or.* 1.6.22.

35. *Ep*. 137.2.6.

36. For discussion of the frequency with which this analogy appears in Augustine's sermons see Cavadini, "Simplifying Augustine."

37. *Ep*. 137.2.7 (CSEL 44.105–6). Cf. *Lib. arb*. 2.14.38.

38. *Ep*. 137.2.8. The theme is repeated later at *Ep*. 137.3.10, and appears also a number of times in his homiletic corpus, e.g. *Serm*. 247.2. Cf. also *Trin*. 3.8.13: following the arguments of Pierre-Marie Hombert, *Nouvelles Recherches de Chronologie Augustinienne* (Paris: Études Augustiniennes, 2000), 62–66, we may note that *Trin*. 3 and *Ep*. 137 are probably contemporary.

39. *Ep*. 137.2.8 (CSEL 44.107).

40. *Ep*. 137.3.11 (CSEL 44.109–10): "Sic autem quidam reddi sibi rationem flagitant, quo modo deus homini permixtus sit, ut una fieret persona Christi, cum hoc semel fieri oportuerit, quasi rationem ipsi reddant de re, quae cotidie fit, quo modo misceatur anima corpori, ut una persona fiat hominis. Nam sicut in unitate personae anima utitur corpore, ut homo sit, ita in unitate personae deus utitur homine, ut Christus sit."

41. *Ep*. 137.3.11 (CSEL 44.110): "verum tamen duarum rerum incorporearum commixtio facilius credi debuit quam unius incorporeae et alterius corporeae . . . ."

42. Thus, for example, the language is considered by Plotinus at *Enn*. 1.1.4. It stems originally from ps.-Plato, *Alcibiades I* 129–30. The best summary discussion of Augustine's language here is John Rist, *Augustine: Ancient Thought Baptized* (Cambridge: Cambridge University Press, 1994), 97–104.

43. Here we see perhaps further confirmation of Rist's arguments in his "Pseudo-Ammonius." In *Ep*. 137 Augustine's discussion of the union of body and soul similarly depends on it being an insoluble paradox, not on any preexisting theory that describes the type of union involved.

44. In response to an earlier draft of this essay, James Wetzel suggested that one might term this the "ironic use" of analogy. Augustine certainly intends us to draw, in a loose sense, an analogy here: and yet the point of the analogy is grasped only when the intentional ironies of its deployment are grasped. In this essay I have not considered Augustine's other uses of the body/soul analogy for the constitution of Christ's person. The analogy in *Ep*. 137 is by far the most developed, but, in many of the other cases in his mature writings, I would argue that Augustine's usage follows the same logic even if the "ironies" he intends are far less clearly drawn out.

45. *Ep*. 137.3.9 (CSEL 44.108): "nunc vero ita inter deum et hominess mediator apparuit, ut in unitate personae copulans utramque naturam et solita sublimaret insolitis et insolita solitis temperaret."

46. *Ep*. 137.3.12 (CSEL 44.113): "scirent hominess tam proximum esse deum pietati hominum ut hominem dignaretur." On the centrality of Christ as

exemplum humilitatis, see Wilhelm Geerlings, *Christus Exemplum: Studien zur Christologie und Christusverkündigung Augustins* (Tübingen: J. C. B. Mohr, 1978), 173–74.

47. Augustine has already noted (*Ep.* 137.3.9) that unless Christ lived a fully human life in which was fully proclaimed the grace of salvation, we would not be able to grasp that God lifts up human nature through a mediator who is both divine and human (and not through any ontological intermediary).

48. R. Dodaro's *Christ and the Just Society in Augustine* (Cambridge: Cambridge University Press, 2004), chaps. 4 and 5, offers an important supplement to the argument here by describing with a new clarity the ways in which Augustine presents the Scriptures as exercising and drawing the mind toward appreciation for the divine mystery.

49. *Ep.* 137.4.15 (CSEL 44.117): "intellectui fides aditum aperit, infidelitas claudit."

50. I have explored one way in which the different senses of *fides* come together somewhat obliquely in my "Augustine on the Rule of Faith: Rhetoric, Christology, and the Foundation of Christian Thinking," *Augustinian Studies* 36 (2005): 33–49.

51. *Ep.* 137.3.12.

52. *Ep.* 137.3.12. We should note that this account also constitutes a further argument in favor of the incarnation: Augustine offers the incarnation as structured to teach a view of the created order of whose coherence and philosophical respectability Augustine has already tried to convince Volusianus.

53. *Ep.* 137.5.17.

54. *Ep.* 137.4.16 (CSEL 44.119–20): "praeclarissima ingenia, cultissima eloquia mirabilesque peritias acutorum, facundorum atque doctorum subiungat Christo et ad praedicandum viam pietatis salutisque convertunt."

55. I am grateful to my colleague Ian McFarland for the phrase "reverse apologetics." Charles Couturier, in his "La structure métaphysique de l'homme d'après saint Augustin," in *Augustinus Magister (Congrès International Augustinien, Paris, 21–24 septembre 1954)* (Paris: Études Augustiniennes, 1954), 1:543–50, argued that Augustine's understanding of the human being's unity was fundamentally governed by his christological premises and is thus best labeled "hypostatic." With some nuance we should, I suggest, reflect carefully on his account. In the course of *Ep.* 137 Augustine seems to present us with a view of the human being as fundamentally resistant to our comprehension because it is a unity brought about by divine power. The argument that Augustine offers involves the Christian in recognizing the extent to which the incarnation provides a model for our contemplation of the creation and of ourselves. We most fruitfully understand the mystery of our composite and yet unified nature by seeing the analogies and distinctions between our existence and that of the incarnate Christ.

10

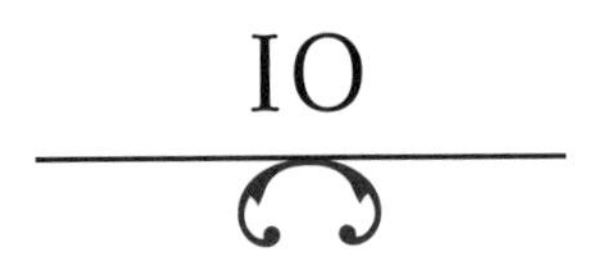

What Was "Wrong" with Augustine?

The Sixth-Century Reception (or Lack Thereof) of Augustine's Christology

David R. Maxwell

A christological controversy erupted in Constantinople in the first decades of the sixth century, which quickly expanded to include a controversy about grace. A group of monks from Scythia, who were in Constantinople to get a hearing for their christological views, fought both fronts of this battle. They relied, however, on separate authorities for each front. For Christology, they drew primarily on the writings of Cyril of Alexandria to oppose what they saw as a Nestorianizing misinterpretation of the Chalcedonian definition. For the doctrine of grace, they drew primarily on the writings of Augustine to oppose a semi-Pelagian understanding of human cooperation in conversion. This division of labor raises the question of why they did not draw consistently on one author or the other. Why did they employ Augustine as a specialist on grace, so to speak, but show little interest in his christological formulations? What was "wrong" with Augustine's Christology that prevented the Scythian monks from relying on him as a primary witness for their own christological position? Briefly, I argue in this essay that when Augustine's Christology was thrust into a new context, that of the Nestorian controversy, his formulations took on a different meaning because they bore a superficial resemblance to certain "Nestorian" formulations, even though they were never intended to address the questions posed by the later controversy.

In order to trace this shift in meaning, I first provide a brief summary of the sixth-century "Theopaschite controversy," which is really a continuation of the Nestorian controversy. After that, I determine which Augustinian texts the Scythian monks had available to them. I am then in a position to describe three features of Augustine's Christology which underwent a transformation and began to look "Nestorian" when they were read in the new context of the Theopaschite controversy. These features are, first, a "rule of interpretation" that Augustine articulated in *De Trinitate;* second, Augustine's account of why Christ is called God; and third, Augustine's inclusion of the concept of grace in his Christology.

The Theopaschite Controversy

In the year 519, a group of monks from Scythia, led by John Maxentius, arrived in Constantinople in order to gain approval from the emperor for their "theopaschite formula," "One of the Trinity was crucified in the flesh." The Scythian monks advocated this formula because they were concerned that many, including their home bishop in the town of Tomi, misinterpreted the Chalcedonian definition in a Nestorianizing direction. Leo's *Tome,* for example, which was endorsed by Chalcedon, states, "Each form [i.e., nature] does what is proper to it in communion with the other, the Word, that is, doing what belongs to the Word, and the flesh carrying out what belongs to the flesh. One of these shines with miracles; the other succumbs to injuries."[1] A statement such as this could easily be taken to posit two different acting subjects in Christ.

The Scythian monks did not believe that Chalcedon or Leo actually intended to divide Christ in two. They themselves were ardent supporters of the Chalcedonian definition, and they culled Leo's letters for evidence that he did in fact believe there is only one subject in Christ. Their concern was that their contemporaries, including a group of monks in Constantinople as well as legates from Rome, were misreading Chalcedon by taking advantage of ambiguities like the above passage from Leo's *Tome* in order to divide the actions of Christ between a human and a divine subject.

The Scythian monks advocated their theopaschite formula as a kind of litmus test to unmask just such a Nestorianizing interpretation of the council. The formula "One of the Trinity was crucified in the flesh" was intended to make clear that everything that Christ underwent, including the crucifixion, was experienced by "One of the Trinity," namely, the Word. If one could confess the theopaschite formula along with Chalcedon, the Scythian monks argued, Chalcedon was defended against a Nestorianizing misinterpretation that would ascribe the sufferings of Christ to some subject other than the Word.

In addition to the controversy about the reception of Chalcedon, a semi-Pelagian controversy erupted in Constantinople at the same time when the North African bishop Possessor attempted to cite Faustus of Riez against the Scythian monks. In response to Possessor, the Scythian monks showed themselves to be ardent Augustinians, affirming original sin and the inability of human beings to will anything pertaining to eternal life without the internal operation of the Holy Spirit.[2]

Corresponding to these two facets of their controversy, the Scythian monks produced a number of documents characterized by a twofold structure. In the first part, they dealt with Christ, and in the second part, they dealt with the doctrine of grace.[3] For Christology, the Scythian monks drew primarily on Cyril of Alexandria in a Latin translation produced for them by Dionysius Exiguus. For the doctrine of grace, they drew primarily on Augustine. As I said earlier, this pattern raises the question of why they did not draw consistently on Augustine for their entire theological argumentation. The implication seems to be that there was something less than helpful about Augustine's Christology.

Augustinian Sources

In order to describe what that problem might be, we must first determine which works of Augustine the Scythian monks knew so that we may have some idea of the christological material from Augustine that was available to them. If we limit ourselves to verbatim or near-verbatim citations, the works of Augustine most frequently cited by the Scythian monks were *De Trinitate* and *De praedestinatione sanctorum*. By my count, they cited *De praedestinatione sanctorum* eight times in their corpus of writings, while they cited *De Trinitate* six times. The other works they cited were *De haeresibus* (three times), the *Enchiridion* (twice), and *Sermo* 80 (once).[4]

Determining what works they cited, however, does not prove that they had access to these works in their entirety. At least two florilegia in existence at the time were relevant to the Theopaschite controversy: the *Exempla sanctorum patrum,* which marshalled evidence in support of the phrase "One of the Trinity," and the *Capitula sancti Augustini,* which dealt with issues of sin, grace, predestination, and anthropology.[5]

By examining more carefully their citations of Augustine, however, it is possible to determine that the Scythian monks did, in fact, have access to the entire treatises from which they cited, at least in the cases of *De Trinitate, De praedestinatione sanctorum,* and the *Enchiridion.* That is because the Scythian monks displayed an awareness of the context of the passages they cited, a context not available to someone relying only on the above florilegia.

This awareness is clearly detectable in their discussion of the one point of Christology for which the Scythian monks did draw on Augustine: their phrase *unus ex Trinitate*. Their opponents charged that this phrase was a novelty that introduced division into the Godhead. In response, the Scythian monks brought forward a number of passages from Augustine that employed similar phrases, and as they cited them, they gave some indication of the context of the passages. For example, when the Scythian monks adduced a passage in the *Enchiridion* that uses the phrase *unus trium* to describe a person of the Trinity, a phrase quite similar to their own *unus ex Trinitate,* they were able to specify that the passage occured in the context of Augustine's discussion of the statement "God the Word was born of the Holy Spirit and the virgin Mary."[6] Again, when the Scythian monks cited two passages from book 2 of *De Trinitate* that employed the phrase *aliqua ex Trinitate persona,* they were able to specify that the second passage occurred "a little later" than the first.[7] Although each of the above-mentioned passages appears in the *Exempla sanctorum patrum,* these contextual cues do not.[8]

The case is even stronger for *De praedestinatione sanctorum.* John Maxentius cited this work numerous times in his response to a letter from Pope Hormisdas. The North African bishop Possessor, who had cited Faustus of Riez against the Scythian monks, wrote Hormisdas, criticizing the Scythian monks. Hormisdas replied with his own stinging criticism of the Scythian monks, but the pope differed from Possessor in one respect: he refused to view Faustus of Riez as an authority. In fact, he declared that the doctrine of the Roman church on free will and grace was found especially in Augustine's work *Ad Hilarium et Prosperum,* referring to the twin work, *De praedestinatione sanctorum* and *De dono perseverantiae.*[9] Maxentius took advantage of this admission and proceeded to discredit Faustus of Riez (and Possessor) by opposing Faustus point for point with passages from Augustine's *De praedestinatione sanctorum*. When Maxentius identified the citations from Augustine he wanted to use, he displayed a knowledge of the passages' contexts. He was able to say, for example, that one passage was found "a little bit after what he says about the beginning of faith."[10] Other contextual cues may be found in a number of places throughout the same work.[11] In the case of these citations from *De praedestinatione sanctorum,* not even the passages, much less the context indicators, are found in either of the florilegia.

These contextual cues, taken together, establish that the Scythian monks were not citing Augustine from florilegia. They were familiar with the contexts in which the passages they cited occurred. At least in the cases of Augustine's *De Trinitate, Enchiridion,* and *De praedestinatione sanctorum,* we can be fairly confident that the Scythian monks had the treatises in their entirety. This fact is significant because these three works have much to say about Christ that the Scythian monks chose *not* to use. I hope the reasons for this decision will become obvious when the polemical context of the Scythian monks is taken into account.

In the three sections that follow, I identify three salient features of Augustine's Christology. First, Augustine articulated a rule of exegesis in *De Trinitate* that correlated different actions of Christ to one or the other of his two natures. Second, he asserted that Christ was called God because God assumed him. Third, in the *Enchiridion* and *De praedestinatione sanctorum,* he employed the term "grace" in his discussion of

Christology. In each of these three cases, Augustine's language would have sounded uncomfortably close to the language that the Scythian monks attributed to their opponents.

Augustine's Rule of Interpretation

A major christological emphasis of Augustine's *De Trinitate,* arising from his anti-Arian concern, was to show that scriptural statements that imply that the Son is less than the Father or that ascribe to Christ obviously human characteristics do not contradict the teaching that he is God. To this end, Augustine applied a rule of interpretation, which he derived from Philippians 2:6, that those statements which imply that the Son is equal to the Father are made on the basis of the form of God in which he was, while those statements which imply that he is less than the Father are made on the basis of the form of a slave which he took on.[12] This rule gave Augustine's Christology a rhetorically balanced shape. Christ did some things according to the form of God, while he did others according to the form of a slave. In that respect, Augustine's Christology would find a later echo in Leo's *Tome,* which stated, as we have already seen above, that "each form does what is proper to it."

This rhetorical balance, however, became a liability in an anti-Nestorian context. Against what they perceived to be a Nestorianizing reading of Chalcedon that posited two acting subjects in Christ, the Scythian monks advocated an asymmetrical Christology in which the Word was the only acting subject. To their ears, the balanced style of Leo's *Tome,* or Augustine's *De Trinitate* (I suggest), while not Nestorian in itself, could easily be taken to imply two subjects in Christ.

Indeed, Augustine was capable of speaking of Christ's human nature in ways that sounded like it was a separate acting subject. He said, for example, "Because the form of God took on the form of a servant, each is God and each is man, but each is God because of God taking on, and each is man because of man taken on [*acceptum hominem*]."[13] Or again, "Accordingly, since the Son is both God and man, God is one substance and the man is another, but it is the man in the Son rather than the Son in the Father [who differs in substance]."[14] The rhetorical balance of these statements, along with their tendency to treat "form of a servant" or "man" as a concrete noun, could easily have suggested that "God" and "man" in the last analysis acted independently from one another.

That is not to say that Augustine actually intended two separate acting subjects in Christ. He stated elsewhere, for example, that "it is the same only begotten Son of the Father who is both in the form of a servant and in the form of God."[15] Because of this identity, Augustine could maintain that the human attributes applied to the only-begotten Son. "For he was crucified as a result of the form of a slave [*ex forma servi*], and nevertheless the Lord of Glory was crucified. For that taking on [of the man by God] was such that it made God a man, and it made the man God."[16]

Nevertheless, Augustine's rule of interpretation partook in the same ambiguity as Leo's *Tome* once *De Trinitate* was read in an anti-Nestorian context. Presumably, the Scythian monks regarded Augustine's Christology in *De Trinitate* like they regarded Leo's Christology: it was orthodox, but its rhetorical balance, assigning some things to God and others to the man, needed to be clarified and shored up against a Nestorianizing misinterpretation.[17]

This need for defense was particularly urgent because Cyril of Alexandria anathematized a similar interpretive procedure on the part of Nestorius. Cyril stated his position most succinctly in the fourth anathema of his third letter to Nestorius:

> If anyone distributes between two persons or *hypostases* the terms used in the evangelical and apostolic writings, whether spoken of Christ by the saints or by him about himself, and attaches some to a man thought of separately from the Word of God, and others as befitting God to the Word of God the Father alone, let him be anathema.[18]

The Scythian monks were well aware of Cyril's position since they had access to this letter through a Latin translation produced by Dionysius Exiguus.

When the emperor Zeno, in 482, attempted to unify the empire on the basis of Cyril of Alexandria's Christology, he issued a statement known as the *Henotikon* that expressed a similar concern. Implicitly correcting, or at least interpreting, Leo's statement that each form does what is proper to it, the *Henotikon* stated, "We say that both the miracles and the passions that he endured willingly in the flesh belong to one [subject]."[19] This unease over Chalcedon was shared not only by the so-called "Monophysites" in the East, to whom the *Henotikon* was intended to appeal, but also by committed Chalcedonians such as the Scythian monks, who recognized an ambiguity in the way that Chalcedon confessed the unity of Christ.

Accordingly, the Scythian monks also stressed that both the miracles and the passions applied to the Word,[20] while they portrayed their opponents as wanting to separate the miracles and the passions, so that God worked the miracles, while (the man) Jesus Christ endured the suffering.[21] The Scythian monks sometimes pressed this point home by reversing the normal rule as expressed by Augustine and Leo; they affirmed that, according to his humanity, *God* was born of a virgin, hungered, thirsted, was crucified, pierced, and so on, and that, according to his divinity, the *Son of Man,* or simply the *man,* was born of the Father before the ages, was one of the Trinity, was eternal life, and so on.[22]

In this context, then, the strategy of referring the sufferings of Christ to the man, which made sense against the Arian argument that the sufferings proved that Christ was not God, was no longer a helpful move once the question had shifted to defending the unity of Christ. The rhetorical balance of Augustine and Leo gave way to an asymmetrical Christology in which the Word was clearly the subject of all Christ's actions.

When the Scythian monks offered their own "rule," they tellingly drew on a statement from Gregory of Nazianzus, not from Augustine. The rule from Gregory, as the Scythian monks cited it, reads, "I admonish you . . . that you indeed ascribe the higher things to the divinity and to that nature which is proven superior to passions and the body, but you attribute the lower things to the composite who for you emptied himself and was incarnate."[23] The Scythian monks cited this passage in support of their contention that after the incarnation, the Word was "composite." However, it is important to note that Gregory was not making a distinction between the divine and human natures of Christ, attributing higher things to the first and lower things to the second. Instead, he was distinguishing between the divinity and the composite, namely, the Word incarnate. In an anti-Nestorian context, the distinction between the two natures, which could sometimes be read as a distinction between two subjects, was often replaced by a distinction between the Word (considered apart from the incarnation) and the Word incarnate. This latter distinction more clearly kept the Word the subject of both the miracles and the sufferings.

Why Christ Is Called God

Beyond the issue of rhetorical balance, one may detect in Augustine's Christology in *De Trinitate* another element that resonated uncomfortably with the opponents of the Scythian monks. This element concerned the basis on which Christ was asserted to be God. Augustine stated, in the passage already quoted above, "Because the form of God took on the form of a servant, each is God and each is man, but each is God because of God taking on, and each is man because of man taken on [*acceptum hominem*]."[24] Here, the man Christ was called God because it was God who assumed him.

In John Maxentius's *Dialogue against the Nestorians,* a similar position was put into the mouth of the character Nestorianus, who represented the position of the papal legates to Constantinople with whom the Scythian monks clashed. In a discussion of the term *theotokos,* Nestorianus stated, "Although I will not hesitate to confess the blessed virgin to be *theotokos,* I confess her to be *theotokos* not because she bore God, but because she bore a man united to God." When Catholicus, the character who represented John Maxentius's position, asked why Nestorianus called her *theotokos* if she bore a man and not God, Nestorianus explained himself by saying that the one born of Mary is called God "by the uniting."[25] In the mind of John Maxentius, to say that the man was called God because he was united to God was tantamount to saying that he was called God merely as a title of dignity or honor.[26] In other words, an appeal to the uniting of God and man as an explanation of why the man deserved to be called God failed to recognize that the word "man" actually referred to the Word and not to an independent human subject. With that failure, the confession of the *theotokos* was compromised.

In Augustine's context, the statement that the man Christ is God because God assumed him was nothing more than an appeal to Christ's unchanging divine nature as the basis for calling him God, without any reflection on the *theotokos* or the mode of union. John Maxentius, on the other hand, laid out the alternatives in the *Dialogue against the Nestorians* as follows: Christ is either God by nature or God by uniting. This was a way of framing the question that Augustine did not have in mind, and it presented a range of possible answers from which Augustine was not attempting to choose. Yet, when one attempts to read Augustine's formulations as an answer to the questions framed by John Maxentius, at least some of those formulations come out sounding uncomfortably close to the position of the character Nestorianus.

Augustine's View of the Incarnation as Grace

A unique element of Augustine's Christology was his argument that the incarnation itself was the premier example of God's grace. This point, however, also underwent a transformation when Augustine was read by those in the sixth century who were attempting to describe the mode of the union of Christ's two natures. Therefore, I will first set Augustine's argument in its own context and then proceed to describe the sixth-century transformation of that context.

Augustine's christological discussion in the *Enchiridion* took place in dialogue most prominently with the Pelagians. Against the Pelagian assertion that salvation was a response on the part of God to human merit, Augustine held up the incarnation as the premier example of grace. "What did the human nature in the man Christ merit," Augustine asked, "that it might be assumed singularly into the unity of person of the only Son of God?"[27] For Augustine, Christ's lack of prevenient human merit set the pattern for salvation by grace apart from prevenient merit for human beings in general. Such glory belonged to human nature without preceding merit, according to Augustine, "so that people may understand that they are justified from sins by the same grace by which it came about that the man Christ could have no sin . . . ."[28]

In *De praedestinatione sanctorum,* Augustine made the same move for the issue of predestination. There he called Christ "the most brilliant light of predestination and grace."[29] Augustine developed his argument in more detail by appealing to the scriptural image of Christ being the head and the church being his body. Since Christ is the head, he is the source of grace, but the same grace applies both to the head and the body.[30]

One might get the impression from Augustine's language about the man Christ being joined to the Word that Augustine subscribed to some sort of adoptionist theory, in which a preexistent human being later becomes Christ. Augustine was aware of this possible misinterpretation and clarified his position in a number of places to exclude it. Augustine held that the creation of the man and the grace of union were coterminous.[31] This fact actually served to strengthen Augustine's argument. Since there was no man Christ before the grace of his assumption by the Word, any talk of prevenient merit bringing about that assumption would be nonsense.

Like Augustine's discussion in the *Enchiridion,* his argument in *De praedestinatione sanctorum* described the incarnation as a grace not in response to a dispute about the mode of union of the two natures, but rather in response to a dispute about the role of merit in human salvation. Augustine's main point with respect to the category of grace in Christology was to maintain God's initiative and execution of the plan of salvation by excluding prevenient human merit not only from Christology but also from every human conversion.

Because the Scythian monks also argued in an anti-Pelagian context, one might expect that Augustine's assertion that the incarnation was a paradigm of grace would be ready-made for the Scythian monks to use against their opponents. The Scythian monks, however, never used this argument. The most likely explanation for this lacuna, it seems to me, is that the Scythian monks, in addition to their opposition to the semi-Pelagians, were also very much focused on the question of the mode of union. They scrupulously avoided all language of grace in their descriptions of the incarnation. In fact, they explicitly rejected the idea that the uniting of the two natures was *secundum gratiam*. They listed this error along with the following erroneous notions of union: "according to affect or grace or dignity or equal honor or authority, or according to name or concord or illustration, or according to interior operation or personal uniting." Instead of these errors, they wished to affirm, with Cyril of Alexandria's third anathema, a "natural union" and, with Gregory of Nazianzus's *Epistle to Cledonium,* that the uniting took place *substantialiter.*[32] According to the way the Scythian monks framed the issues, there were two basic christological positions: the uniting of the two natures occurred either by grace or by nature. If by grace, then there really was no union at all. If by nature, then there was truly one person, whom they identified as the Word.

The Scythian monks found a different way of excluding merit from Christology. They made the point over and over again that God became Christ, Christ did not become God.[33] For them, this guaranteed that merit has no place in Christology because it ruled out the position, which they attributed to their opponents, that Christ became God "by advancement, not by nature" (*per provectum non per naturam*).[34] The suggestion here was that their opponents thought that the man somehow merited becoming God.

Even though the Scythian monks shared, then, Augustine's ultimate purpose to exclude prevenient merit both from the incarnation and from human salvation in general, Augustine's way of making this case, by speaking of a role for grace in the incarnation, created a dissonance with the Christology of the Scythian monks because they were apt to understand assertions of christological grace to refer to the mode of union, a concern which Augustine in his original context was not primarily addressing.

Conclusion

In the anti-Nestorian context of the sixth-century Theopaschite controversy, two concerns arose that distinguished this controversy from Augustine's original context. First, the Scythian monks were concerned to make the point that all Christ's actions and experiences, especially his most humiliating one, the crucifixion, applied to "One of the Trinity," that is, the Word. Second, the Scythian monks were concerned to show that the mode of the christological union was ontological rather than based on grace or good will.

Augustine must have sounded Nestorian when he was read with these questions in mind. His interpretive rule expressed in *De Trinitate,* which was originally intended to defend the deity of Christ, in the new context sounded like it was designed to separate out Christ's actions between two subjects. Second, his statement that Christ was called God because it was God who assumed him lacked the clarity that the Word was the only subject in Christ. Finally, his description of the role of grace in the incarnation, originally intended to exclude merit from Christology as well as soteriology, could have sounded like he was describing a mode of union based on good will rather than on an ontological foundation. It is no surprise, then, that the Scythian monks chose not to rely on Augustine as a primary authority for their christological position. Because the Scythian monks did not discuss these passages of Augustine, we cannot be certain whether they read them this way or whether they were sophisticated enough to place them in their original context. In any case, the problem was not Augustine himself, but the way his formulations could be interpreted in their new context. Regardless of their commitment to Augustine, the Scythian monks simply could not afford to use quotations from him that appeared uncomfortably close to what their opponents were saying.

This historical example of the way in which theological formulations change meanings when thrust into a new context has direct relevance for the struggle over the course of the last century to classify Augustine as either "Antiochene" or "Alexandrian."[35] In order to claim Augustine for one side or the other, one must read Augustine as if he were addressing the questions posed by the controversy between these two schools of thought.[36] The example of how Augustine fared in the Theopaschite controversy, however, suggests that such a procedure ultimately falsifies Augustine.

Notes

1. Leo, *Tome* 4 (in T. Herbert Bindley, ed., *The Oecumenical Documents of the Faith,* 4th ed. [Westport, Conn.: Greenwood, 1980], 170, lines 125–28). All translations are my own unless otherwise indicated.

2. *Libell. fid.* 29–34 (CCSL 85A, 23–25.361–413 [pp. 23–25, lines 361–413]).

3. The following documents follow this pattern: *Libellus fidei, Capitula,* and *Epistula ad episcopos*.

4. I am not including the *Capitula sancti Augustini* in this count because, although Cappuyns identifies John Maxentius as its compiler, I am trying to establish which works of Augustine the Scythian monks possessed in their entirety. A citation in a florilegium does not establish this. On the identity of the compiler, cf. D. M. Cappuyns, "L'origine des 'Capitula' d'Orange 529," *Recherches de Théologie Ancienne et Médiévale* 6 (1934): 135. For another view, see Glorie's introduction to the *Capitula sancti Augustini* in CCSL 85A, 246.

5. These are found in CCSL 85, 83–129, and CCSL 85A, 247–73, respectively.

6. *Libell. fid.* 9.15 (CCSL 85A, 15.193–94).

7. *Libell. fid.* 9.16 (CCSL 85A, 15.200–206).

8. *Exempla ss. patrum* 20 (CCSL 85, 90–91.120–26), *Exempla ss. patrum* 3–4 (CCSL 85, 85–86.17–26). For a more thorough discussion of the relationship between this florilegium and the Scythian monks, see Berthold Altaner, "Zum Schrifttum der 'skythischen' (gotischen) Mönche: Quellenkritische und literarische Untersuchungen," *Texte und Untersuchungen zur Geschichte der altchristlichen Literatur* 83 (1967): 489–506.

9. *Ep. Papae Hormisdae* 15 (CCSL 85A, 120–121.105–7).

10. *Resp. adv. epist.* 45 (CCSL 85A, 145.653).

11. "denique mox, post illam sententiam" (*Resp. adv. epist.* 48 [CCSL 85A, 146.690]), "inter initia antedicti primi libri sui" (*Resp. adv. epist.* 50 [CCSL 85A, 147.715–16]), "in eodem libro" (*Resp. adv. epist.* 53 [CCSL 85A, 149.766]), "post aliquanta" (*Resp. adv. epist.* 54 [CCSL 85A, 150.789–90]).

12. *Trin.* 1.7.14 (CCSL 50, 45.25–28): "Non itaque immerito scriptura utrumque dicit, et *aequalem patri* filium, et patrem maiorem filio. Illud enim propter *formam dei*, hoc autem propter *formam servi* sine ulla confusione intellegitur." *Trin.* 1.11.22 (CCSL 50, 60.1–4): "Quapropter cognita ista regula intellegendarum scripturarum de filio dei ut distinguamus quid in eis sonet secundum *formam dei* in qua est et *aequalis* est *patri*, et quid secundum *formam servi* quam accepit et *minor* est *patre*." *Trin.* 2.1.2 (CCSL 50, 81.4–6): "[Teneamus] tamquam canonicam regulam quomodo intellegatur *dei filius* et *aequalis patri* secundum *dei formam* in qua est et *minor patre* secundum *servi formam* quam accepit . . . ."

13. *Trin.* 1.7.14 (CCSL 50, 46.44–46). Translation by Edmund Hill, *The Trinity,* in *The Works of St. Augustine: A Translation for the 21st Century,* I/5 (Brooklyn, N.Y.: New City Press, 1991), 75.

14. *Trin.* 1.10.20 (CCSL 50, 57.35–37).

15. *Trin.* 1.7.14 (CCSL 50, 45.20–21). Translation by Hill, p. 74.

16. *Trin.* 1.13.28 (CCSL 50, 69.5–7).

17. In much the same way as I have offered unitive christological statements from Augustine to counterbalance the ones that seem to describe two acting subjects in Christ, the Scythian monks locate a unitive christological passage in Leo's epistles to counterbalance the *Tome*. See *Libell. fid.* 24 (CCSL 85A, 20.310–18).

18. Bindley, *The Oecumenical Documents,* 114.287–92. Translation by Edward Hardy, *Christology of the Later Fathers,* Library of Christian Classics (Philadelphia: Westminster, 1954), 353.

19. The text is found in Evagrius Scholasticus, *Ecclesiastical History* 3.14.113.9–11.

20. *Libell. fid.* 13.26 (CCSL 85A, 21.329–32).

21. *Dial. contra Nest.* 2.11 (CCSL 85A, 90.511–13).

22. *Prof. brev.* 3–4 (CCSL 85A, 34–35.14–36). Cf. *Ep. ad episc.* 8–9 (CCSL 85A, 162–163.128–56). The qualifications "according to his humanity" and "according to his divinity" do not change the fact that God (the Word) is the subject of Christ's human experiences. Such qualifications are meant to specify the means by which the Word is capable of undergoing human experiences. Cf. David Maxwell, "Crucified in the Flesh: Christological Confession or Evasive Qualification?" *Pro Ecclesia* 13 (2004): 70–81.

23. *Ep. ad episc.* 6 (CCSL 85A, 161.119–23).

24. *Trin.* 1.7.14 (CCSL 50, 46.44–46). Translation by Hill, p. 75.

25. *Dial. contra Nest.* 1.2 (CCSL 85A, 56–57.71–82).

26. Cf. *Dial. contra Nest.* 1.2 (CCSL 85A, 57.83–87).

27. *Enchir.* 11.36 (CCSL 46, 69.2–4).

28. *Enchir.* 11.36 (CCSL 46, 70.16–18).

29. *Praed.* 15.30 (PL 44, col. 981D).

30. *Praed.* 15.31 (PL 44, col. 982C).

31. *Praed.* 15.30 (PL 44, col. 982A). Cf. also *Arian.* 6.8: "ipsa assumptione creatur."

32. *Libell. fid.* 12 (CCSL 85A, 12–13.145–61). The Scythian monks understand "natural union" to imply not one nature, but rather that the union is composed of natures. Thus, when they reject a "personal" union in this context, they are rejecting a uniting of two persons.

33. *Cap.* 7 (CCSL 85A, 30.29–30), *Libell. fid.* 25 (CCSL 85A, 20.319–20), *Dial. contra Nest.* 1, cap. 8 (CCSL 85A, 53.19–20), *Ep. ad episc.* 11 (CCSL 85A, 163.168–69).

34. *Ep. ad episc.* 11 (CCSL 85A, 163, 170–71). Cf. *Libell. fid.* 25 (CCSL 85A, 20.322–23).

35. For a summary of the history of this debate, see John A. McGuckin, "Did Augustine's Christology Depend on Theodore of Mopsuestia?" *Rivista di storia e letteratura religiosa* 25 (1989): 444–48.

36. Joanne McWilliam Dewart, for example, seems to read Augustine this way when she assumes that Augustine's language in *Letter* 187 about God being present to Christ by grace is intended to define the mode of union and, that by affirming a union by grace, Augustine is denying a substantial union. See Dewart, "The Influence of Theodore of Mopsuestia on Augustine's *Letter 187*," *Augustinian Studies* 10 (1979): 118. Though Augustine is concerned with the way God is present, there is nothing in the context of *Letter* 187 to suggest that Augustine is attempting to define the mode of the union, or, even if he is, that he is attempting to choose between a union by grace and a substantial union. Both the question of mode of union and the range of possible answers are part of the framework of the struggle between Antioch and Alexandria that is being imposed upon Augustine. Cf. McGuckin, "Did Augustine's Christology Depend on Theodore of Mopsuestia?" 454.

II

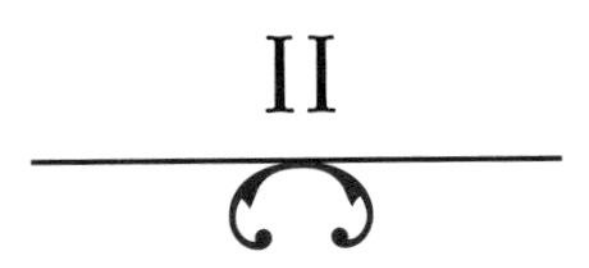

The Persistence of Decay

Bodily Disintegration and Cyrillian Christology

John J. O'Keefe

In one of the most memorable scenes from Fyodor Dostoyevsky's magisterial work *The Brothers Karamazov,* Alyosha's mentor, the monk Zosima, dies. Because of his exemplary life, many in the monastery and around the village in which the monastery is located expect that Zosima's death will be accompanied by some kind of miracle. Perhaps, some wonder publicly, he might even be one of those given the grace of incorruptibility, donning in death an even more public witness to the sanctity that he had exhibited in life. Scandalously, however, this is not to be: even before the prayers for the dead can be completed, the unmistakable odor of decay escapes from inside the dead monk's coffin. Zosima's "corruption" provokes feelings of bitter disappointment in his friends and quiet glee in those who disliked him. None of the observers exhibit indifference.

When I read that passage for the first time in my late teens I knew nothing about theology, but unlike most Americans, who are insulated from decay, I knew something of corruption. When I was ten or eleven years old my family took a trip to St. Croix, in the United States Virgin

Islands. I befriended the person who worked at the beach shack, selling cokes and passing out surfboards. One morning a terrible stink was coming from the shack, and I watched my new friend look around for the source. After a few minutes he moved some objects and discovered a decomposing rat sitting on the shelf. The rat was oozing with maggots, and it was quickly returning to the dust of the earth. This was my first experience of "corruption."

Years later when I began my studies in patristics, I did not immediately associate the word "corruption" (a standard translation of *phthora*) with the decay I had seen in the rat. To my untrained mind corruption meant moral turpitude, of the sort found in a "corrupt" cop or a "corrupt" politician. Certainly there are moral overtones in the meaning of *phthora,* but it would be erroneous to think that this was the primary meaning of the term in early Christian theological reflection. This fact has not been lost in modern Bible translation. Indeed, the loss of the sense of corruption as "decay" offers strong arguments for the translation of Romans 8:20–21 that appears in the new RSV: "for the creation was subjected to futility, not of its own will but by the will of the one who subjected it, in hope that the creation itself will be set free from its bondage to decay and will obtain the freedom of the glory of the children of God." This translation conveys the sense of physical decomposition far better than the English word "corruption." Similarly, when Paul wrote in 1 Corinthians 15 with respect to the resurrection of the dead that "what is sown in corruption is raised in incorruption," he meant primarily decay and lack of decay and not moral failure.

This may seem an odd way to begin an essay discussing later developments in the Christology of Cyril of Alexandria. However, such a beginning offers us the opportunity to explore a neglected side of the christological controversy. Elsewhere I have argued that in that debate Cyril advanced a christological argument that allowed him to maximize language defending the incarnation even when such language seemed to endanger a robust doctrine of divine impassibility.[1] This conviction led him into direct conflict with Nestorius, who found Cyril's emphasis on incarnation overly reckless and insufficiently attentive to the immutability of the divine nature. I do not wish to rehearse those arguments here. Instead, I will explore the later Christology that Cyril exemplifies from a slightly different angle. Rather than focus on Cyril's texts that highlight the identity of the Son of God and that attempt to explain how he could really become a flesh-and-blood human being without compromising his divinity, I focus on the human side of Cyril's christological thinking. It was not, in my view, simply a conceptual puzzle that motivated Cyril's efforts to defend the truth of God's presence in Jesus. Rather, Christ gave hope that the human race would one day be able to escape from the violent force of bodily corruption, putrefication, and decay.

Attention to the problem of decay and corruption can help modern readers access that hope more concretely. It can also help students of classical Christology break free of the tendency to dismiss Alexandrian Christology as "high." In contemporary theological discourse, high Christologies are thought to be "bad" because of their alleged inattention to experience and overemphasis on philosophical categories. We often fail fully to realize, however, that in making these distinctions we emphasize a particular kind of human experience over another. Modern low Christologies seek to emphasize the sacredness of the human here and now, as well as the way in which Christ sanctified human physical life as it is by means of his true humanness. Such an emphasis includes an eschatology that focuses on the realized elements of the Christian hope and, as such, fits comfortably in the modern Western world, where material prosperity facilitates a more favorable assessment of physical creation than was possible in the ancient world.

There is no space here to offer a full evaluation of the cultural roots of a theological insistence on low Christology. However, we serve the ancient Christian past poorly if we claim that only a low Christology of the modern sort can access human desire and flow from human experience. In fact, we have every reason to believe that ancient Alexandrian Christology was deeply and profoundly driven by particular human experience and particular human hopes. That these differed somewhat from our own should neither surprise nor scandalize us.

As already noted, early Christian concern with decay goes all the way back to Paul, for whom incorruption is a key component of the resurrected life. We would be hard-pressed to claim that this constitutes a major theme in Paul's work. However, as with many passages in Scripture, some take on a life of their own in a surprising manner. A classic example is the preoccupation with Romans 7 that has heavily determined Western debates about human freedom and God's grace. Similarly, preoccupation with Paul's reference to corruption and incorruption significantly influenced the development of classical Christology in the patristic tradition. The context of this essay does not allow for a comprehensive survey of the patristic reception of Paul's interest in incorruption. However, since Cyril was heavily influenced by Athanasius, and Athanasius in turn by Irenaeus,[2] a brief consideration of the presence of this theme in Irenaeus and Athanasius will help us to understand its impact on later christological thinking.

Corruption in Irenaeus and Athanasius

In Irenaeus's *Against the Heresies,* we frequently encounter the scandal of corruption. Significantly, references to the problem are not limited to Irenaeus's discussion of Christ's redemptive role. They also appear in the context of his discussion of the value systems of his Gnostic opponents. These, it would appear, were constructing their schemes of salvation on the assumption that corruption was a human evil that could not be overcome because it was intrinsically linked to the world of matter. According to Irenaeus, these individuals maintained that matter "is incapable" of receiving the spiritual and that "it is impossible that spiritual substance should ever come under the power of corruption."[3] This Gnostic antithesis between spirit and matter is hardly surprising, but the connection between Gnostic revulsion at material life and the reality of material decay is worth noting. Irenaeus certainly did so. Thus, in book 2, to cite another example, Gnostic views of salvation fall under scrutiny when they claim material substance falls "of necessity" into corruption and that Jesus came to transfer humanity out of this corruption-prone materiality to a place of spirit.[4]

For many ancient authors, even some Christian authors who vigorously defended the resurrection of the body, the Gnostic revulsion at decay would not have stirred much debate. According to Caroline

Walker Bynum, "horror at decay"[5] was a common sentiment. Citing a variety of ancient sources, Bynum captures some of the emotion that corruption and decay could arouse:

> Body is worse than dung, asserted the pagan Celsus (quoting Heraclitus); it is "a disgusting vessel of urine" and "bag of shit," said the Christian apologist Arnobius. It is perpetual mutation, explained the theologian Basil. It can be the food of fish or carrion beasts or even of human beings, said Cyril of Jerusalem and Macarius (quoting pagan objections); how then will it be reassembled? Who would want it back, asked Ambrose; it is only a wretched prison for the soul, which aches to escape from pain.[6]

Context could soften some of these judgments against bodily life, but probably not by very much. Bodily life was hard; according to historian Peter Brown,

> [Ancient society] was more helplessly exposed to death than is even the most afflicted underdeveloped country in the modern world. Citizens of the Roman Empire at its height, in the second century A.D., were born into the world with an average life expectancy of less than twenty-five years. Death fell savagely on the young. Those who survived childhood remained at risk. Only four out of every hundred men, and fewer women, lived beyond the age of fifty.[7]

In such a context of disgust, how can we account for the expectant optimism that accompanies the death of Dostoyevsky's Zosima? Alyosha Karamazov and many others clearly expect that some form of miraculous liberation from the bondage to decay will be materially visible on the body of the dead monk. They would not have been satisfied with an allegorical translation of "incorruption" into the language of the soul's escape from material bondage. The unfortunate arrival of Zosima's stink disappoints them precisely because of their implicit dissatisfaction with such rhetoric. Zosima's corruption reminds them painfully of their own approaching dissolution and challenges their hope that they will transcend it in resurrection. That the people have hope at all for a miraculous sign of saintly incorruption derives, at least in part, from the ancient vision of Irenaeus and the Christology that flows from it.

While Irenaeus's opponents may have been revolted by corruption and decay, Irenaeus himself made hope in its demise a centerpiece of his Christian vision. Nowhere is this more clear than in book 5 of *Against the Heresies.* Here, Irenaeus, like all of his contemporaries, defended the immortal character of the soul and recognized that the body is the aspect of human life that suffers from the sting of corruption. "For to die is to lose vital power," Irenaeus writes, "and to become henceforth breathless, inanimate, and devoid of motion, and to melt away into those component parts from which also it derived the commencement of its substance." This dissolution cannot happen to the soul, for it is "simple and not composite, so that it cannot be decomposed."[8]

One might expect that with such a traditional sense of the soul's immortality, Irenaeus would be tempted to reduce humanity to its soulish character, but he does not. Instead, he argues forcefully that the full weight of biblical revelation points to a salvation that includes the complete human, both the soul and the body. Indeed, it was the aim of saving physical creation itself, which includes humans with their bodies, that prompted the Son to become incarnate in the first place. For Irenaeus, when the Scriptures speak of death, "it is in reference to the flesh," the very same flesh that Paul promised would be restored when he declared with respect to our bodies that they are "sown in corruption, but raised to incorruption."[9]

This aspect of Irenaeus's teaching is well known. However, we can still miss the existential force of his commitment to this position. Readers of many works that describe Irenaeus's impact are less likely to be reminded of it than of the fact that he developed the notions of "apostolic succession" and "the rule of faith." Irenaeus's vision, however, reached far beyond his concerns about authority. Recall that one of the central tenets of the Gnostic worldview was revulsion at the idea of bodily life. Tertullian captures this sentiment well in his treatise *On the Flesh of Christ.* Reflecting upon what those with Gnostic sensibilities found unworthy in the idea of incarnation, he notes how much they hate the idea of the birth itself—"the filth of the generative seeds within the womb, of the bodily fluid and the blood; the loathsome, curdled lump of flesh which has to be fed for nine months off this same muck."[10] Irenaeus shared Tertullian's contempt for those who rejected Christ's flesh, and we must understand that this contempt was rooted in a profoundly different vision of what Christianity was about and of what Jesus had come to do.

The resurrection of the body out of corruption into an incorrupt, restored creation defines Irenaeus's central concern far better than worries about authority. He says what he says about authority in order to protect his core vision. For "inasmuch as the opinions of certain persons are derived from heretical discourses, they are both ignorant of God's dispensations, and of the mystery of the resurrection." They know nothing of the "earthly kingdom which is the commencement of incorruption" and in which the just will gradually take on characteristics of the divine nature. The resurrection of the dead will take place in the context of a creation renewed. This will be "that very creation in which they toiled or were afflicted, being proved in every way by suffering."[11] According to Irenaeus, "neither is the substance nor the essence of the creation annihilated, for faithful and true is He who has established it."[12] Indeed, when this world ends, as Irenaeus explains at the conclusion of his long book against the heresies, and all creation "flourishes in an incorruptible state . . . there will be a new heaven and a new earth in which the new man will remain forever, always holding fresh converse with God."[13]

Ireneaus's eschatological vision bore the marks of a literal millenarianism that did not appeal to succeeding generations of Christian thinkers. The presence of this literalism has led some to pay insufficient attention to the central core of his vision and the impact that it would have on succeeding Christian generations who, like Alyosha, tried to give an account of the "hope that was in them." However, if we pay attention, we can discern the persistence of this theme in the emerging Greek tradition.

Athanasius was clearly dismayed by the reality of death and decay. Because ancient writers generally do not reveal their inner feelings, it is dangerous to speculate about their motivations. However, to assume that the lack of explicit self-disclosure indicates an internalized apatheia would seem to miss the mark. Athanasius's *On the Incarnation,* although lacking first-person intimacy, displays considerable pathetic energy. We are surely not extracting more than that text can offer if we sense in chapter 6 a desperation at the human condition and a profound hopefulness in the face of God's dramatic intervention: "the race of men was being destroyed, and man who was rational and who had been made in the image was being obliterated; and the work of God was perishing." Indeed, Athanasius continues, "it would have been improper that what had once been created rational and had partaken of his Word, should perish and return again to non-existence through corruption."[14]

This text seems to anticipate the language of Saint Ignatius of Loyola. Writing centuries later, he also meditated on the sorry state of the human race when he asked those making the spiritual exercises to contemplate "how the three divine persons looked at all the plain or circuit of the world, full of men." We should, he added, consider "how seeing that all were going down to hell," the blessed Trinity determined that "the Second Person shall become man and save the human race . . . ."[15] Clearly, Ignatius lived in a vastly different age than Athanasius. He intended his *Spiritual Exercises* to move the heart and excite the retreatant to conversion. Athanasius's world was different, but to the extent that we can assume a continuity of human experience, we do a disservice to our account of past theological reflection if we fail to consider the human side of the equation: theology is not always constructed upon calculated syllogisms and the rigid application of logic. Life and death, love and desire, joy and loss—all of these are intangible factors that drive and motivate, even if unseen and unarticulated.

Thus, in a way, Athanasius's sense of the pathos of corruptible humanity influenced his lifelong quest to ensure the full divinity of the Son of God. It would not be unfair to say that Athanasius, like Irenaeus, was obsessed with bodily survival. Chapter 8 of *On the Incarnation* captures this. Because of the pervasive disease of human corruption, "the incorporeal and incorruptible and immaterial Word of God came to our realm." He did this "because he saw that the rational race was perishing and that death was reigning over them through corruption." Seeing this, God noted how improper such destruction was, and "he had pity on our race, and was merciful to our infirmity, and submitted to our corruption, and did endure the dominion of death." For this reason, Athanasius explains further, "he took to himself a body, and that not foreign to our own."[16]

Studies of the development of doctrine tend to concentrate on the inadequacy of Athanasius's christological imagery. Surely no Christology that imagines Jesus as God wearing humanity as a slipcover can be adequate to the task of taking seriously the human dimension of the incarnation. Defenders of modern ascending Christologies necessarily object. While these observations raise legitimate concerns, they can also deflect attention from the primary insight that Athanasius would have us grasp: corruption has grabbed, crippled, and devoured humanity, and only the invasions of God's divinizing power can correct our inevitable slide into nothingness. Athanasius himself explains:

> And this he did in his loving kindness in order that, as all die in him, the law concerning corruption in men might be abolished—since its power was concluded in the Lord's body and it would never again have influence over men who are like him—and in order that, as we had turned to corruption, he might turn them back again to incorruption and might give them life for death, in that he had made the body his own, and by the grace of the resurrection had rid them of death as straw is destroyed by fire.[17]

Such a transformation of human bodily existence could, in Athanasius's view, be effected only by the radical invasion of divinity into the creation. Death, like some kind of personified demon, clung to human bodies and dragged them down to corruption.[18] In response, only God, who is life by nature, could cling to bodily nature and drag it up, as it were, to incorruption.

Given this conviction about the human predicament and the divine cure, we should not be surprised at the energy with which Athanasius attacked the theology of Arius. A Son who is anything less than God could never hope to achieve this dramatically physical transformation in the human person. Far from evincing a revulsion at human bodily life, Athanasius's defense of the Son's complete divinity reveals his deep commitment to a vision of a humanity transformed.

Corruption in Cyril of Alexandria

If the Irenaean thread is present in Athanasius, can we say the same of Cyril of Alexandria? What, if any, are the clues that would indicate that the fifth-century patriarch of Alexandria conducted his own theological reflection with a similar revulsion at the destructive forces of corruption? This side of Cyril can be difficult to discover. Much of the academic discussion detailing his contribution has become entrenched in a distinction between Antiochene Christology and Alexandrian Christology, which depicts the Antiochene tradition as interested in the humanity of Jesus and the Alexandrian tradition as interested only in the divinity. Moreover, Cyril's behavior as bishop irritated even his defenders. The persecution of local Jews, his willingness to sanction violence against traditional temples, and his callous disregard for the lives of his opponents make efforts to describe him sympathetically seem imprudent at best and reckless at worst.

The dark side of Cyril (like the dark side of Athanasius, or even the dark side of Augustine) certainly exists and should not be ignored in any comprehensive assessment of his contribution to the formation of ancient Christian theology. Yet, we should also take care that our attention to his deficits not blind us from seeing his other side. If we are attentive we can discover the contours of a person with passionate convictions about the nature of God's promise and the gift that Christ brings to the human race.

Like Athanasius and virtually all patristic authors with the notable exception Augustine, Cyril does not directly reveal his inner world. We have no easy access to his hopes and fears or to his joys and sorrows, but we do have some access if we notice the clues. I have long been fascinated by an obscure passage from Cyril's *Third Letter to Nestorius.* After spending some time meditating on the divine origins of the Son and the sublime dignity of the Holy Spirit, Cyril abruptly shifts direction to the glories of the incarnation and the mystery of Mary, the mother of God. She is so named, not because the Son had a beginning in her womb, but because "he substantially united humanity with himself, and underwent fleshly birth from her womb." He did this "to bless the very origin of our existence." Indeed, "through a woman's giving birth to him united with flesh," he meant that

> the curse on the whole race which dispatches our earthly bodies to death should cease as well as the words (from now on rendered null and void by him) "in sorrow you shall bear children" (Gen 3:16), and he intended to prove true the prophet's utterance, "Death waxed strong and swallowed and again God took away every tear from every countenance" (Isa 25:8). This is our reason for affirming of him that he personally blessed marriage by his Incarnation as well as by responding to the invitation to leave for Cana in Galilee along with the holy apostles.[19]

In reading this passage, it would be tempting to dwell on possible insufficiencies in Cyril's description of the relationship between the divine and human natures in the one man Jesus. Alternatively, we could ponder the growing sophistication of Cyril's concept of hypostatic union. In both cases we would be asking good questions. However, if we focus only on dominant melodies we may fail to hear significant descants.

Clearly, Cyril developed a more sophisticated way to account for the union of humanity and divinity in Jesus as a result of Nestorius's challenge to his less sophisticated early account. Yet, we cannot conclude that Nestorius's challenge drove Cyril's vision. That vision existed before any theological confrontation. In the passage cited above, we see it coming to the surface: we glimpse a primordial insight that the later theology was designed to defend, not the other way around. Consider the close connection between the assertion of blessing on the origin of human existence—Christ's incarnation in the womb of Mary as a human person—and the "curse . . . which dispatches our earthly bodies to death." Note how quickly this is followed by the quotations from Genesis and Isaiah emphasizing the invasion and removal of sorrow from the human condition. These sentiments reveal something about Cyril himself.

Single instances rarely inspire trust, but this one does not stand alone. Such sentiments appear in Cyril's writing well before the christological controversy. For example, in the *Commentary on John,* possibly one of Cyril's earliest works,[20] we encounter the following, which is worth quoting at length:

> It was not otherwise possible for man, being of a nature which perishes, to escape death, unless he recovered that ancient grace, and partook once more of God who holds all things together in being and preserves them in life through the Son and the Spirit. Therefore, his only-begotten Word has become a partaker of flesh and blood (Heb 2:14), that is, he has become man, though being life by nature, and begotten of the life that is by nature, that is, of God the Father, so that, having united himself with the flesh which perishes according to the law of its own nature . . . he might restore it to his own life and render it through himself a partaker of God the Father . . . . And he wears our nature, refashioning it to his own life.[21]

The extent to which Cyril's vision of salvation depends upon an appropriation of divine life made possible by the Son's incarnation has been documented in an excellent study by Daniel Keating.[22] This particular passage from the *Commentary on John* aptly captures this dimension of Cyril's understanding. Human beings are born with a corruptible nature—"a nature which perishes." Only the intervention of a nature that does not perish is sufficiently powerful to alter our trajectory toward dissolution. We should not be confused here: Cyril, like Athanasius, and, more remotely, Irenaeus, was not thinking about perishing in an amorphous moral sense. To perish meant to succumb to decay.

Keeping this in mind helps to contextualize some of Cyril's remarks that could lead one to think that in his theology the humanity of Jesus was a ruse. For example, in his *Dialogues on the Trinity,* Cyril frequently explains that the nature of the Son is far from those beings on earth who are subject to corruption.[23] Reading these passages without due reference to the soteriological implications fundamentally distorts Cyril's point. The incorruptibility of the Son is necessary to ensure the transformation of the person from corruption to incorruption. Further passages in the dialogues make this connection explicit: the Son "ascended after having destroyed the bonds of death. He brought us to a state of sanctification" by establishing "anew" the ancient beauty of nature and by the bestowal of the Holy Spirit.[24]

Cyril's approach can also clearly be seen in his famous dialogue *That Christ Is One.* To cite an example, Cyril is eager to show that the Son's incarnation must be taken literally. He argues against those who claim that we should take this language metaphorically. When Paul in Galatians and 2 Corinthians asserts that Jesus became a "curse" and "sin" for us, they maintain, he clearly did not mean this literally; it has to do with Christ's power to undo the curse and to undo sin. So also, they say, language about the Word becoming flesh should not be taken literally. Cyril's response is instructive:

> In that case, if it is true that the Word became flesh in exactly the same way that he became curse and sin, which is how they understand it, then surely he must have become flesh for the suppression of flesh? But how would this serve to exhibit the incorruptibility and imperishability of flesh which he achieved, first of all in his own body? For he did not allow it to remain mortal and subject to corruption, thus allowing the penalty of Adam's transgression to continue to pass on to us, but since it was his own and personal flesh, that of the incorruptible God, he set it beyond death and corruption.[25]

These sentiments appear throughout the text, and, when observed in their soteriological context, they offer evidence against an easy characterization of Cyril's Christology as hopelessly naive about Christ's humanity. Christ's divine humanity transforms our corruption into his incorruption. Incorruption is the true, intended form of human nature.

Cyril's commentaries were, of course, directed to a fairly sophisticated audience. However, we can also observe similar themes permeating official patriarchal messages directed to his entire flock. The *Festal Letters* provide the best vantage point from which to observe this in action. Following ancient tradition, each year of his episcopate Cyril composed a festal letter whose primary purpose was to announce the date of Easter and the beginning of Lent. These letters also provided him with the opportunity to reflect pastorally on the state of his diocese. Fortunately for those who study Cyril, we possess letters from nearly every year of his episcopacy. In these letters the themes of corruption and deliverance from corruption make frequent appearances. Particularly striking is a text from *Letter* 5, written in preparation for Easter of 417:

> What is it, then, that makes this joyful noise so timely and decides that we must exult and lift up to the Savior his death as something sacred? I know that you know, but I will explain it anyway. Death has been conquered, which refused to be conquered. Corruption has been made new. Invincible suffering has been destroyed. Hell, stricken with insatiable greed, and never satisfied with those who had died, has learned, all unwillingly, what it could not bear to learn earlier. For it does not strive to get hold of those who are still falling, but has already disgorged those already taken, having suffered a wonderful desolation by the Savior's power. For he paid it a visit with the words, "Come out! You in the darkness, show yourselves!" And having made his proclamation to the spirits in hell, who had once disobeyed, he ascended victorious, having raised up his own temple as a kind of first-fruits of our hope, made resurrection from the dead a way on which nature can travel, and performed for us other good things as well.[26]

The rhetorical juxtaposition of contrasting themes evokes strong emotions: death is conquered; corruption is made new; the invincible is destroyed; hell the desolator is desolated. Those who heard Cyril's words would recognize the experience that they evoke and relish the hope that they offered. Christological explanations of the mechanism by which death is desolated are, in many ways, secondary to the profound human experience that drives them.

Similar examples in the festal letter are not difficult to find. *Letter* 10, especially, delivers the whole package, from the evocation of the pathos of death to the transforming power of the incarnate Son of God. However, one particular passage stands out. In *Letter* 10, Cyril reflects on corruption and resurrection in conjunction with an interpretation of the deeper meaning of "manna from heaven." "After shaking off the corruption dwelling in our bodies," he notes, paraphrasing Paul, "we will put on instead the glory of incorruptibility." This will not happen by denying our physical human nature; rather, it will be in a "refashioning" that captures the "honor of incorruptibility." This truth about our transformation, Cyril argues, is rooted in the Scriptures themselves and not just in Paul. The story in Exodus 16 about the manna from heaven functions as a type of the resurrected body. Cyril notes that when the Israelites tried to keep the manna overnight for themselves (Exod 16:20), it became corrupted, according to its nature. However, when God commanded that some be kept as an example for future generations (Exod 16:33–34), it was not corrupted because it was placed in God's presence. "That this is what will happen to us too I think no one will doubt." When Christ places us "in the presence of God the Father," our bodies will become incorruptible. "For we will no longer be subject to corruption, but rather will remain forever. The manna was taken as an example of this reality." This reflection on the transforming power of God, typified in the manna, leads Cyril to an immediate reflection on the significance of the incarnation:

> Let us reflect, then, that being by nature God, since he even appeared from God, shining forth ineffably and incomprehensibly from God the Father's very substance, he is for this reason quite reasonably regarded as completely in his form and in equality with him, as is in fact true; and yet "he humbled himself," as scripture says, "taking the form of a slave" (Phil 2:7) and becoming as we are, that we might become as he is, refashioned by the activity of the Spirit into his likeness by grace. Since then he is one of us, he is a human being like us because of us; but he is God because of himself and the one who begot him, both before the Incarnation and when he became a human being. For it was not possible that he who is from God by nature should not be God, even if "he became flesh," as John says (Jn 1:14).[27]

In this text we can easily discern some of the passages from the New Testament that Cyril uses most frequently in the articulation of his Christology.[28] However, it is worth emphasizing that Cyril quoted these texts not as part of some abstract argument about the divine nature of the Son of God. Rather, they appear in a pastoral letter and function to build up the hope of his hearers that death will not have the final word. In other words, a human experience drives his insight, the human experience of death and dissolution.

Conclusion

More examples could be assembled to support the point I have been emphasizing in this essay. However, these here should suffice to show the extent to which easy dismissals of Cyril's (or Athanasius's) Christology as irredeemably "high" miss the human realities that motivated its development and articulation. Alexandrian Christology may not embody contemporary sensibilities about the value of ordinary human life and subjective human experience, but it does embody actual sensibilities about actual human lives. We should recall that this ancient Alexandrian diagnosis of the human problem, along with the prescribed cure, had tremendous staying power in the subsequent Christian tradition. Indeed, in the nineteenth century it was still actively firing the imagination of one of the world's greatest authors. Alyosha Karamazov knew nothing about the modern quest to raise up the ordinary, but he did know something about God's promise to transform that which was broken and consigned to decay. If we recognize this, we can understand the disappointment caused by Zosima's decay, and, in recognizing the source of Alyosha's bitterness, we may come to reverence the depth of the hope that was in those ancients who heard Paul's promise of transformation and received it in their hearts.

Notes

1. John J. O'Keefe, "Impassible Suffering? Divine Impassibility and Fifth-Century Christology," *Theological Studies* 58 (1997): 39–60.

2. K. Anatolios, "The Influence of Irenaeus on Athanasius," in *Studia Patristica* 36 (Louvain: Peeters, 2001), 463–76.

3. Irenaeus, *Against the Heresies* (*Haer.*) 1.6.2. All translations from *NPNF,* vol. 1.

4. *Haer*. 2.24.6.

5. Caroline Walker Bynum, *The Resurrection of the Body in Western Christianity, 200–1336* (New York: Columbia University Press, 1995), 84.

6. Ibid., 61.

7. Peter Brown, *The Body and Society: Men, Women, and Sexual Renunciation in Early Christianity* (New York: Columbia University Press, 1988), 6.

8. *Haer.* 5.7.1.

9. *Haer.* 5.7.1.

10. Richard A. Norris, *The Christological Controversy* (Philadelphia: Fortress, 1980), 67.

11. *Haer.* 5.32.1.

12. *Haer.* 5.36.1.

13. *Haer.* 5.36.1.

14. Athanasius, *On the Incarnation* (*Inc.*) 6.15 (the translation is from *Contra Gentes and De Incarnatione,* ed. and trans. Robert W. Thomson [Oxford: Clarendon Press, 1971], 147–49).

15. Ignatius of Loyola, *The Spiritual Exercises* 102. The translation is from David L. Fleming, S.J., *Draw Me into Your Friendship: The Spiritual Exercises, A Literal Translation and a Contemporary Reading* (St. Louis: The Institute of Jesuit Sources, 1996).

16. Athanasius, *Inc.* 8.1–18.

17. *Inc.* 8.28–35.

18. *Inc.* 8.44.

19. Cyril of Alexandria, *Third Letter to Nestorius* 11. The translation is from Cyril of Alexandria, *Select Letters,* ed. and trans. Lionel R. Wickham (Oxford: Clarendon Press, 1983), 29.

20. For a discussion of the dating of Cyril's corpus, cf. G. Jouassard, "L'Activité littéraire de Saint Cyrille d'Alexandria jusqu' à 428: Essai de Chronologie et de Synthèse," in *Mélanges E. Podechard: Études des sciences religieuses offertes pour son émériat au Doyen Honoraire de la Faculté de Théologie de Lyone* (Lyon: Facultés Catholiques, 1945), and his "La date des écrit antiarien de saint Cyrille d'Alexandrie," *Revue Bénédictine* 87 (1977): 172–78.

21. *Jo.* 14.20 (Cyril of Alexandria, *Sancti Patris Nostri Cyrilli Archiepiscopi Alexandrini in D. Joannis Evangelium,* ed. Philip E. Pusey, vol. 2 [Oxford: Clarendon, 1872], 485–86, as quoted by Daniel Keating, *The Appropriation of Divine Life in Cyril of Alexandria* [Oxford: Oxford University Press, 2004], 1). Cf. also Cyril's *Commentary on the Gospel according to John,* Pusey, vol. 2, 314, 315, 317–18, and 321.

22. See previous note for reference to Keating's study.

23. Cf. Cyril of Alexandria, *Dialogues sur la Trinité,* ed. and trans. G. M. de Durand, SC 231 (Paris: Cerf, 1976), 206.3ff. (412a); 216.21ff. (415c); 242.39ff. (423e).

24. Cyril of Alexandria, *Dialogues sur la Trinité,* ed. and trans. G. M. de Durand, SC 237 (Paris: Cerf, 1977), 108.25–39 (494c–d).

25. Cyril of Alexandria, *Deux dialogues christologiques,* ed. and trans. G. M. de Durand, SC 97 (Paris: Cerf, 1964), 720b–c. The translation is from John A. McGuckin, *St. Cyril of Alexandria on the Unity of Christ* (Crestwood, N.Y.: St. Vladimir's Seminary Press, 1995), 57.

26. Cyril of Alexandria, *Lettres festales: I–VI,* ed. and trans. P. Evieux, W. H. Burns, and L. Arragon, SC 372 (Paris: Cerf, 1991), 284.26–42.

27. Cyril of Alexandria, *Lettres festales: VII–XI,* ed. and trans. P. Evieux, SC 392 (Paris: Cerf, 1993), 10.470–92.

28. Cf. John J. O'Keefe, "A Letter that Killeth: Toward a Reassessment of Antiochene Exegesis," *Journal of Early Christian Studies* 8 (2000): 83–104.

12

Mystery or Conundrum?

The Apprehension of Christ in the Chalcedonian Definition

John A. McGuckin

I remember once, in an interdisciplinary meeting of university professors and graduate students, mainly from Classics and Religion, the sardonic remark that New Testament "types"[1] had so trampled their small number of texts into the ground, with such vast tonnage of commentary compressing them into an impenetrable density, that any hope for a sensible future of exegesis seemed ill-grounded. I cannot remember a satisfying answer being returned on the occasion. Chalcedon seems, in many respects, a similar battleground for patristic "types." Hardly anyone can be found who has not something to say on the subject, in and outside the discipline. A serious Chalcedonian bibliography would need an industrial truck to move it around campus, even if one ignored the near-infinite number of books that had at least a passing pundit's reference to that council. One is reminded of Gregory of Nyssa trying to concentrate while his bath attendant (so he complains) insisted on telling him the ins and outs of trinitarian *perichoresis*.[2] (That, incidentally, must be the most well-repeated aphorism about patristics of the modern age, apart from Origen's alleged self-castration, which was highly unlikely). Most have taken Gregory's complaint at face value, smiling at the presumptuousness of a water-boiler instructing one of the most learned men of his generation, and smiling too at the class-ism of the Cappadocian bishop. But we moderns ought not to presume we understand all the ramifications of his joke, nor feel smug in a putatively class-less superiority, especially when we consider that his greatest opponents in the city where he was hoping to have his bath were Aetios (a former repairer of water boilers) and Eunomius (who had just presided over the canonization of Aetios as a thaumaturg, while denouncing Basil, Gregory's recently deceased brother, as a charlatan). Here, as is usually the case in all theological and historical writing, context matters. Scores were being settled in the real world; people were being held to account. Whether it concerns Gregory's bath attendant, or the infinitely greater complexity of the Council of Chalcedon, without the proper context one reads the various melodies as disastrously as a musician who accidentally inverts a medieval score that does not have give-away tails for the correct orientation of the notes. What Gregory meant, I propose, was not that the average person in Byzantium spent the day discoursing about theology (*pace* Yeats), but that the Neo-Arians had done their groundwork well, and he was signaling to his friends in advance that the outcome of the Council of Constantinople 381 was far from secure, simply because Theodosius I was himself a Nicene.

For its part, the message of Chalcedon has been decried by theologians of every stripe, as a prime example of mechanistic befuddlement, as a relic of patriarchal obscurantism, as a hopeless enmeshment in historical compromising (thereby betraying an unconscious debt to the Chalcedonian fathers that immiscibility is a "consummation devoutly to be wished"). Harnack even called it "the bankruptcy of Greek theology." The loudest critics of all, however, often turn out to be those who have no Greek, sometimes no connection with the context, or even text, of Chalcedon itself, beyond the digests of the symbolic statement that are presented in standard history of doctrine textbooks, and mostly of the type that were written in that period of European patristic study where it was fashionable to decry the aridity of such "Byzantine" obscurantism. The implicit racism of such views of the "Greeks" remains to be excavated, of course, but that is a topic for another day. Few are they who have been able to master the nuances of the languages, the historical contexts, and the many varieties of true religious and ethical passion that were the real origination of those difficult texts which remain before us as our historical record (and for several of us as the authoritative statements of our faith). Brian Daley has certainly been one of these *aves rarae,* and it is an honor to offer this brief essay as a *festschriftliche* tribute to someone whose work has, across many years, illuminated all that to which he has turned his attention, especially the christological domain which has been such a focus of his labors.

The Road to Chalcedon

The enterprise of the Council of Chalcedon, considered for its theological purpose, can be briefly stated.[3] At the time of the death of Theodosius II,[4] which precipitated the calling of a new synod, there was a widespread desire among the bishops to rein in what was seen as the atrocious high-handedness of Dioscorus, the bishop of Alexandria. Less enthusiasm was felt among the Eastern bishops to remedy the latter's apparent disregard for the careful "ecumenical" dialogue that Cyril had agreed to (brokered by Proclus and the Constantinopolitan court) in the years after Ephesus I. That settlement, culminating in 433 in the *Formula of Reunion,*[5] had come into crisis following the death of its chief negotiators: Cyril himself, Proclus of Constantinople, John of Antioch, and most recently Theodosius II. Only Theodoret (the probable author of the *Formula*) remained, which is why he was a special target for many in the conciliar proceedings in 449.[6] Even before Ephesus II, that ecumenical settlement had always represented only a tentative peace. In private writings at the end of his life Cyril had expressed unwavering scorn for the "great lights" of the Syrian tradition, Diodore and Theodore of Mopsuestia, indicating that Theodore ought to be regarded as much a heretic as Nestorius. It did not need much of a perceived slight to set the furor off all over again, and this was exactly what the trial of Eutyches provided, and why this apparently small incident in turn set off the forest fires that led not only to Ephesus in 449, but Chalcedon in 451, and Constantinople II in 553.

Eutyches was, by that stage, an old and revered archimandrite, protected by the grand chamberlain Chrysaphios and the emperor himself, but hated by empress Pulcheria, who was bent on the downfall of the powerful eunuch who had closed her out of state counsels. Pulcheria was thus more than happy to orchestrate the opposition to her brother's religious policy, if by doing so she could diminish the political credibility of her rival[7] and weaken the patronage the equally-despised Empress Eudoxia was exercising, at a distance, through her separate alliance with him. More Cyrilline than Cyril himself, Eutyches was a walking target for many powerful factions. It was he who had been the first to cast a stone in the old days, by raising complaints against the new archbishop, Nestorius, in 428, very shortly after the latter's installation. Popular imagination too trustingly accepts Pope Leo's caricature of him as a dim old man. Eutyches was far from that. But while his theological "extremism" was not necessarily popular in the Great City (and certainly not with the Syrians or Romans), many of the Greek bishops outside Egypt were as loathe to condemn him as they were to exonerate him. This is exactly why Flavian's tepid censure of the old man at an internal synod in Constantinople brought down on his own head the wrath of Pope Leo. What the Romans were not aware of, or were perhaps choosing to ignore, was that the Greeks knew the situation had radically altered between the possibility of the Constantinopolitan settlement of 433, and the realities operative on the eve of Chalcedon. Most of the "non-involved" Greek bishops attending both councils at Ephesus in 449 and Chalcedon in 451 were deeply aware of the lively possibility of a major rift that threatened to tear the Eastern church into three parts, dividing all its patriarchates from each other: Syria, Constantinople, and Alexandria, together with the considerable territories each also represented. This is of course exactly what would happen in the Chalcedonian aftermath, though probably no one in their wildest imaginings then ever thought that a temporary incapacity to reconcile differences would endure into a schism that would last for a millennium and a half. Dioscorus's excessively robust attempt to settle the matter as he thought Cyril would have done it, was both politically and theologically inept. His blatant siding with Eutyches, and his disregard of the legitimate concerns of Syria and Rome, when added to his high-handed dealings at the synod of 449, were significant in pushing away chances at reconciliation.

When the opportunity for a fresh consideration of the christological problem presented itself, with Pulcheria and Marcian's willingness to address the complaints of the papacy in late 450, the hearts of many of the Greek bishops must have sunk. It was not as if the Roman agenda was not already known. Leo had already sent the *Tomus Ad Flavianum* to be read out at Ephesus 449, and had been infuriated when Dioscorus had suppressed it. Battle lines had been drawn up very clearly. To most of the easterners the prospect was simply that of an all-out war between christological positions that had, by attrition, been hardening into a straightforward conflict over terminology understood in the narrowest of parameters. By "narrowest" I mean the entire dispute being focused on the question of a "one or the other" kind of answer to the question: "One nature or two natures after the Union?" European church history books have long been used to seeing this whole intellectual line of development through the lens of the Western tradition, and in particular, the figure of Leo. It is almost a cliché to see Leo's "clarity" contrasted with the political and intellectual shenanigans of the Greeks. But this is a long-standing lens that is necessary to resist. Clear, Leo may well have been. Even admirable may have been the intent to impose a stark matrix over the ins and outs of the christological puzzle: but the terms of the Roman settlement were, it could equally be argued, too abrupt, and too disconnected from the reality of the delicate ecumenical balance that constituted the affairs of the easterners in the mid-fifth century. This is not to advocate fudge (as many an emperor and patriarch would do in the years after Chalcedon); it is rather to state that the process of approaching a christological settlement in the Roman manner gave too high a valency to logical clarity, over the more ancient patterns of thinking that had gone on at the many former synodical processes of the Eastern church, always working on the principle that a conciliar gathering was not about forming new doctrine, simply about stating the basic parameters of the ancient doctrine in a suitably reverential way that addressed new crises, through a pattern of already, popularly validated doxological confession.

The Spirit of the Creeds: A Thesis

I will return to this notion in due course. It concerns the ancient synodical belief that the *vox episcoporum* in synodical assembly is a prophetic one that restates the church's doxological confession. The first recourse to synodical "statement" (we can think of the Councils of Nicaea I and Constantinople I as examples) elevated the Creed as the fundamental statement of faith, and did so insofar as it was understood as a very basic catechumenal confession of praise: a recitation in faith of the simplest form of restating the salvation story. We may tend to regard Creeds today as doctrinal summaries, but they began life as liturgical prayers, and were still being used as such when they were admitted into the conciliar record (indeed this was the intent of Justinian when they were inserted into Eucharistic liturgy, as well as baptismal liturgy, after the sixth century). So when occasion demanded more precision, as at Nicaea, a baptismal prayer was brought forward, and a few *clausulae* were added to refine it—but not to the extent that the prayer itself lost its primary status. The insistence was always retained: theological articulation of the faith, at important synods, must needs be doxological. In short, what was required in times of crisis, by the assembled episcopate, was not the resolution of theological conundrums, but the restatement of the soteriological mystery in doxological form that would provide the correct lens for approaching such problems. This is a critical point. For I would like to suggest the thesis subsequently, that this is exactly where Leo's *Dogmatic Epistle to Flavian* (the *Tome*) falls short, and that it was for this reason (as well as reasons of politically wishing to avoid inflaming antagonisms in the East) that most of the Chalcedonian bishops at first were reluctant to admit it beyond the very broad acclamation, "Leo and Cyril think alike." When pressed, by imperial authority, to a more exact statement, the long stalling arguments that took up the dogmatic sessions of Chalcedon were entirely about shifting away from Leo's terms until as much restatement and distance could be managed as possible. The eventual restatement of the Chalcedonian *symbolon* is something that the easterners felt more at ease with—and this (not least) because it had more of the character of a doxology than the Leonine *Tome*.

In its origins the christological controversy was largely about settling on agreed semantics. Through much confusion, the different parties had moved through the various possibilities presented by "new christological terms," such as *physis, prosopon, hypostasis,* and complexly vying structures of christological models such as *synapheia, krasis, mixis,* and *henosis.* We may now take all of these major shifts in terminology in our stride, but to have argued the way through the thicket of semantic difficulties of this order, with a terminology that was still in process of being created (and notions of personhood that had not yet existed in classical philosophy),[8] is little short of miraculous. That such a wonderful development and coherent progress toward international communion should be so strictly relegated to the question, "One nature or two natures after the union?" was a tragic eventuality, whose impact still remains to damage the international communion of the Christians, and is especially felt in the East, where a profound spirit of harmony exists liturgically, and spiritually, among churches who continually sense their common unity, while being perennially faced with doctrinal and jurisdictional separation.

Why the issue should have "threatened" polarization in this way is largely to be laid at the door of a major fault line having developed between Alexandrian and Antiochene traditions of thought in the mid-fourth century. Enough has already been written on this theme to have established clearly enough, however, that the "Two Sons" theory of the Syrians was not what the Alexandrians heard it to be, and takes on an entirely different aspect when read in Syriac, than when read in Greek translation. If the "Assumed Man" in Syriac means no more than the "human nature" in Greek, then we begin to see to what extent confused semantics can be blamed for much of the crisis of the fifth century. Even if this is too rosy a view, and we were to conclude that Theodore and Diodore really did have a defective understanding of the composite unity of the God-man, then so clear and passionate and profound a theologian as Theodoret could still show definitively that by the early fifth century the Syrian church was ready to move on from its earlier "Sons" language, in the cause of international communion, and adopt the substance of the single-subject Christology which was increasingly emerging as the point of contention. By the end of his life, as instanced in the *Eranistes* (by all accounts a serious and unremitting assault on Eutyches' position in theology), the same Theodoret who as a young man had expressed grave doubts about Cyril's sanity, as well as his incipient Apollinarism, all because the Alexandrian had dared use the word "hypostasis," was himself using hypostatic language as the powerful medium of his message. What does this suggest? That the christological fault line between Alexandria and Syria was healing, if not healed, and would have merged in a generation or less—so long as precipitate action had not been taken to press a point that perhaps did not need to be insisted on.

What I mean to suggest here, of course, is that Chalcedon proved to be the last straw for many in the East, not because of the ongoing argument between the Syrians and the Alexandrians but because a new element had been stirred into the mix: precisely the narrowing of the question down to "One or two natures after the Union?" This focused all eyes on the interpretation of the concept of "nature" (*physis, ousia, natura*) in a way that brought with it also the unavoidable corollary that the Romans who pressed this agenda had to be listened to for what they had to say about that concept of "nature." And they had a lot to say. Being an ancient tradition, they had much to quarry from, as they instinctively reached back into their own comparatively isolated patterns of thought for a definitive answer, instead of listening to the contemporary debate as it had been unfolding in the rich decades from 431 to 452. This default mechanism of turning back to a distinctively Roman past (as opposed to being open to the more messy ecumenical consensus of all the traditions and languages of the East) was understandable, but fatal for the cause of unity. It was, after all, what Rome was famed for: a traditionalist and secure source of ancient practice. On this basis Rome had built up its large prestige in Christian antiquity. But its weakness was that when Leo quarried far and wide among the Latins for the sources of his *Tome to Flavian*[9] he introduced into the debate a mechanistic, typically Latin, idea of person, that took its origins in the Latin language's conception of person as "that factor which stands as possessor of a generic nature." The highly practical language of the Romans approached individual identity through the legal notion of possession. This explains why the *Tome* (and its literary and intellectual remains in the Chalcedonian statement) is very good at conceiving "balances" and "delimitations" (the separate rights and characters of the two natures possessed by the Logos, for example), but is comparatively tone deaf to the central notion that had been driving the christological problem in the East—which was the way the natures mysteriously ran into consilience: the word "mysteriously" signifying here exactly what the ancients meant by it—sacramentally or salvifically. After the era of the Cappadocians, consilience into unity was the central issue of all Greek religious discourse on Christ, and this because that consilience was commonly regarded as the absolute paradigm of how the Word of God, within the great and sacred mystery of the incarnation, caught up the entirety of humanity's "nature" and deified it; that is, how humanity, through Christ, had a consilience into God; or put another way—how Christology functioned always as soteriology, if it was to be authentic.

Possession was about something else: about keeping things intact. Consilience to union is about a view of natures as themselves fluidly capable of being reconfigured. Cyril had deeply impressed this on most of Greek theology from decades before. His point was that the human nature of Jesus was not just common, unredeemed, human nature, or Adamic nature. It was the nature of a New Adam. The common spittle of this God-Man was sight-restoring. The "mere" human flesh of this God-Man was (eucharistically) life-endowing; the simple word of this God-Man was life-restorative (as in the Lazarus episode). As much as he was truly human, therefore, he was "New Creation humanity." His own New Creation humanity. This was a dynamic notion that the Greeks wished to preserve, for it was at the heart of all they understood by the principles of incarnational soteriology. Being strict about possessions seemed singularly ill-fitting a response to the Lord who voluntarily emptied himself out as a pauper, and so lavishly enriched the dying and destitute mortal race. Possession here gave way to gift and grace. The correct response to which, in turn, was the doxology of the praise of the church which recognized the mystery of life-giving faith, even through the vagaries of semantic problems.

And this is where we return, for our ending, to the issue stated earlier: that bishops in synod were traditionally expected to produce not new theology, but old doxology that would illuminate new difficulties. The imposition of Leo's language, written from a different perspective that had no liturgical embeddedness in it at all, but was simply a cut-and-paste job from the old and prestigious teachers of the Latin world, threw the Chalcedonian fathers slightly off balance, but did not derail them. They ultimately refused to make Leo's language the sole outcome of Chalcedon. This was not, as has sometimes been suggested, Greek *hybris* holding out against Roman stubbornness. I propose that it was traditional Greek elevation of liturgical doxology, over legal semantic precision.

Doxology and Chalcedon

We thus end with the central terms of the Chalcedonian settlement. But instead of deconstructing the *symbolon* to see what its origins were, or to make some form of intellectual or literary "balance" between the *clausulae* (and how many commentators have simply presumed this was all about balance?), let us see what different perspective we gain if we isolate the doxological skeleton (just as the baptismal creed was the skeletal structure of Nicaea) from the occasional *scholia* that were felt to be necessary for this particular occasion (again by comparison to Nicaea, such as the *Homoousion,* or the intruded *anathemata*). This is, I suggest, what we get if we stop looking at the Chalcedonian marginal notes and look at the doxological core, the "Prayer to the Savior."

The prolegomena to the synodical statement (lines 1–35) describes a fundamentally important context that ought not to be excised as if it were simple blather: that the Chalcedonian settlement is simply the faith of the Creeds of Nicaea and Constantinople. It offers no new creed to replace these cardinal statements of faith. In addition, it endorses the precise christological settlement that was achieved at Ephesus I. The bishops quote both creeds (Nicaea and Constantinople) in full, and then go on (lines 87–100) to endorse the (Ephesine) christological *Epistles* of Cyril and the *Tome to Flavian* as authoritative writings, the one for refuting Nestorius, the other for censuring Eutyches. After that point it makes its final *ekthesis* in the words we know so well. In what follows here, I have recast that *symbolon,* taking it out of the language of *anathema* and restoring it to the doxological *stasis* from which it originated. Although they have said that their creed is no different from Nicaea or Constantinople, their utterance makes it slightly nuanced, nonetheless. In a positivist light it would run like this, with the issue of "two natures before and one after?" being the pivot of the confessional statement, and thus set in the doxology to hem it in and contextualize how to exegete the question:

We believe in the single Son.
We believe in the impassible deity of the Son.
We believe that the Son does not mix up or confuse natures.
We believe that the Son took up our form, as the form of a servant.
We believe that there were not two natures before the Union,
  becoming a new nature after it.
We believe what the Fathers believed.
We believe in One Son, the Lord Jesus Christ.
We believe that he is perfect in deity and humanity, truly God and Man.
We believe that he has a rational soul and body.
We believe that he is consubstantial with the Father in Godhead
  but consubstantial with us in humanity.
We believe that the Son is like us in all things except sin.
We believe that the Son was eternally begotten of the Father, as God,
And that he was born in history of Mary the Virgin Theotokos for our salvation.
We believe in the unity of the Christ, the Son, the Lord, the Only Begotten,
  As this is made known [*gnorizomenon*] without confusion,
    without change,
    without division,
    without separation;
A union that does not remove the distinctions,
But preserves the characteristics of humanity and godhead,
As each comes together in one person [*prosopon*] and one subsistence [*hypostasis*].
We do not believe that he is separated and divided as two persons.
We believe he is One Son, the Only Begotten God, Word, and Lord, Jesus the
  Christ.

For this is what the prophets have taught us.
This is what the Fathers have taught us in the creeds.
This is what the Lord Jesus himself has taught us.

This (with only minimal edits) is pure doxology. It is pure credal prayer, affirmation, celebration of the good news of Christ, and to that extent evangelical confession. How startlingly different the Chalcedonian formula appears in this guise (or rather, once its guise of *anathema* has been stripped off). It becomes more clear, I suggest, how the patristic enterprise was not to solve a christological puzzle, but to protect a salvific mystery, so that it might continue to evoke wonderment, and continue opening the doors of mystery to the faithful.

In this light Harnack's statement (that here we have the bankruptcy of Greek theology), is patently fallacious. Even when pressed to the wall, the Greek fathers can rise, in the end, to sublime christological praise. Chalcedon is, then, not a silly conundrum, but rather the prayerful celebration of the mystery of the Union—the soteriological reunion of God and his mortal creatures in the mystery of unity that Christ himself represents.

Notes

1. Also worth noting here is the remarkable disconnection in the past between the disciplines of Classics, History, Theology, and New Testament Studies!

2. Gregory of Nyssa, "On the Divinity of the Son and the Holy Spirit," *GNO* 10.2, 121.7–14.

3. For more on this, see Alois Grillmeier, *Christ in Christian Tradition,* vol. 1, 2nd ed. (London: Mowbrays, 1975), 520–57; for a brief context, cf. also J. A. McGuckin, "Il Lungo Cammino Verso Calcedonia," in *Il Concilio di Calcedonia 1550 Anni Dopo,* ed. A. Ducay (Vatican: Libreria Editrice Vaticana, 2003), 13–41.

4. He died on July 28, 450, by breaking his neck after a fall from a horse. Theodosius was inclined to allow the theological settlement of Ephesus II, 449 to stand (reiterating the Cyrilline settlement of Ephesus I, 431) despite the political

behavior of Dioscorus, though many factions in the Constantinopolitan aristocracy were bent on revenge for the perceived slight against them in the person of Flavian, their patriarch. Dioscorus's fate would be sealed once he was taken out of his environment and adjudicated in the suburbs of Constantinople itself.

5. See T. H. Bindley, ed., *The Oecumenical Documents of the Faith,* 4th ed. (London: Methuen, 1950), 138–48. This *Letter* (39) attributed to Cyril is actually Cyril's return, with signature of agreement, of the formulary of faith that would establish the resumption of communion between the patriarchates of Antioch and Alexandria (broken after the Council of Ephesus 431) that had been sent to him through the intermediary services of the Constantinopolitan chancery. The actual terms of settlement were largely sketched out by Theodoret, on behalf of John of Antioch. Dioscorus believed (along with a few other Egyptian bishops) that Cyril's judgment had lapsed in signing this document, and proceeded up to Ephesus II, 449, as if the formulary did not exist. *Letter* 39 ought to be read in the immediate context of Cyril's post-Ephesine correspondence, especially the *Letter to Eulogios* and the two *Letters to Succensos*. For these, cf. J. A. McGuckin, *St. Cyril of Alexandria and the Christological Controversy* (New York: St. Vladimir's Seminary Press, 2004), 343–63; see also 227–43.

6. Chalcedon made a very large statement in its early sessions, before even considering the theological statement that was expected from it, by making two very revealing canonical, that is judicial, decrees: one to rehabilitate Theodoret (deposed at Ephesus 449), and the other to depose Dioscorus himself, who had secured Theodoret's deposition, bent as he was on the downfall of the only surviving Syrian theologian of international weight. Dioscorus's deposition at Chalcedon was ostensibly based on his behavior at Ephesus in 449, but the real motive was the more complex "clearing of the ground," theologically speaking, that was needed to roll the clock back to the last settlement that included Antioch, Constantinople, Rome, and Alexandria: and that was the one represented in the *Formula of Reunion*.

7. When she assumed regnant power in 450 she solved the problem more directly with his arrest and execution.

8. Aristotle, for example, had embedded in the mind of Greek antiquity that 'person' was an accidental characteristic that did not illuminate the fundamental philosophical datum of the genus (*physis*) or nature (*ousia*). When Christian theologians at this period were speaking about the movement of the divine *hypostasis* into history, through the incarnation, and consequently elevating the idea of the Person of the God-man to center stage, metaphysically and anthropologically, they effectively created an entirely different philosophical concept of Person as a substantive. This moment was an axis point of ancient thought, and is one of the unsung aspects of the maligned Council of Chalcedon.

9. Ambrose and Augustine are major contributors to the *Tome*'s doctrine. The list also includes Hilary, Jerome, Ambrose, and Ambrosiaster. The prime

position of Tertullian as a source (*Adv. Praxean* 27.11) ought no longer to be simply "presumed" (though it should not be entirely ruled out in my estimate). And one of the "unstated" or silent sources has to be the work of Cassian, whose report on Nestorian Christology Leo himself had commissioned when he was secretary to Pope Celestine at the time of the Ephesine crisis. One of the best synopses of the Latin sources that comprise this pastiche of Leo's is by H. R. Drobner, "Fonti teologiche e analisi della formula calcedoniana," in Ducay, *Il Concilio,* 42–58.

13

From Doctrine of Christ to Icon of Christ

St. Maximus the Confessor on the Transfiguration of Christ

Andrew Louth

Throughout the Eastern Christian theological tradition—from its first flowering with St. Irenaeus in the second century to the gathering up of the tradition by St. Gregory Palamas in the fourteenth century, and beyond—the mystery of the transfiguration has been central.[1] We find Irenaeus's most famous utterance in the course of a series of reflections focused by the mystery of the transfiguration: "gloria enim Dei vivens homo: vita autem hominis visio Dei" (for the glory of God is a live human being: and human life is the vision of God).[2] Origen pondered on the transfiguration long and frequently.[3] In the Makarian Homilies, the transfiguration of Christ is seen as a prefiguration of the precisely *bodily* transformation that the saints will finally experience.[4] Patristic homilies generally dwell on the way in which the transfiguration reveals the doctrine of the Trinity and the mystery of the incarnation and foreshadows—both in what is said and who is there—the mystery of the agony in the garden and the paschal mystery of death and resurrection; but they also see it as prefiguring the future hope—a hope that embraces both soul and body—of those who follow Christ. The mystery of the transfiguration in these homilies concentrates the whole of Christian faith and hope in a single image.[5] Depictions of the transfiguration in sacred art are important and striking as well: one thinks of the apse of S. Apollinare in Classe in Ravenna, where the transfiguration is depicted symbolically as bordering on paradise; or the spare and arresting apse in the monastery of St. Catherine on Sinai, which has been so illuminatingly interpreted by Jaś Elsner as the culmination of a spiritual ascent modeled on that of Moses, who appears—standing before the burning bush and receiving the Law in the cleft of a rock—in roundels on either side of the apse.[6] Beneath this apse worshipped John of Sinai, the author of the *Ladder of Divine Ascent* (hence called John Climacus), the most influential work in the Byzantine monastic tradition. As John reaches the final step of the ladder, he says, with a plausible allusion to the mystery of Mount Tabor (maybe even an allusion to the depiction in the apse):

> And now, for the rest, after all that has been said, there remain these three, binding tightly and securing the bond of all: faith, hope, and love. And the greatest of these is love, for God is so called. But I, so far as I can understand, see one as a ray, one as light, one as a disc, and all as one radiance and one brightness . . . .[7]

The transfiguration is also central to the vision of St. Symeon the New Theologian at the turn of the millennium.[8] For the Byzantine hesychasts—monks who claimed that in their prayer the Uncreated Light of the Godhead was revealed to them—the transfiguration became a central symbol of the reality of that transfiguring vision of the Uncreated Light, defended by St. Gregory Palamas.[9]

This is the dominant tradition concerning the transfiguration in the Byzantine East. And it is easy to think that it is the only tradition, but this would be a mistake. In Origen there is another interpretation of the transfiguration with a rather different emphasis. In his *Contra Celsum* we read:

> Although Jesus was one, he had several aspects; and to those who saw him he did not appear alike to all. That he had many aspects is clear from the saying, "I am the way, the truth and the life," (Jn 14:6) and "I am the bread," (Jn 6:35) and "I am the door," (Jn 10:9) and countless other such sayings. Moreover, that his appearance was not just the same to those who saw him, but varied according to their individual capacity, will be clear to people who carefully consider why, when about to be transfigured on the high mountain, he did not take all his disciples, but only Peter, James, and John. For they alone had the capacity to see his glory at that time, and were able also to perceive Moses and Elias when they appeared in glory, and to hear them conversing together, and the voice from heaven out of the cloud.[10]

The emphasis on the way in which Christ appeared to different people in different forms, according to their spiritual aptitude, reflects Origen's concern to make credible the idea of a finite manifestation of the infinite: the infinite is manifest in manifold ways, and we can see this in the case of the incarnation, the transfiguration being a crowning example. But a corollary is that there can be no adequate image, or icon, of Christ. This is the line taken by Eusebius of Caesarea, the proud inheritor of Origen's tradition, in his letter to Constantia Augusta, the Emperor Constantine's half-sister, who had requested a picture of Jesus. Eusebius's reply is that the different forms in which Jesus appeared during his earthly ministry belong to the past, while his present glorified form was prefigured by the transfiguration, in which his appearance was so transformed that the apostles could not look upon him because of the splendor that, in its ineffability, surpasses the measure of any eye or ear and consequently cannot be depicted by lifeless colors and shades.[11] This letter is preserved because it was cited by the eighth-century iconoclasts in a patristic florilegium and thus found its way into the *Acta* of the Seventh Ecumenical Council. Georges Florovsky saw in this letter evidence of an Origenist tradition, native to Greek theology and hostile to icons.[12]

My central concern in this essay is St. Maximus the Confessor, who, I shall argue, should be understood as inheriting and in fact reconciling both these traditions of interpreting the transfiguration. Until very recently Maximus the Confessor was known, if at all, as the "Confessor," the Eastern monk who in the seventh century, together with Pope Martin I, resisted the imperial policy of monothelitism, the last of the classical christological heresies, ultimately at the cost of his life. Over the last few decades—mainly as a result of the work of Hans Urs von Balthasar, a Swiss Catholic, Polycarp Sherwood, an American Benedictine, and Lars Thunberg, a Swedish Lutheran—a much fuller picture of Maximus has become known in the West.

Maximus, born in 580, educated probably in Constantinople, and briefly a very senior civil servant in the early years of Herakleios's reign, became a monk in his early thirties and remained one for the rest of his long life. Until he was drawn, with some reluctance, into theological controversy, all his works grew out of that vocation: his theological vision is grounded in his commitment to and understanding of the Christian life, lived in his case as a monk.

We find Maximus's reflections on the transfiguration in his writings composed long before the outbreak of the monothelite controversy. In fact, in his writings on Christology, the mystery of Christ that lies at the center of his reflections is not the transfiguration but rather the closely related mystery of the agony in the garden. Maximus turns to the transfiguration in three works that cannot be exactly dated, but that belong to the decade from the mid-620s to the mid-630s, During this period Maximus left his monastery on the Sea of Marmara, close to Constantinople, in flight before the marauding troops of the Persians, and settled in North Africa, where he was to remain for fifteen years or so.

The first treatment of the transfiguration is found in the second "century" of his *Centuries on Theology and the Incarnation*—"centuries" refers to a monastic genre in which thoughts, both theological and ascetical, were presented in brief paragraphs for meditation. At the end of II.13, Maximus introduces the transfiguration as God's final manifestation in his own form. For, he says, there are differences among those who stand before the Lord, and the Lord appears in different forms "according to the measure of each person's faith." The Mount of the Transfiguration is a symbol of the spiritual life: at its foot the Lord appears in the form of a servant, at its summit in the form of God, "the form in which he existed before the world came to be." The meaning of the transfiguration is stated very briefly: the Lord's face shines like the sun, and his garments appear white, "that is to say, the words of the Gospel will then be clear and distinct, with nothing concealed." Maximus briefly comments on the significance of Moses and Elias—they signify the law and the prophets—and the three tents, in which Maximus sees a reference to the three stages of salvation: virtue, spiritual knowledge, and theology, typified by Elias, Moses, and the Lord, respectively.

The extent of Maximus's debt to Origen here is unmistakable: note the emphasis on the chameleon-like nature of the Word made flesh, the way the garments of Christ symbolize the gospel, and the identification of Moses and Elias with the law and the prophets.[13] The three stages represented by virtue, knowledge, and theology are also found in Origen.[14]

In Maximus's other two attempts to expound the mystery of the transfiguration, however, we find something that we might even call original—not what one expects in Byzantine writers. Origenist themes are still developed, but we begin to hear Maximus's own voice.

The first of these attempts occurs in questions 191 and 192 of the newly discovered *Questions and Answers* (*Quaestiones et dubia,* as its first editor called it). Question 191[15] begins by addressing the discrepancy between the Gospels about when the transfiguration took place: whether after six days, as in Matthew and Mark, or after eight days, as in Luke. The six days, Maximus argues, indicate the six days of creation, so that "after six days" signifies passing beyond *ta phainomena,* the created order as it appears to our senses. Luke's eight days, by contrast, include a beginning and an end: "the first day in which the Lord spoke and the last of the transfiguration."[16] But both ways of reckoning are taken up in the spiritual interpretation (*kata tên theôrian*), which Maximus presents as follows:

> Since the human being through transgression has been reduced to a state opposed to nature, it is necessary that one who wants to ascend by the Word to the mount of theology first, as it were on one day, passes beyond what is opposed to nature and, as it were in six

> days, traverses nature and comes into a state beyond nature, that is the eighth, for this underlies time and characterizes the state that is to come.

Here Maximus affirms one of the basic principles of his theology, namely, the integrity of the natural, which has been established by God: our normal state, fractured by the Fall, is unnatural, and redemption and asceticism are concerned to restore a natural state.

After reflecting on the apostles Peter, James, and John, who signify the three virtues of faith, hope, and love, Maximus considers the transfiguration itself:

> The Word leads those who possess faith, hope, and love up on to the mountain of theology and is transfigured before them, so that to call him God is no longer to affirm that he is holy, king, and suchlike, but to make denial of him according to the fact that he is beyond God and beyond holy and everything said of him transcendently.

What Maximus is doing here is assimilating the ascent up the Mount of the Transfiguration—Mount Tabor—to Moses' ascent of Mount Sinai, as it is interpreted by Gregory of Nyssa[17] and especially by Dionysius the Areopagite in his *Mystical Theology,*[18] as a symbol of the ascent of the soul to God. (In this, he follows the suggestion of the mosaics in the apse of the monastic church of the Monastery of the Burning Bush—as it was called in his day, now the Monastery of St. Catherine—on Mount Sinai, though there is no reason to suppose that Maximus ever saw these mosaics.) Both Gregory and Dionysius make the point that, as Moses ascends the mountain, he passes beyond affirming those images and concepts in which God is revealed—symbolized by the sounding of the trumpets and the light flashing from the summit—and enters the dark cloud that shrouds the summit, where he can no longer see anything: this is a symbol that he can now only know God by rejecting what his senses can perceive and his mind grasp. Dionysius had borrowed Neoplatonic terminology and called the theology of affirmation "kataphatic theology," and the theology of denial "apophatic theology." Maximus uses this language to describe the ascent of the Mount of the Transfiguration: one passes from saying things about God derived from our knowledge of the created order and of God's revelation ("that he is holy, king, and suchlike") and is led to the rejection of images and concepts, and thus to silent wonder. In the blinding radiance of the divinity of the transfigured Christ, manifest on Mount Tabor, the disciples are reduced to silence, the silence of apophatic acknowledgment of the transcendence of divinity.

But when Maximus goes on to remark that "the face of the Word, that shone like the sun, is the characteristic hiddenness of his being," I think we should pick up an allusion to something deeper. The Greek word I have translated as "face" (*prosôpon*) could equally well be translated "person," and what Maximus is alluding to is the fact that the radiant face of Christ reveals the divine person that He is: "the face of the Word . . . is the characteristic hiddenness of his being," that is, of the being of God. The Council of Chalcedon in 451 had endorsed a definition according to which, in the incarnate Christ, there are two natures—the divine and the human—united in a single person. The fifth ecumenical council (of Constantinople, in 553) clarified this by affirming that that one person is divine, "one of the Trinity." In a way that seems typical of Maximus, the precise words he uses allude to the exact distinctions of the Christology of the councils. But there is more; if, on the Mount of the Transfiguration, the blinding radiance of the face/person of the Word reveals the "characteristic hiddenness" of the being of God, then apophatic theology—the theology of denial—is our acknowledgment of the divinity of Christ. The language of apophatic and kataphatic theology is the language of Dionysius, but the use to which it is put, and thus the meaning, is Maximus's own. For Dionysius, apophatic and kataphatic theologies spelt out the dialectic involved in our predicating attributes or names of God: the dialectic of affirmation and denial steered a way between the twin errors of anthropomorphism and agnosticism in our attempt to say something about God. But for Maximus, the terminology of apophatic and kataphatic theology seems to be bound up with our confession of the union of divine and human natures in the single divine person of the incarnate Word: acknowledgment of the divine radiance of the face of Christ draws us into apophatic theology, since the dazzling radiance of the face of Christ is beyond affirmation and can only be regarded in silent—apophatic—wonder. In Maximus's novel use of Dionysius's terminology of apophatic and kataphatic theology, there is what I would like to call a "christological turn."

This is confirmed as Maximus considers Christ's body and garments that became resplendently white in the transfiguration. The body refers to the "substance of the virtues" and the garment to the words of Scripture, or to the works of the cosmos: the whiteness of the garments means that both the divine words of Scripture and the divine works in the cosmos become transparent to those who have ascended to contemplation of Christ, and their beauty is revealed. But to understand the words of Scripture and the works of the cosmos is precisely what is involved in affirmative—kataphatic—theology. So while the face of Christ draws us into apophatic theology, the body and the garments of Christ speak of kataphatic theology. The "christological turn" means that the terminology of apophatic and kataphatic, formulated by Dionysius to describe the dialectical nature of our knowledge of God, is applied by Maximus to express the truth of the union of the divine and human natures in the divine person of the Son. The whole of our knowledge of God, therefore, is summed up in the apostles' beholding of Christ on the Mount of the Transfiguration.

Question 192 follows from this and considers the meaning of the three tents Peter thought should be set up.[19] They signify—as in the *Centuries on Theology and Incarnation*—the three stages of the Christian life, only here Maximus uses the more traditional terminology for these stages that goes back to Evagrius, the late-fourth-century Origenist and theorist of the eremitical life of the Desert Fathers: namely, *praktiké* (the active life of ascetic struggle), *physiké* (contemplation of the natural order), and *theologia* (theology as contemplation of God). Elias corresponds to *praktiké,* Moses to *physiké,* and the Lord himself to *theologia*. Maximus does not elaborate, and therefore it would be rash for us to do so; however, it is clear that this comment entails an understanding of the transfiguration as embracing the whole span of the Christian life.

These two early questions are relatively brief, amounting to about two and a half pages. The Origenist background is evident, but two factors are, I think, striking: first, the use of the terminology of the developed Byzantine Christology of the sixth century set out in the decrees of the fifth ecumenical council, and, second, Maximus's strikingly original use of the Dionysian distinction between apophatic and kataphatic theology in relation to our understanding of Christ. The apophatic points to the *person* of Christ: it is in a personal relationship with the incarnate Word that God's unknowability is not only registered but experienced. Origen had reconciled God's ineffability with his manifestation in the incarnation by emphasizing the manifold ways in which the manifestation of God is apprehended, with the consequence, drawn explicitly by Eusebius in his letter to Constantia (quoted earlier) that the notion of the inexhaustibility of God rules out any true depiction of the Incarnate One. For Maximus, on the contrary, the ineffable, the inexhaustible, is actually found in the face-to-face, person-to-person experience disclosed by the incarnation. This "christological turn," then, transforms the theology of negation: apophatic theology is an acknowledgment of the overwhelming *reality* of the person of God, rather than a principle of denial that qualifies and limits our affirmation of the revealed images and concepts of God.[20]

The final attempt of Maximus to expound the mystery of the transfiguration is found in the fifth and longest of his *Ambigua,* or *Difficulties,* so called because all of the questions concern difficult passages in the writings of Gregory of Nazianzus or, in the single case of *Ambiguum* 5, of Dionysius the Areopagite. The transfiguration forms the center of gravity of this long and fascinating question-and-answer passage.[21] The central thread of this "difficulty" concerns what is meant by "passing over"—*diabasis*. Maximus tackles this question from a bewildering variety of perspectives, including a long list of examples from the Bible (mainly the Old Testament), culminating in the transfiguration.

Maximus's treatment of the transfiguration[22] begins by focusing on the face of Christ: the natural focus in any icon of the transfiguration, or indeed any icon at all. This comes as no surprise after what we have already seen in the *Questions and Answers*. We know how much is concentrated in the image of the face of Christ, the *prosôpon* or (divine) person of Christ. The radiance from the face signifies Christ's divinity, and that divinity dazzles—it both reveals and blinds. Maximus then explains why he has evoked the transfiguration in *Ambiguum* 10: this "difficulty" is concerned with *diabasis* (passing over), and in the transfiguration the disciples "passed over" from seeing Christ as "without form or beauty" (Isa 53:2) to seeing him as "fair with beauty beyond the sons of men" (Ps 44:3)—an Origenist theme we have already encountered.[23] Maximus interprets this as a passing over from understanding Christ primarily as the "Word made flesh" to understanding him as the "One in the beginning, with God, and God"—a passage from the end of the Johannine prologue to its beginning, so to speak. He unfolds a little more what was contained in a single brief allusion in the earlier *Questions and Answers.* He calls this "passing over" from the "Word made flesh" to the "Word, in the beginning, with God" a movement of *apophasis,* negation or denial, and this *apophasis,* he says, the disciples have learnt from—or perhaps better, experienced in beholding—the blinding radiance of the face of the transfigured Lord. He then moves on to interpret the whitened garment of Christ, which—as we saw in *Questions and Answers*—he takes as referring to the words of Scripture or to creation itself, and is led into a long digression in which he expounds the parallelism of Scripture and cosmos. The cosmos is like a book, and the Bible is like the cosmos: both consist of words, *logoi,* which, though diverse, when read with understanding form a single harmonious whole, the meaning of which is the mind of God Himself. Maximus insists very strongly on the absolute equivalence of the written law and the natural law: the written law does not mark an advance on the natural law, it simply reveals what has been obscured as a result of the Fall. This idea of the cosmos and Scripture as mutually reflecting each other—an idea that extends both to what they mean and how we are to understand them—is central to Maximus's thought: he returns to it in the introductory chapters of his *Mystagogia*.[24]

Maximus then explores further the two sides of the transfiguration, symbolized by the two figures who appeared with Jesus, Moses and Elias.[25] He does so at length, in seventeen meditations. Some of his discussion is already familiar, such as Moses and Elias symbolizing the law and the prophets, much of it is arcane and fascinating, but I shall skip everything save for a few points in the last six meditations. There is an exposition of the difference between apophatic and kataphatic theology, in very Dionysian terms. This is followed by what I have already called the "christological turn," in which the distinction between apophatic and kataphatic theology is focused on the person of Christ, the silent wonder of *apophasis* being a response to the dazzling radiance of Christ's face. Here Maximus says that, through accepting a human form, the Word has become a "symbol of himself," in order

> through this manifestation of himself to lead to himself in his complete and secret hiddenness the whole creation, and while he remains quite unknown in his hidden, secret place beyond all things, unable to be known or understood by any being in any way whatever, out of his love for humankind he grants to human beings intimations of himself in the manifest divine works performed in the flesh. (*Amb*. 10.31c: PG 91.1165D–1168A)

Note that what Christ grants to humankind he grants for the sake of the whole creation—a characteristically Maximian stress on the cosmic. The next meditation affirms the primacy of apophatic theology in christological terms: "the light from the face of the Lord, therefore, conquers the human blessedness of the apostles by a hidden apophatic theology" (*Amb*. 10.31d: PG 91.1168A). Three meditations then explicitly expound kataphatic theology in terms of the cosmic dimension of the Word made flesh (*Amb*. 10.31 e–g: PG 91.1168B–D).

In this *Ambiguum,* then, Maximus sees in the transfiguration a thoroughly Christocentric theology, a theology that leads to and from the person of Christ, and finds in everything illumined by the uncreated light of his radiance the revelation of Christ in nature and in Scripture. But it is also theology expressed in an icon, so to speak: it is a series of meditations on aspects of the mystery or picture contemplated, all held together by the central figure of Christ.

At the beginning of this essay, I pointed out that while the dominant interpretation in the Eastern Christian tradition holds that the transfiguration is one of the most profound icons of Christ, an Origenist interpretation used the transfiguration as prime evidence of the manifold forms taken by the incarnate Word, to show that there could now be no icon of Christ. When controversy eventually broke out in the

Byzantine world about the legitimacy of icons and their veneration, the letter written by the Origenist Eusebius to Constantine's half-sister, Constantia, was cited as key evidence of patristic disapproval of icons by the iconoclasts.

Maximus's interpretation of the transfiguration shows, I think, that without denying the Origenist approach to this mystery, he sets it in a different context. The manifold manifestations of the ineffable God belong to the theology of affirmation, or kataphatic theology: everything in Scripture and the created cosmos reveals some aspect of the inexhaustibility of God. But the ineffable, inexhaustible nature of God is more surely revealed in the dazzling radiance of the face, or divine person, of Christ: beholding that, we pass beyond utterance and gaze in silent wonder—we enter the realm of apophatic theology. This approach does not discard the icon as inadequate, but rather affirms its validity by underlining the central significance in theology of beholding, looking, and contemplating. The "christological turn," understood in this manner, effects a transition from the doctrine of Christ, carefully honed by the definitions of the councils, to the icon of Christ, the symbol—in the fullest sense—of encounter with Christ, and in this transition the doctrine is not left behind. Far from it: rather, the carefully honed doctrine of Christ guides our understanding of the icon.

If there is such a transference of the doctrine of Christ to the icon of Christ in the theology of St. Maximus, then we are well on the way to understanding why the icon was invested with such profound significance by Byzantine Christians, and in particular, why the question of the icon, when it became a matter of controversy, was understood as a matter of precisely *christological* controversy. We cannot enter into this question now, but let me suggest two hints of the connections that I think exist between Maximus's theology and the icon as a central symbol of the incarnation.

First, a key passage occurs in Maximus's interpretation of the transfiguration in *Ambiguum* 10. There he says, and I quote more fully a statement quoted above:

> For it was necessary,[26] without any change in himself, to be created like us, accepting through his immeasurable love for humankind to become the *type and symbol of himself,* and from himself

> symbolically to represent himself, and through the manifestation of himself to lead to himself in his complete and secret hiddenness the whole creation . . . . (*Amb.* 10.31c: PG 91.1165D)[27]

In the incarnation, the Word became a "type and symbol of himself." One can perhaps hear an echo of this phrase in one of the central iconophile arguments of St. Theodore of Stoudios, who, together with the deposed patriarch Nikephoros, became the most important champion of the veneration of the icons in the second period of iconoclasm in the first half of the ninth century. Theodore argues that, in the incarnation, Christ becomes "the archetype of his own image," *prototypos tês heautou eikonos*.[28] It follows that it is not simply *possible* for there to be an image of Christ, and it is not simply *possible* for an artist to depict an image of Christ, through which Christ can be encountered and worshipped: because Christ is manifest in the incarnation as "the archetype of his own image," acknowledgment of the incarnation actually makes *necessary* the making of images to continue the access to the archetype entailed in the incarnation.[29] The premise of Theodore's argument is, it seems to me, provided by Maximus when he says that the Word became a "type and symbol of himself."

Another hint is found in Maximus's use of studied ambiguity—almost a play on words—when referring to the *prosôpon* of Christ: either "face" or "person." When we look at the face of the transfigured Christ, from which radiance flows, we behold the person of the Godhead: that is why the radiance dazzles, and that is why apophatic theology interprets the vision here.[30] Many years ago, in his *Der Logos am Kreuz,*[31] Alois Grillmeier drew attention to the depiction of the crucified Christ in the sixth-century Rabbula Gospels, where Christ is depicted on the cross with his eyes open. Grillmeier suggested (drawing, among other things, on the *Physiologus,* which mentions the legend that the lion sleeps with its eyes open and applies this to the idea of Christ as the "lion of Judah" [cf. Gen 49:9; Rev 5:5]) that the open eyes indicate the divinity of Christ awake, while the humanity of Christ submits to death.[32] If the eyes make the face, then St. Maximus's interpretation of the transfiguration is strikingly analogous to the iconography of the "Logos on the Cross."

What we find, then, in Maximus's attempts to unfold the meaning of the mystery of the transfiguration is a fascinating interweaving of a spiritual theme, a theological theme, and a philosophical theme. The spiritual theme treats the transfiguration as emblematic of the fullest possible human encounter with God; the theological theme is drawn from the councils of the church, where the technical language of the conciliar decrees suggests a bold interpretation of the radiant face of the transfigured Christ; the philosophical theme, drawn from Dionysius the Areopagite, of the distinction between apophatic and kataphatic theology, is focused on the person of the Incarnate One. In the mutual illumination of these themes, there emerges the icon of Christ in whose contemplation is found the fullness of theology. Theology as doctrine draws those addressed into theology as contemplation: doctrine of Christ yields to contemplation of the icon or image of Christ.

Notes

1. I acknowledge my debt, especially for the insight into the christological turn of apophatic theology in Maximus, to the brilliant essay by Ysabel de Andia, "Transfiguration et théologie négative chez Maxime le Confesseur et Denys l'Aréopagite," in *Denys l'Aréopagite et sa postérité en orient et en occident: Actes du Colloque International, Paris, 21–24 septembre 1994,* ed. Ysabel de Andia, Collection des Études Augustiniennes, Série Antiquité 151 (Paris: Institut d'Études Augustiniennes, 1997), 293–328, which I heard at the colloquium in 1994. My essay was written, however, before I had sight of the published version, and I have made no attempt to take account of it here, as my approach is, for the most part, rather different from De Andia's.

2. Irenaeus, *Haer.* 4.20.7

3. Origen, *Comm. Matt.* 12.36–43; cf. *Cels.* 1.48, 2.64–65, 4.16, 6.68, and *Hom. Gen.* 1.7.

4. Makarios, *Hom.* 15.38, cf. 20.3, 1.3 (from the standard collection, Collection II: H. Dörries, E. Klostermann, and M. Kroeger, eds., *Die 50 Geistliche Homilien des Makarios,* Patristische Texte und Studien 4 [Berlin: Walter de Gruyter, 1964]).

5. For a collection of translated extracts from the Fathers on the transfiguration from Irenaeus to John of Damascus (and Gregory Palamas at the end of the Greek section), with an introductory part, mainly on the New Testament

text and its interpretation, but including a brief chapter on patristic interpretation, cf. J. A. McGuckin, *The Transfiguration of Christ in Scripture and Tradition,* Studies in the Bible and Early Christianity, vol. 9 (Lewiston, N.Y.: Edwin Mellen, 1986).

6. Jaś Elsner, *Art and the Roman Viewer: The Transformation of Art from the Pagan World to Christianity* (Cambridge: Cambridge University Press, 1995), 99–123.

7. John Klimakos, *Ladder of Divine Ascent* 30.1. My translation from Ioannou tou Sinaïtou, *Klimax,* ed. Fr. Sophronios (Athens: Astir, 1979), 167.

8. Cf., for instance, the autobiographical *Catechesis* 22 (B. Krivochéine and J. Paramelle, eds., *Catéchèses 6–22,* SC 104 [Paris: Cerf, 1964), 364–92], or, even more significantly perhaps, the title of Archbishop Krivochéine's book on Symeon: *Dans la lumière du Christ,* Collection Témoins de l'Église indivisé, vol. 1 (Gembloux: Éditions de Chevetogne, 1980).

9. Cf. Saint Gregory the Sinaïte, *Discourse on the Transfiguration,* ed. David Balfour (off-print from the Athens quarterly *Theologia* 52.4–54.1 [1981/83], Athens, 1983), and Gregory Palamas, *Hom.* 34 (PG 151.423–36), translated in McGuckin, *Transfiguration of Christ,* 225–34.

10. *Cels.* 2.64. Translation by Henry Chadwick in Origen, *Contra Celsum* (Cambridge: Cambridge University Press, 1965), 115.

11. Paraphrase of Eusebius's letter to Constantia, in H.-J. Geischer, ed., *Der Byzantinische Bilderstreit,* Texte zur Kirchen- und Theologiegeschichte, vol. 9 (Gütersloh: Gerd Mohn, 1968), 15–17.

12. Georges Florovsky, "Origen, Eusebius, and the Iconoclast Controversy," *Church History* 19 (1950): 77–96 (reprinted in his *Collected Works,* vol. 2 [Belmont, Mass.: Nordland, 1974], 101–21 [notes on 236–40]).

13. Cf. the passages from Origen translated by John McGuckin, *Transfiguration of Christ,* 151–64.

14. Cf. my *Origins of the Christian Mystical Tradition: From Plato to Denys* (Oxford: Clarendon Press, 1989), 57–61.

15. Maximus, *Quaestiones et dubia,* ed. José H. Declerck, CCSG 10 (Turnhout: Brepols, 1982), 132–34.

16. Note the rather different interpretation provided by St. John Damascene in his sermon on the transfiguration, where 6 is a perfect number and 8 is a type of the age to come (*Homilia in Transfigurationem* 8, in *Die Schriften des Johannes von Damaskos,* 5 vols., ed. P. Bonifatius Kotter, O.S.B., Patristische Texte und Studien, vol. 29 [Berlin: W. de Gruyter, 1988], 446–47).

17. Cf. Gregory of Nyssa, *Life of Moses* 152–69 (J. Daniélou, ed., SC 1, 3rd ed. [Paris: Cerf, 1968], 202–16).

18. Cf. Dionysius the Areopagite, *Mystical Theology* 1 (G. Heil and A. M. Ritter, eds., Patristische Texte und Studien, vol. 36 [Berlin–New York: W. de Gruyter, 1991], 141–44).

19. *Quaestiones et dubia,* ed. Declerck, 134–35.

20. This understanding of apophatic theology is very much that of Vladimir Lossky: "La voie apophatique de la théologie orientale est le repentir de la personne humaine devant la face du Dieu vivant" (*Essai sur la théologie mystique de l'Église d'orient* [Paris: Aubier, 1944], 237).

21. *Ambiguum* 10 can be found in PG 91.1105C–1205C; English translation in my *Maximus the Confessor,* Early Church Fathers (London: Routledge, 1996), 96–154.

22. *Amb.* 10.17: PG 91.1125D–1128D (English trans., Louth, *Maximus the Confessor,* 108–10).

23. Cf. also Origen, *Cels.* 6.77, where the citation from Isaiah is related to the disciples' experience at the transfiguration.

24. Maximus the Confessor, *Mystagogia* 1–7, esp. 7 (C. Sotiropoulos, ed., 2nd ed. [Athens, 1993]; English translation by G. C. Berthold, in *Maximus Confessor, Selected Writings,* Classics of Western Spirituality [Mahwah, N.J.: Paulist Press, 1995], 183–225).

25. Maximus the Confessor, *Amb.* 10.31: PG 91.1160B–1169B (English trans. Louth, *Maximus the Confessor,* 128–34).

26. Amending (on the suggestion of my former pupil Adam Cooper) *eidei* to *edei*.

27. PG 91.1165D: my translation (modified) from *Maximus the Confessor,* 132 (emphasis added).

28. Theodore of Stoudios, *Antirrheticus* 2: PG 99.356A; 3: PG 99.428C (I translate *prototypos* as "archetype," because the English "prototype" means something different). I owe this reference to my former pupil the Reverend Dr. Gary Thorne.

29. Cf. Kenneth Parry, "Theodore Studites and the Patriarch Nicephoros on Image-Making as a Christian Imperative," *Byzantion* 59 (1989): 164–83.

30. Cf. the interpretation of *Questions and Answers* 191 and *Ambiguum* 10.17 earlier in this chapter.

31. Alois Grillmeier, S.J., *Der Logos am Kreuz* (Munich: Max Hueber, 1956).

32. Cf. also Karl-Heinz Uthemann, "Christ's Image *versus* Christology: Thoughts on the Justinianic Era as the Threshold of an Epoch," in *The Sixth Century: End or Beginning?* ed. Pauline Allen and Elizabeth M. Jeffreys, Byzantina Australiensia, vol. 10 (Brisbane: Australian Association for Byzantine Studies, 1996), 197–223, esp. 216–20.

The Works of Brian E. Daley, S.J.

Books, Translations, and Monographs

"Die Soteriologie in der Heiligen Schrift." In *Handbuch der Dogmengeschichte,* edited by M. Schmaus, A. Grillmeier, L. Scheffczyk, and M. Seybold, III/2a, 1–54. Freiburg: Herder, 1978.

"Patristische Eschatologie." In *Handbuch der Dogmengeschichte,* edited by M. Schmaus, A. Grillmeier, L. Scheffczyk, and M. Seybold, IV/7a, 84–248. Freiburg: Herder, 1986.

Companions in the Mission of Jesus: Texts for Prayer and Reflection in the Lenten and Easter Seasons, edited by Brian E. Daley, S.J. New York: Georgetown University Press for the New York Province of the Society of Jesus, 1987.

The Hope of the Early Church: A Handbook of Patristic Eschatology. Cambridge: Cambridge University Press, 1991. Second edition, Peabody, Mass.: Hendrickson, 2003. First edition translated into Portuguese: *Origens da Escatologia Cristã: A esperança da Igreja primitiva,* translated by Paulo D. Siepierski. São Paulo: Paulus, 1994.

On The Dormition of Mary: Early Patristic Homilies, translated by Brian E. Daley, S.J. Crestwood, N.Y.: St. Vladimir's Seminary Press, 1998.

Hans Urs von Balthasar, *Cosmic Liturgy: The Universe according to Maximus the Confessor,* translated by Brian E. Daley, S.J. San Francisco: Ignatius Press, 2003.

Gregory of Nazianzus, introduction and translation by Brian E. Daley, S.J. The Early Church Fathers. London: Routledge, 2006.

Articles (Excluding Reviews)

"The Origenism of Leontius of Byzantium." *Journal of Theological Studies* 27 (1976): 333–69.

"Apokatastasis and 'Honorable Silence' in the Eschatology of Maximus the Confessor." In *Maximus Confessor: Actes du Symposium sur Maxime le Confesseur. Fribourg, 2–5 septembre 1980,* edited by F. Heinzer and C. Schönborn, 309–39. Fribourg: Éditions Universitaires, 1982.

"Ordination: The Sacrament of Ministry." *America* (December 11, 1982): 365–69.

"Boethius' Theological Tracts and Early Byzantine Scholasticism." *Mediaeval Studies* 46 (1984): 158–91.

"'In Ten Thousand Places': Christian Universality and the Jesuit Mission." *Studies in the Spirituality of Jesuits* 17.2 (1985).

"The 'Closed Garden' and the 'Sealed Fountain': Song of Songs 4:12 in the Late Medieval Iconography of Mary." In *Medieval Gardens,* edited by E. B. MacDougall, 255–78. Washington: Dumbarton Oaks Research Library and Collection, 1986.

"Councils, Christian." In *Encyclopedia of Religion,* edited by M. Eliade et al., 125–32. New York: Macmillan, 1987.

"A Humble Mediator: The Distinctive Elements in St. Augustine's Christology." *Word and Spirit* 9 (1987): 100–117.

"The Ministry of Disciples: Historical Reflections on the Role of Religious Priests." *Theological Studies* 48 (1987): 605–29.

"Splendor and Wonder: Ignatian Mysticism and the Ideals of Liberal Education." In *Splendor and Wonder: Jesuit Character, Georgetown Spirit, and Liberal Education,* edited by William J. O'Brien. Washington, D.C.: Georgetown University Press, 1988.

"Eschatology," "Millenarianism," "Henri Leclercq." In *Encyclopedia of Early Christianity,* edited by E. Ferguson et al. New York: Garland, 1989.

"Structures of Charity: Bishops' Gatherings and the See of Rome in the Early Church." In *Episcopal Conferences: Historical, Canonical and Theological Studies,* edited by T. J. Reese, 25–58. Washington, D.C.: Georgetown University Press, 1989.

"Feasts of Mary." In *A New Dictionary of Sacramental Worship,* edited by P. E. Fink. Collegeville, Minn.: Liturgical Press, 1990.

"The Ripening of Salvation: Hope for Resurrection in the Early Church." *Communio* 17 (1990): 27–49.

"Born of a Virgin." *The Tablet* (December 19–26, 1992): 1598–1603.

"Christ and the Catholic University." *America* (September 11, 1993): 6–14.

"The Giant's Twin Substances: Ambrose and the Christology of Augustine's *Contra sermonem Arianorum*." In *Augustine: Presbyter Factus Sum,* edited by J. T. Lienhard et al., 477–95. New York: Peter Lang, 1993.

"Position and Patronage in the Early Church: The Original Meaning of 'Primacy of Honor.'" *Journal of Theological Studies* 44 (1993): 529–53.

Section on "Eschatology." In *Commentary on the Catechism of the Catholic Church,* edited by Michael J. Walsh, 205–24. Collegeville, Minn.: Liturgical Press, 1994.

"How Should We Pray? Five Guiding Principles." *Crisis* (March 1994): 28–32.

"A Mystery to Share In: The Trinitarian Perspective of the New Catechism." *Communio* 21 (1994): 409–36.

"'A Richer Union': Leontius of Byzantium and the Relation of Human and Divine in Christ." *Studia Patristica,* edited by Elizabeth A. Livingstone, vol. 24, 239–65. Leuven: Peeters, 1994.

"Apollo as a Chalcedonian: A New Fragment of a Controversial Work from Early Sixth-Century Constantinople." *Traditio* 50 (1995): 31–54.

"'To Be More Like Christ': The Background and Implications of 'Three Kinds of Humility.'" *Studies in the Spirituality of Jesuits* 27.1 (1995).

"What Did 'Origenism' Mean in the Sixth Century?" In *Origeniana Sexta: Origène et la Bible: Actes du Colloquium Origenianum Sextum, Chantilly, 30 août–3 septembre 1993,* edited by G. Dorival and A. Le Boulluec, 627–38. Leuven: Peeters, 1995.

"'Bright Darkness' and Christian Transformation: Gregory of Nyssa on the Dynamics of Mystical Union." In *Studia Philonica Annual: Studies in Hellenistic Judaism,* edited by David T. Runia, vol. 8 (1996): 83–98. Also in *Finding God in All Things: Essays in Honor of Michael J. Buckley, S.J.,* edited by Michael J. Himes and Stephen J. Pope. New York: Crossroad, 1996.

"Headship and Communion: American Orthodox-Catholic Dialogue on Synodality and Primacy in the Church." *Pro Ecclesia* 5 (1996): 55–72.

"Divine Transcendence and Human Transformation: Gregory of Nyssa's Anti-Apollinarian Christology." In *Studia Patristica,* edited by Elizabeth A. Livingstone, vol. 32, 87–95. Peeters: Leuven, 1997. Reprinted in *Modern Theology* 18 (2002): 497–506; also in *Re-Thinking Gregory of Nyssa,* edited by Sarah Coakley, 67–76. Oxford: Blackwell, 2003.

"Judgment Day or Jubilee? Approaching the Millennium." *America* (May 31, 1997): 8–21. Also published as pamphlet by Pauline Editions, 1998. Also translated into Spanish: "¿Día del Juicio o Jubileo? En vísperas del tercer milenio." *Selecciones de teología* 38 (1999): 191–200.

"Leontios von Byzanz," "Leontius von Jerusalem." In *Lexikon für Theologie und Kirche,* 3rd edition, edited by Walter Kasper et al. Vol. 6. Freiburg: Herder, 1997.

"The Pursuit of Excellence and the 'Ordinary Manner': Humility and the Jesuit University." In *For That I Came: Virtues and Ideals of Jesuit Education,* edited by William J. O'Brien, 11–35. Washington, D.C.: Georgetown University Press, 1997.

"Apocalypticism in Early Christian Theology." In *Encyclopedia of Apocalypticism,* edited by Bernard McGinn, vol. 2, 3–47. New York: Continuum, 1998.

"Constantinople II," "Communication des idiomes," "Apocatastase." In *Dictionnaire critique de théologie,* edited by Jean-Yves Lacoste. Paris: Presses Universitaires de France, 1998.

"Heaven," "Hell." In *Guide to the Late Antique World,* edited by Peter Brown et al. Cambridge, Mass.: Harvard University Press, 1998.

"Origen's *De Principiis:* A Guide to the Principles of Christian Scriptural Interpretation." In *Nova et Vetera: Patristic Studies in Honor of Thomas Patrick Halton,* edited by John Petruccione, 3–21. Washington, D.C.: Catholic University of America Press, 1998.

"1998 NAPS Presidential Address. Building the New City: The Cappadocian Fathers and the Rhetoric of Philanthropy." *Journal of Early Christian Studies* 7 (1999): 431–61.

"Christology," "Incarnation," "Resurrection." In *Augustine through the Ages: An Encyclopedia,* edited by Allan Fitzgerald and John C. Cavadini. Grand Rapids: Eerdmans, 1999.

"'At the Hour of our Death': Mary's Dormition and Christian Dying in Late Patristic and Early Byzantine Literature." *Dumbarton Oaks Papers* 55 (2001): 71–89.

"Revisiting the 'Filioque': Roots and Branches of an Old Debate. Part One." *Pro Ecclesia* 10 (2001): 31–62; "Revisiting the 'Filioque.' Part Two: Contemporary Catholic Approaches." *Pro Ecclesia* 10 (2001): 195–212.

"Training for the 'Good Ascent': Gregory of Nyssa on Psalm 6." In *In Dominico Eloquio/In Lordly Eloquence: Essays on Patristic Exegesis in Honor of Robert Wilken,* edited by Paul Blowers et al. Grand Rapids: Eerdmans, 2001.

"'Heavenly Man' and 'Eternal Christ': Apollinarius and Gregory of Nyssa on the Personal Identity of the Savior." *Journal of Early Christian Studies* 10 (2002): 469–88.

"'A Hope for Worms.' Early Christian Hope." In *Resurrection: Theological and Scientific Assessments,* edited by Ted Peters, Robert John Russell, and Michael Welker, 136–64. Grand Rapids: Eerdmans, 2002.

"Is Patristic Exegesis Still Usable? Reflections on Early Christian Interpretation of the Psalms." *Communio* 29 (2002): 185–216; shorter version in *The Art of Reading Scripture,* edited by Ellen F. Davis and Richard B. Hays, 69–88. Grand Rapids: Eerdmans, 2003.

"Nature and the 'Mode of Union': Late Patristic Models for the Personal Unity of Christ." In *The Incarnation: An Interdisciplinary Symposium,* edited by Stephen T. Davis, Daniel Kendall, S.J., and Gerald O'Collins, S.J., 164–96. Oxford: Oxford University Press, 2002.

"The Fullness of the Saving God: Cyril of Alexandria on the Holy Spirit." In *The Theology of St. Cyril of Alexandria: A Critical Appreciation,* edited by Thomas G. Weinandy and Daniel A. Keating, 113–48. London: T. & T. Clark, 2003.

Translation of, and comment on, Maximus the Confessor, *Quaestiones ad Thalassium* 22. In *Corpus Christianorum 1953–2003: Xenium Natalicium: Fifty Years of Scholarly Editing,* edited by Johan Leemans and Lucas Jocqué, 288–91. Leuven: Brepols, 2003.

"A Response to Robin Darling Young, 'The Eucharist as Sacrifice according to Clement of Alexandria.'" In *Rediscovering the Eucharist: Ecumenical Conversations,* edited by Roch A. Kereszty, 92–103. New York: Paulist, 2003.

"Adoration of the Blessed Sacrament." In *Awake My Soul: Contemporary Catholics on Traditional Devotions,* edited by James Martin, S.J., 143–54. Chicago: Loyola Press, 2004.

"Death, the Afterlife, and Other Last Things: Christianity." In *Religions of the Ancient World: A Guide,* edited by Sarah I. Johnston, 493–95. Cambridge, Mass.: Harvard University Press, 2004.

"Finding the Right Key: The Aims and Strategies of Early Christian Interpretation of the Psalms." In *Psalms in Community: Jewish and Christian Textual, Liturgical, and Artistic Traditions,* edited by Harold W. Attridge and Margot E. Fassler, 189–205. Atlanta: Society of Biblical Literature, 2004.

"'He Himself is our Peace' (Eph 2:14): Early Christian Views of Redemption in Christ." In *The Redemption: An Interdisciplinary Symposium on Christ as Redeemer,* edited by Stephen T. Davis, Daniel Kendall, and Gerald O'Collins, 149–76. Oxford: Oxford University Press, 2004.

"Rebuilding the Structure of Love: The Quest for Visible Unity among the Churches." In *The Ecumenical Future. Background Papers for: In One Body through the Cross: The Princeton Proposal for Christian Unity,* edited by Carl E. Braaten and Robert W. Jenson, 73–105. Grand Rapids: Eerdmans, 2004.

"Resurrection," "Eschatology." In *The Westminster Handbook to Origen,* edited by John A. McGuckin. Louisville: Westminster John Knox, 2004.

"Saint Gregory of Nazianzus as Pastor and Theologian." In *Loving God with Our Minds: The Pastor as Theologian: Studies in Honor of Wallace M. Allston,* edited by Michael Welker and Cynthia A. Jarvis, 106–19. Grand Rapids: Eerdmans, 2004.

"Universal Love and Local Structure: Augustine, the Papacy, and the Church in Africa." *The Jurist* 64 (2004): 39–63.

"Forty Years of Orthodox-Catholic Dialogue (in Memory of John Long, S.J.)." *Origins* 35 (November 10, 2005): 363–70.

"The *Nouvelle Théologie* and the Patristic Revival: Sources, Symbols, and the Science of Theology." *International Journal of Systematic Theology* 7 (2005): 362–82.

"Word, Soul and Flesh: Origen and Augustine on the Person of Christ." *Augustinian Studies* 36 (2005): 299–326.

"'The Human Form Divine': Christ's Risen Body and Ours according to Gregory of Nyssa." *Studia Patristica*, edited by F. Young, M. Edwards, and P. Parvis, vol. 41, 301–18. Leuven: Peeters, 2006.

"Incorporeality and 'Divine Sensibility': The Importance of *De Principiis* 4.4 for Origen's Theology." *Studia Patristica,* edited by F. Young, M. Edwards, and P. Parvis, vol. 41, 139–44. Leuven: Peeters, 2006.

"'One Thing and Another': The Persons in God and the Person of Christ in Patristic Theology." *Pro Ecclesia* 15 (2006): 17–46.

"The Acts and Christian Confessions: Finding the Start of the Dogmatic Tradition. A Review Essay of Jaroslav Pelikan's *Commentary on Acts*." *Pro Ecclesia* 16 (2007): 18–25.

"The Cappadocian Fathers and the Option for the Poor." In *The Option for the Poor in Christian Theology*, edited by Daniel G. Groody, 77–83. Notre Dame, Ind.: University of Notre Dame Press, 2007.

"Eschatology in the Early Church Fathers." In *The Oxford Handbook of Eschatology,* edited by Jerry L. Walls, 91–109. Oxford: Oxford University Press, 2007.

Contributors

Khaled Anatolios is associate professor of historical and systematic theology at the Boston College School of Theology and Ministry. Among his publications is *Athanasius: The Coherence of His Thought* (Routledge, 1998).

Lewis Ayres is associate professor of historical theology in the Candler School of Theology and the Graduate Division of Religion at Emory University. His works include *Nicaea and Its Legacy* (Oxford University Press, 2004) and *Augustine and the Trinity* (Cambridge University Press, forthcoming).

Carl L. Beckwith is assistant professor of divinity at Beeson School of Divinity. He has authored several articles on Hilary of Poitiers, including "The Condemnation and Exile of Hilary of Poitiers at the Synod of Béziers (356 C.E.)," *Journal of Early Christian Studies* 13 (2005): 21–38.

Christopher A. Beeley is the Walter H. Gray Assistant Professor of Anglican Studies and Patristics at Yale Divinity School. He is the author of *Gregory of Nazianzus on the Trinity and the Knowledge of God: In Your Light We Shall See Light* (Oxford University Press, 2008).

D. Jeffrey Bingham is chair and professor of theological studies at Dallas Theological Seminary. He is the author of several works, among them *Irenaeus' Use of Matthew's Gospel* (Peeters, 1997).

Andrew Louth is professor of patristic and Byzantine studies at the University of Durham (England). Among his numerous books are *Maximus the Confessor* (Routledge, 1996) and *St John Damascene: Tradition and Originality in Byzantine Theology* (Clarendon Press, 2004).

Michael C. McCarthy, S.J., is assistant professor of religious studies at Santa Clara University. He has authored several articles, including "An Ecclesiology of Groaning: Augustine, the Psalms, and the Making of Church," *Theological Studies* 66 (2005): 23–48.

John A. McGuckin is professor of early church history at Union Theological Seminary of Columbia University. He has authored numerous books, including *St. Cyril of Alexandria: The Christological Controversy* (Brill, 1994) and *St. Gregory of Nazianzus: An Intellectual Biography* (St. Vladimir's Seminary Press, 2000).

Peter W. Martens is visiting assistant professor of theology at Yale Divinity School. His articles include, "Why Does Origen Refer to the Trinitarian Inspiration of Scripture in Book 4 of *Peri Archon?*" *Vigiliae Christianae* 60 (2006): 1–8, and "Revisiting the Allegory/Typology Distinction: The Case of Origen," *Journal of Early Christian Studies* 16 (2008): 283–317.

David R. Maxwell is assistant professor of systematic theology at Concordia Seminary in St. Louis. He has published "Crucified in the Flesh: Christological Confession or Evasive Qualification?" *Pro Ecclesia* 13 (2004): 70–81.

John J. O'Keefe is professor of theology at Creighton University. Among his publications are "'A Letter that Killeth': Toward a Reassessment of Antiochene Exegesis, or Diodore, Theodore, and Theodoret on the Psalms," *Journal of Early Christian Studies* 8 (2000): 83–104, and (with R. R. Reno) *Sanctified Vision: An Introduction to Patristic Exegesis* (Johns Hopkins University Press, 2005).

KELLEY MCCARTHY SPOERL is department chair and associate professor of theology at St. Anselm College. She has authored numerous articles on Apollinarius, including "Apollinarian Christology and the Anti-Marcellan Tradition," *Journal of Theological Studies* 45 (1994): 545–68.

BASIL STUDER, O.S.B., is a monk at Engelberg Abbey in Switzerland. He was professor of the history of ancient Christianity and patrology at the Collegio di San Anselmo and the Instituto Patristico Augustinianum, both in Rome. He is the author of numerous works, including *Trinity and Incarnation: The Faith of the Early Church* (Liturgical Press, 1994) and *Schola Christiana: Die Theologie zwischen Nizäa (325) und Chalzedon (451)* (Schöningh, 1998).

ROWAN DOUGLAS WILLIAMS is the Archbishop of Canterbury and former professor of theology at Oxford University. Among his numerous publications are *Arius: Heresy and Tradition,* rev. ed. (Eerdmans, 2002), *Resurrection: Interpreting the Easter Gospel* (Pilgrim Press, 2003), and *Tokens of Trust: An Introduction to Christian Belief* (Westminster John Knox, 2007).

General Index

Scripture Index

Thanks to Scott D. Moringiello for compiling the indices.